# Our Founding Foods

# Our FOUNDING Foods

## Classics From the First Century of American Celebrity Cookbooks

### Jane Tennant

with S.G.B. Tennant, Jr.

WILLOW CREEK PRESS

Minocqua, Wisconsin

LHF Billhead Typeface Collection used on the cover and interior
© Letterhead Fonts/www.letterheadfonts.com

Published by Willow Creek Press
P.O. Box 147, Minocqua, Wisconsin 54548

For information about custom editions, special sales, premium and corporate purchases,
please contact Jeremy Petrie at 800-850-9453 or jpetrie@willowcreekpress.com.

Editor/Design: Andrea Donner

Library of Congress Cataloging-in-Publication Data

Tennant, Jane.
  Our founding foods : classic recipes from the first century of American celebrity cookbooks /
Jane Tennant with S.G.B. Tennant, Jr.
      p. cm.
  Includes bibliographical references and index.
  ISBN 978-1-59543-591-0 (pbk. : alk. paper)
  1. Cookery, American--History. 2. Cookery, American.  I. Tennant, S. G. B. II. Title.
TX715.T304 2008
641.5973--dc22
                    2008007389

Printed in the United States of America

*This cookbook is for our friends who have tasted
the recipes and given their opinions.
Jo and Michael,
Wendy and Irvin,
Helen and Sandy,
Mary Anne and Tom,
Dedie and Lonn,
and, for their special contributions,
always, Elise and Phileda.*

# TABLE OF CONTENTS

# On the Printed Page

## The first 100 years of American cookery books

*by S.G.B. Tennant, Jr.*

The first cookbooks in America weren't American at all! They came over the ocean from the homeland with the rest of the emigrants, stuffed in luggage and packages. All the early cookbooks came from Europe, and in every case those books and handwritten manuscripts were the last echoes of home cooking, a thread back to the old world for families seeking a new beginning.

From 1620 to 1796, the strangers arriving on the east coast were predominantly English. Without question, diverse and important travelers of other origins were also crossing at the same time, landing in a variety of places that later became America. The Dutch in New Amsterdam, the Spanish in the West, and the French in New Orleans were, of course, all tied for first place. Then came the German, African, and Irish as well. The early settlers brought cookbooks ranging from the Dutch *Sensible Cook & Housekeeper* (1669) to the French *Le Vrai Cuisiner* (1651).

From the outset each native voice began to choir, heralding its own foods and customs and expectations, and melding with the New World's challenges and opportunities. For the most part, however, the books were in English, printed in London, and announced the traditional canon of English food at the time.

For the Plymouth Colony in Massachusetts, there arrived two copies of *The Compleate Cook* (1671) by Dame Alys of Asthorne Glen, and for the Virginia Colony at Jamestown, two copies of Gervase Markham's *The English Hus-Wife* (1615) about which much will be said.

With the growth of the early settlements, there developed markets for all the goods from "merry olde England" and beyond. Step by step, a market for cookbooks grew and a new "trade" flourished, so much so that by the early 18th century, book publishing had become a rough and tumble commercial experience. This book, then, is the story of that first century of American cookbook publishing, as it was set down in this country on the printed page.

## THE EARLY CANON OF AMERICAN FOOD

The books that formed the canon, or base, of accepted English food conventions in the early Colonial era of the 17th century were written by larger-than-life characters such as Gervase Markham, a contemporary of William Shakespeare. Markham compiled *The Complete Hus-Wife* in 1615, and between its pages put down everything there was to know about homemaking, from roasting venison on an open fire to brewing small beer, and baking manchet bread. His work represented the known and accepted body of food knowledge at the time. Many have since wondered at this broad range of interests in a single man, and some have suggested that his inspiration may have been the diary/manuscripts kept by his patron Frances, Dowager Countess of Exeter. Markham himself said as much in the dedication contained in the 2nd edition of *The Huswife* in 1623. Seventeenth century attitudes toward the use of sources were in any case a lot more relaxed. Shakespeare himself used plots borrowed from other writers.

As settlers of every religious persuasion sailed over the Atlantic, the population numbers in the colonies rocketed upward; what today we call New York grew from a population of 500 in 1700 to 12,000 in 1720. The other settlements and business interests grew apace, and were quick to see a market for printing and publishing books. By 1750, books, pamphlets, hand-bills and "broadsides" had become a profitable occupation for the eager and the lucky.

The risks and rewards of unrestrained publishing meant that as early as 1733 Benjamin Franklin would churn out 1,000 copies of his famous *Poor Richard's Almanac*, sell them as fast as he could in his Philadelphia neighborhood, then revise and reissue a slightly amended "Second" edition and carry on, all in the same year.

There was no shortage of new material. Franklin freely made use of his contemporaries' work and later boasted that pilfering clever aphorisms from others was better than offering his own thin jokes.

The protection of an author's work, commonly known today as "copyright" had a slow and uneven history in the "dog catch dog" world of Colonial publishing. Following the British *Statute of Queen Anne*, promulgated in 1709, protections were selectively identified and then gradually extended, but the practice of plagiarizing whatever fit the page was more the standard. A century later Mark Twain was still struggling with British pilfering of his *Adventures of Huckleberry Finn*, and he was forced to produce numerous "editions."

In such an environment it was sometimes difficult to tell whose "venison pasty" came first. Recipes were lifted wholesale, back and forth between successive editions without scruple or remedy. The first American born cookbook author, Amelia Simmons, borrowed from her English counterparts. Her pioneering work, *American Cookery* (1796), both gained and suffered from the looting by others. Her English contemporary, Hannah Glasse, was notoriously the "author" of recipes and even entire chapters that were borrowed whole cloth from an early 17th century work called *The Whole Duty of a Woman*.

Simultaneously, the American Colonial kitchen fires were nurtured by a treasure trove of handwritten recipes, medicinal cures, and manuscripts of daily life written by homemakers and passed on, one generation to the next. These keepsakes were not printed and bound, but continued the traditions and received wisdom of the times, much like the diaries of the Countess of Exeter upon which Gervase Markham relied.

The old ways were preserved in these kitchen notebooks, but it was the rush of hungry publishers chasing the market potential of "big sales" that brought out the would-be famous authors. To meet the burgeoning market, English authors Eliza Smith, Susannah Carter, and the previously mentioned Hannah Glasse all produced cookbooks in England that were printed, shipped, released, and sold in American cities. Likewise the Dutch *The Sensible Cook and Housekeeper*, first anonymously published in Amsterdam in 1669, was subsequently translated into English and rushed to what is now New York for a partisan market.

These books were all of a piece. They restated established themes of meats and breads, and were cobbled together and rushed to market, reflecting a total absence of embarrassment at purloined recipes, and the ineffectualness of copyright laws. For many small publishers their sole ambition was to get a book into print and out the door.

The first of these English food mavens to test the book market over the water was Eliza Smith. Her book, *The Complete Housewife* (London 1727), was published in the same year as the first performance of Handel's *Messiah*. The book had developed a fifteen year publishing history in England and was optimistically reissued in Williamsburg, Virginia, in 1742. The new "American" edition contained a "ketchup" recipe, without tomatoes, and itself became the object of much subsequent pirating by the likes of Hannah Glasse and others.

Hannah Glasse, once described as quintessentially American, in fact never visited the Colonies. Her name was "like glitter," however, and her publishers added a "New World Supplement" containing cornmeal recipes that was published posthumously in the Alexandria, Virginia, edition of 1805.

Another food savant with a disposition toward publishing, Brillat Savarin (*Le Philosophie de Gout*, Paris 1825) had found himself at this time in the company of many French chefs touring America in search of new employment. The collapse of the Ancien Regime in Paris made that city too hot for the aristocracy—and their chefs—and America beckoned. Brillat Savarin was in Boston in 1792, playing his violin for old French friends and sampling the cities best restaurants, surprised at the urbane enthusiasm of the new nation. New food and fine food were on everyone's mind, and as Brillat Savarin later wrote, "Tell me what you eat, and I will tell you what you are."

Everywhere the cookbooks on offer were foreign made. *The Frugal Housewife* (London, 1765, and Boston, 1772) was written by another Englishwoman, Susannah Carter, who had never set foot in America. This was the most popular cookbook in America in 1776, and twenty years later, Amelia Simmons "borrowed" significantly from the text.

On the cusp of the 18th century, many other English cookbooks were notable for their success including *The New Art of Cookery* (Philadelphia, 1792), a 557 page encyclopedia by the Englishman Richard Briggs, and *The Sportsman's Companion or An Essay on Shooting* (Harrisburg, Pa. 1783), by "a gentleman." This last quoting at length from Gervase Markham's advice on "shooting flying" as the newly minted sport of hunting over dogs and shooting birds on the wing in 1615 had been dubbed.

The culinary bar was raised with each incoming ship and its load of books. At a time when the American population reached to just over 1.5 million souls in thirteen colonies, a French chef, Honore Julien, was presiding over the kitchen in the White House at the invitation of President Thomas Jefferson, and the American publishers were eager to cook up a storm.

## The One and Only Amelia Simmons, Writing on Her Kitchen Table

Amidst this enthusiastic ambience the native child, Amelia Simmons, a self described orphan, strode into a provincial print shop in Hartford, Connecticut, in 1796 and made a simple proposition. She would produce a cooking manuscript of undeniable quality, giving as she said "...the art of dressing Viands, Fish, Poultry and Vegetables." The printer, for his part, would get paid for his ink and labor as the books sold, the standard "Ben Franklin" operating rules. The book was to be called *American Cookery*, the year was 1796, and the horses, as they say, "were off."

Later the same year, Amelia Simmons imposed on another printer in Albany, New York. The second printing, nearly identical except for the addition of an interloper's "preface," and with some errors corrected, was produced and sold in the Hudson River Valley of New York.

Amelia's cookbook was thorough, local, and full of the foods that Americans ate, particularly her follow-up editions, of which there were several. She gave recipes for corn meal, such as Indian Pudding and Hoe Cakes, and she spoke of cooking by the wood fire with a spit. Her style was direct, if not actually laconic, and to the point. On roast beef, she said, "rare done is the healthiest and the taste of this age." She also pioneered the use of pearlash in her recipes for baked goods, including gingerbread and cakes.

The success of Simmons' *American Cookery* was noticed by the publishing trade. In quick succession competitive books by various anonymous "cooks" were printed in Boston, Harrisburg, Philadelphia, Williamsburg, and beyond.

As a last grab for market share, the established but fading English authors Susannah Carter and then, in turn, Hannah Glasse, each added a "corn meal appendix" to their books in the form of identical recipes using indiginous American ingredients meant to tempt buyers in the American market.

These last English books to see significant sales in America tried every gimmick they could muster, including engraved frontispiece illustrations by the now famous Paul Revere, but it was all too late. The enthusiasm created by the first true American book, *American Cookery* by Amelia Simmons, whipped the hometown horses past the post. American publishers were quick to welcome the market for American cookbooks. This marked the effective end of transatlantic publishing of cookbooks in America. After 1805 the trend reversed. Some of the most important American authors would publish their books in England.

### THE HOME TOWN GENIUSES: MARY RANDOLPH AND ELIZA LESLIE

Mary Randolph lived in Virginia and she wrote the first Southern cookbook in 1824. *The Virginia Housewife* (Washington, D.C., 1824) not only emphasized the importance of good household management, a skill that Mary Randolph had inherited from her mother, but gave a recipe for polenta made from corn, and gazpacho made with tomatoes. These were two novel inclusions for the time, not previously included in the "corn meal appendix," and that have since become the world's recognized standard.

It is significant that polenta, the dish synonymous with rural Italian cuisine, had for centuries been made with barley flour, or some other substitute. But only with the introduction of corn-meal did the dish in its modern form become possible. Mary Randolph wrote it down first.

The culinary applications of tomatoes, no less portentous, was another case in point. The fruit was well known by this time and served in the better restaurants, but very few were brave enough to eat it at home. To prove a point, one forward thinker in New Jersey, Col. Robert Gibbon Johnson, gathered a crowd and ate a raw tomato on the steps of the Salem County, New Jersy, courthouse to no apparent ill effects in 1826. Within a matter of years tomato growing, canning, drying, and consumption were rampant nationwide.

Mary Randolph strengthened the case for tomatoes by offering a Spanish Gazpacho using tomato, which she may have learned from the Continental cookbooks of Juan de la Mata published in Madrid several generations earlier. And from there it was only a step to her recipe for ketchup, discussed later. There can be little doubt where Mary Randolph learned her practical experience roasting meat, however; it was over an open fire. Her directions are in the American "tradition," succinct, spare, and confident: "No meat can be well roasted except on a spit turned by a jack, and roasted before a steady clear fire—other methods are no better than baking."

Predictability and order were the watchwords in Mary Randolph's book, and she quickly assumed the status of protector of the American hearth. "The prosperity and happiness of a family depend greatly on the order and regularity established in it," she announced with absolute certainty. As the matriarch of an old Virginia family, she had come by her status the time-honored way.

Mary Randolph was innovative at the time for many of her

dishes such as catfish, okra, and gumbo. Her recipes were both solid and artful, and I can point with pride to her pan reduction sauce for teal, which I still use today and that includes the use of whole peppercorns in the duck sauce, anticipating Escoffier by 75 years. Here are her directions for *Sauce for Wildfowl*:

> *Take a gill of claret, with as much water, some grated bread, three heads of shallots, a little whole pepper, mace, grated nutmeg, and salt; let them stew over the fire, then beat it up with butter, and put it under the wild fowl, which being a little roasted, will afford gravy to mix with this sauce.*

*The Virginia Housewife* was a huge success and enjoyed 19 printings, the first coinciding with the nationwide celebration of the 50th anniversary of the American Revolution and the triumphant Farewell Tour of the French General Lafayette. The old hero of the American Revolution was wined and dined across the fledgling nation, visiting some of the dozens of towns named after him, and enjoying banquets of enormous scale turned out by grateful Americans. The feasting never seemed to stop and venison, snipe, seabass, and waterfowl were on every menu; the culinary standard far removed from the sod cabin and sustenance frontier vittles of earlier times.

It was in this era, also, that the American food world was becoming more business-like and predictable. "Pork in brine" had become an industry in Cincinnati by 1818, with cured meat shipped around the country. The Erie Canal opened in 1825 and revolutionized the nation's commercial distribution system, including The Fulton Fish Market, which had opened its doors in New York in 1822, and by then sold every fish, turtle, bird, and beast known to be in existence in the area.

With the confidence of two successful wars against Britain behind them, Americans were justifiably assertive of their autonomy, and it began to show in their cookbooks. With her elbows firmly planted on her Boston kitchen table, the next publishing leader, Eliza Leslie, threw down the kitchen towel in a challenge to all of Europe in 1827: "There is much difficulty in following directions in English and French books. Not only from their want of explicitness, but from the difference in the fuel, fire places, and cooking utensils generally used."

Thus inspired, and supported by her brother, Leslie wrote *Seventy Five Receipts for Pastry, Cakes and Sweetmeats* (1828) and *Directions for Cookery* (1837), both published from Boston, which had become a cosmopolitan center. With aplomb, Leslie offered Sea Coast Pie, Missouri Cake, and Roasted Canvasback Duck. This incomparable diving duck later found its culinary icon status in the novel *The Age of Innocence* (1899) by Edith Wharton, and was later raved about by George Escoffier on his first trip to America.

Eliza Leslie became a well-known and easily recognized name in the burgeoning "home economics" industry in America. Her books endured many editions, and were a trusted friend in many pioneer kitchens. In an interesting turn-around in publishing history, she even wrote a cookbook, *The Indian Meal Book* (1846), that was intended to introduce Britain to corn and corn meal.

## WAGON WHEELS ROLLING WEST

With the onset of the 19th century, free land warrants and a burgeoning population pushed the American dream over the Allegheny Mountains and into Ohio, Indian Country, and the new "West."

There was a rush to print following the success of *American Cookery*, but the record keeping was notoriously ill reported. We do know from the work of well-regarded cookbook bibliographer Louis Pitschmann that between 1742 and 1860, 800 different titles were published in the exploding American market.

The American self-image was split between the frugal pioneer in Ohio and Indiana, and the imagined grandees of Virginia and Boston. It was at this time that Robert Roberts, a successful major D'omo/butler in Boston, wrote and published *The House Servant's Directory* (Boston, 1827), as a model of household management, intending to promote the proper discharge of domestic duties. Roberts showed the management style of grand and well-ordered living in an upper class urban setting even though he happened to be a black butler, free, and very proud of his professional skills.

At the other end of the economic scale, Lydia Maria Child wrote for a modest household focused on economy. *The Frugal Housewife* (1832) came out only eight years after *The Virginia Housewife* and raised many issues of household economy. Sarah Josepha Hale, influential editor of *Godey's Lady's Book*, called Child's view "cheap living" to distinguish it from Dr. Kitchener's "good living." Home economics writers played to the contrasts, and continued to produce recipes for a varied readership spread across America. They invited readers to contribute their own favorites, and Sarah Josepha Hale became the Queen of the "out reach authors" while she edited *The Lady's Magazine*. Before Mr. Godey moved in to buy up the title, Hale's cookbook *The Good Housekeeper* (1841) sold 2,000 copies in its first month of publication. Up to this time, all commercial sales had been of books, bound volumes, and sturdy tomes. But the magazine publishers were testing this model. It was in the run-up to secession, and at a time of national dialogue fraught with the Fugitive Slave Act and John Brown in Bloody Kansas that magazines first came of age. Harriet Beecher Stowe serialized *Uncle Tom's Cabin* and lifted the small weekly magazine *National Era* to world significance in 1850, producing a book that eventually outsold every book in English save the Bible.

During this era, distinctive voices recently arrived from other parts of Europe began to assert themselves. George Girardey, an American of Alsatian/Swiss extraction, wrote and published a *Manuel of Domestic Economy* (Cincinnati, 1841), with recipes in German which was then translated into English and sold throughout the "German Belt" of middle America.

Girardey's book is extremely rare these days, but in addition to its vast ethnic offerings there is included a recipe for "Tomato Catsup." While some critics argue that Girardey's early recipe is just "tomatoes added to stew," it brings up the entire catsup history, which is an intriguing example of the emergence of our founding foods in print.

What started out as a fishy sauce made of anchovies, shallots, wine, vinegar, and spices, created by the Chinese and imported to Britain by homecoming sailors, was faithfully reported by the early English writer Eliza Smith (*The Compleat Housewife*, 1742). The English thereafter developed dozens of types of ketchup, including mushroom, walnut, and cucumber, but none of them remotely similar to tomato ketchup.

As startling as "tomato ketchup" would have been to the 19th century reader, the prospect of "walnut ketchup" draws even fewer takers today. Eliza Smith's early 18th century recipe was taken directly from the Chinese and endured as the standard until after the 1820s when Thomas Jefferson and his cousins, the Randolphs, wrote the tomato into everything from Brunswick Stew to "ketchup."

Even the spelling of the word has been an artistic football. Jonathan Swift declared it "catsup" (1730); Eliza Smith used "katchop" (1727); neither contained tomatoes. The spelling and the ingredients continued to change until they reached the hands of H.J. Heinz in America in 1876, and there things stopped for the foreseeable future.

*The Sugar House Book* (1801) had perhaps the first recipe for tomato ketchup in America, but a more influential and popular recipe for tomato ketchup was given by Mary Randolph in *The Virginia Housewife*. By the time Sarah Josepha Hale was writing *The Good Housekeeper*, tomato ketchup had found what seemed a natural place in the condiment chapter and vinegar was included in the recipe. Ketchup was now bottled and corked and ready for use in every conceivable dish.

## AROUND THE EDGES

Although New Orleans was not formerly a part of the United States by 1840, the French language cookbook, *La Cuisiner Habile*, takes pride of place as the first cookbook printed in New Orleans. Although some date the book later, it appears to be based in part on the French cooking treatise, *Le Tresors des Menages*, first published in France in 1825 and imported by emigrants to the Crescent City. As we incorporated the Big Easy and its gustatorial enthusiasm into the national fabric, the contributions of Creole and Cajun cuisine, quite distinct at the outset, became at first legendary, and then difficult to distinguish.

It was shortly before mid-century, in 1849, that gold was discovered at Sutter's Mill in California, and the previous light scale trading and commercial exchanges between the opposite ends of the national geography were washed aside in the resulting gold rush. The consequences for every aspect of American life, not the least of which was culinary, were such that by 1870 San Francisco was the tenth largest city in America. The first Californian cookbook by a Hispanic, Encarnacion Pineda, in which she memorializes her native "colonial" cuisines, was not to see print, however, until 1898.

## Cooking Becomes an Institution

The devastation of the Civil War brought a momentary hiatus in the cookbook publishing avalanche, but inevitably, the pace resumed, because getting a cookbook into print was widely seen as a key to fame and fast fortune, whether for individuals, charities, or well-meaning institutions.

The widely successful *Buckeye Cookery and Practical Housekeeping* (Community published in 1877) sold 27,000 copies in its first year and then catapulted itself into high gear and went on to sales of over one million by the turn of the 19th century, extolling the Buckeye chauvinism of burgeoning Ohio.

George Girardey, mentioned earlier, had been so successful with the German-Americn market that the field was ripe for another teutonic import. Henriette Davidis and her *Praktisches Kochbluch* had enjoyed fifteen successful editions in Germany, when a sharp-eyed publisher in Milwaukee made his move. Davidis's book was translated and refitted with a new title, *The Practical Cook Book* (1897), and she soon became a household name in German America. More than a generation following George Girardey's success in Cincinnati, Davidis encountered the same ethnic appeal of Americans searching to reaffirm their roots with the old country while steadfastly adopting the mores and ingredients of the new.

One familiar signpost of the old European traditions was the small breweries dotted across the Midwest. Essential to the fabric of these communities, the tiny breweries sprang up wherever farmers found the rich soil tillable and the inhabitants accommodating. In a supportive community of fellow immigrants, a working family could turn 2,000 bushels of local wheat and 1,000 pounds of local hops into 50 barrels of beer a month. What more could one ask from the richness of America?

It was among one of these rich and insular farmer communities that Antonin Dvorak arrived in Spillvile, Iowa, in 1895 to celebrate the New World and its many freedoms. Glowing reports still circulate in the Czech community there of the long summer evenings spent in song and remembrance with the maestro on farm porches, pilsner in hand. Dvorak wrote the *New World Symphony* from this experience, and you can hear the echoes of the American countryside in his melodies.

In rural America, the wood-fired household stove came into common use about mid-century and became a familiar object in rooms set aside for cooking, despite its squat 200- to 300-pound cast iron bulk. Every house had one, but the monsters were still regarded with suspicion. When President Fillmore installed the first iron stove in the White House kitchens, his chef walked out in protest.

At a time when the average British family ate only two to three hot meals a week due to the exorbitant price of fuel, the American cookbook publishers rushed to offer new books loaded with instructions on taming the flues and dampers of red hot ovens. In skilled hands, the new "range" was promised to turn out a vast array of "...cakes, pies and... etc...," all of which were made possible by the convenient, and usually wood burning home stove, or "range."

The first full-blown kitchen gas ovens operating on a professional level were installed by that Chef/Impresario Alexis Soyer to glamorize his Reform Club in London, about 1841. Those kitchen ovens were an anomaly, of course, the gas fuel being not only exclusive but expensive, and emphasizing the disparity between home and restaurant cooking worldwide.

By 1850 there were over 2,000 commercial bakers in the principle American cities, each using one form or another of the modern cooking stove or oven. Even so, most bread was still cooked at home and so the cookbooks of that era exploded with offerings of unique breads using modern commercial, or "store bought," flours.

With the comparative ease of use of the modern stoves and ovens came ambition. No longer were the prospects of a square meal for the family burdened with the prospect of hours beside a wood fire, tending the brazier and the coals. This was "modern" living, and in response to the growing middle class with more stoves and more cooking capacity, recipes themselves began to be written in an efficient and orderly way, giving reproducible measurements and expecting standardized results.

## The Last Frontiers

Much of the charm and variety of this great smorgasbord that is America's cookbook history is found in the isolated pockets or hotspots of her distinctive cuisines. One of these surely was the distinction between Creole and Cajun food in Louisiana.

In modern times, there have been any number of academic distinctions drawn between the Creole traditions, emphasizing tomatoes, and the Cajun presentation of foods rich with flour roux from the Bayou country. The former come from the slave and French culture of the early 18th century, and the latter from the mysterious Arcadian immigrants settling in the fish- and game-rich swamps.

The great chef Paul Prudhomme recently had the final word when he announced that in his kitchen, the two traditions had "intermarried," and they were no longer distinguishable.

For the record, however, we do remember that at an earlier time, the African slaves residing in Louisiana informed the rural French cooking. Near the Melrose Plantation, overlooking the Natchitoches River in Louisiana, the French Creole traditions were announced, and then adopted local ingredients such as the savory native bay laurel leaf, much stronger than the Mediterranean bay leaf, and animated by the indigenous chili petines, file (or sassafras root), and the imported okra. In spite of the paucity of cookbooks from this insular community, the very distinctive *Melrose Plantation Cookbook*, now itself quite rare, is a glimpse into that ante-bellum culture, where English was a foreign language. This book was dictated by the nearly illiterate Marguerite Hunter, the daughter of slaves, to the nearly blind French historian and cultural artifact collector, François Mignon. The book came to life on the heels of Hunter's fame as the "black Grandma Moses" in the middle of the 20th century. Its value for us is as a steady guide into her post Civil War childhood kitchen on a great plantation, true to the authentic Creole/African cuisine of 18th century Louisiana.

On the eve of the 20th century, the great Eastern cities stewed up a flurry of cooking schools and instructed the middle class with a high moral imperative. "This was the way to run a kitchen," said the New York Cooking School, the Boston Cooking School, and the Philadelphia Cooking School. Enrollment soared and cookbooks came pouring forth. Authors Fannie Farmer, Mary Lincoln, and Sarah J. Rorer traveled all over the country giving cooking demonstrations. They were part of the emerging Domestic Science movement that emphasized level measurements and sound nutritional advice.

Between them, these ladies took American cooking writing into the 20th century. At the same time, let us not forget the enormous contribution of food-centered magazines with a growing number of advertisements for new convenience foods and equipment that wove together the now animated body politic of the kitchen and made the life of American cooks more fascinating. Books, magazines, and concerted literary effort, generations before television and the Internet, together provided a network across the miles of prairie, and over and beyond the sometimes shrill and competitive commercial picket lines.

Communication, in its many forms, is what sustained our fragile culinary consensus and solidified our sense of shared purpose during the first century of American cookbooks; because of this, the march has always been forward, informed, and reflective. Cooking scholars, and now the rest of us, can confidently declare that American cooks and American cookbooks have established a new canon, our founding food, broad as a rainbow and as close as the sky. It was all done with simple ideas, fresh ingredients, and a practical determination that sparkled on the printed page.

## CHAPTER ONE

# THE FIRST COOKBOOK

Gervase Markham, *The English Huswife*, London 1615
Molen-Willebrands, Ed. *The Sensible Cook and Housekeeper*, 1669
Eliza Smith, *The Compleat Housewife*, Williamsburg 1727, 1742
Hannah Glasse, *The Art of Cookery Made Plain and Easy*, 1747, 1805
Martha Washington, *The Booke of Cookery*, 1749 (1981)
Susannah Carter, *The Frugal Housewife*, Boston 1765, 1772
Amelia Simmons, *American Cookery*, Hartford 1796

The women who made the journey to America in the seventeenth century were mostly British. They brought with them a well-established tradition of cooking and a small number of trusted cookbooks that would remain, for the century after Plymouth Rock, the only cookbooks in America.

Gervase Markham's *The English Huswife* was one of the best known. A contemporary of Shakespeare, Markham was a prolific author who wrote on every aspect of household management. His housewife was "a complete woman," who was expected not only to cook meals but weave and dye cloth, run a dairy, brew beer, make candles and soap, and distill the medicines used for "perfumery and physick."

The *English Huswife* was shipped to Jamestown in 1620 for the colonists who looked to its pages for guidance and reassurance. However, only the well-to-do could afford to buy a book and, more to the point, only a few women at the time could read or write.

It was for such a gentlewoman that William Parks had the bright idea of importing another British title, *Compleat Housewife* by Eliza Smith, which was published in Williamsburg in 1742.

Eliza Smith was decidedly English, and she had been cook to fashionable and noble families. Her book offered more than 600 recipes, which she said were "suitable for English constitutions and English palates." It was in this book, also, that the fashion for announcing a multitude of cures and remedies for every ailment, from a pimpled face to the bite of a mad dog, became a cookbook fixture.

There was no mention of the Native American foods in Eliza's recipes. Neither beans, corn, squash, cranberries, nor pumpkin made an appearance. This was no surprise, for Eliza Smith had never been to America.

Neither had fellow countrywoman Susannah Carter, whose *The Frugal Housewife* was published in Boston in 1772. The "receipts" were in the English manner. The thrifty colonial house-wife would be very much at home preparing familiar dishes such as roast breast of mutton, eel pie, or marmalade.

Another source of guidance came from handwritten collections of receipts that were passed down in families. Just such a treasured possession was *The Booke of Cookery*, inherited by Martha Washington in 1749. A recipe from the pages of the First Lady's cookbook was a prized possession amongst well-connected families in Virginia.

Martha Washington's receipts were hand-me-downs and patch-me-ups, and included both elaborate dishes and everyday fare. Many were adapted to take advantage of the fish, game, and vegetables available at Mount Vernon. At Martha's death, *The Booke of Cookery* was bequeathed to her precious granddaughter. Among other treasures in her estate was another classic English cookbook by Hannah Glasse. *The Art of Cookery Made Plain and Easy* was popular amongst well-to-do colonial families.

Modern eyes will view these 18th century receipts as hopelessly vague and anachronistic. Cooking was done over the hearth and it was impossible to give cooking times. The best that could be recommended was cooking until "done." Essential instructions and precise measurements were also few and far between; their absence is attributable as much to secrecy as to a lack of scientific jargon, and also because cooks were expected to know how much of each ingredient to include.

Here's an example, taken from Susannah Carter's *The Frugal Housewife* (1772). She is cooking Gooseberry Pie, an old English favorite: "Make a good crust, lay a little around the sides of your dish, throw sugar at the bottom and lay in your fruit and sugar at the top. Bake it in a slack oven" reads the receipt. "Take as much creame and new milk as you please and put to it as much runnit as will make it come" and "when they are well baked in yr oven, soe serve them up."

Breads, pies, and cakes were baked in a brick oven built into the hearth, a Herculean task that demanded an experienced eye and great dexterity with the long-handled peel that was used to remove hot pans from the glowing oven. Timing was crucial. As the oven temperature decreased, successive dishes were cooked. Breads went in first, then pies and, finally, when the oven was coolest, delicate cakes.

The British cookbooks continued to dominate the market and American needs went unanswered until the publication of a groundbreaking book called *American Cookery* in 1796. The author, Amelia Simmons, was an orphan and not well educated. Her modest background was announced on the title page of her book. This was a shrewd marketing ploy. Thus far, no cookbooks had been written for ordinary American folks.

Amelia favored a direct writing style; her instructions were easy to follow and she used foods that were available to Americans. Amongst other traditional dishes, she included recipes for perennial favorites such as roast turkey and cranberry sauce, pumpkin pie, Indian pudding, hoe cake, and molasses gingerbread.

Her baked recipes were especially popular as they used pearl ash, the earliest form of baking powder. A spoonful of the chemical leavening agent added to the batter made light work of what had been a labor intensive task: some early recipes instructed the overworked cook to beat eggs for 45 minutes.

*American Cookery* was such a success that publishers at once rushed to press with American appendix attached to cookbooks. Susannah Carter's *The Frugal Housewife* and Hannah Glasse's *The Art of Cookery Made Plain and Easy* both received the makeover treatment.

Amelia Simmon's appearance on the stage of culinary history was tantalizingly brief. *American Cookery* was her only book, but it was a major publishing event. The scope of the work was modest, but its appeal was huge. No writer had previously used American ingredients and written in such an approachable manner as Amelia.

The dishes in this chapter span the important influences in American food ways. English, Dutch, French, and German dishes all find a place. Some are elegant entrées that graced the aristocratic dining tables at Mount Vernon and Monticello. Others would be at home on a scrubbed wooden table in a farmhouse kitchen. They all shared the distinction of having been prepared over an open fire.

The American housewife risked singed eyebrows, burned fingers, and a permanent backache as she hung a heavy pot on a crane suspended over the flames, or turned a roast on a spit, or emptied coals into a brazier so that she could simmer a sauce. The wonder was not that she turned out an edible meal, but the variety and elegance of many dishes prepared under such circumstances.

# MARTHA WASHINGTON'S LEG OF LAMB

Adapted from: Martha Washington's, *The Booke of Cookery*, 1749, p. 52

**M**artha Washington's *Booke of Cookery* was not published until 200 years after she used it in the kitchens at Mount Vernon and then it was hailed as a historical treasure that offered insight into the lives of the old guard. The manuscript was far more than a cookbook. As precious as the recipes was the section on "sweetmeats," "medicinal waters" and "physicks." Martha Washington and other 18th century housewives were their family's physicians and the advice given was the accumulation of many years of received wisdom. When George and Martha married she was a widow with two children, and a prominent legacy in the Custis family of old Virginia. Frances Parke Custis may have started this keepsake manuscript, but it was cherished and added to by Martha and generations ever since.

*1 leg of lamb, 7 lbs., boned, not split, with shank removed*
*salt and freshly ground black pepper*
*1 cup white wine for basting*

## STUFFING

*4 tablespoons pork fat, chopped and rendered in butter (alt: corn oil)*
*1 tablespoon anchovy paste*
*4 tablespoons parsley, chopped*
*2 teaspoons capers, chopped*
*1 teaspoon thyme, crumbled*
*1 teaspoon lemon peel, finely grated*
*1 cup white breadcrumbs*
*1 cup onions, chopped*
*2 garlic cloves, minced*
*½ cup white wine*
*1½ cups chicken stock*

 Preheat oven to 450°F. Prepare the stuffing in a large mixing bowl by combining the butter and all other ingredients, thoroughly, and reserve. Close the opening at the shank end of the leg of lamb using kitchen twine, leaving access to the pocket in the meat behind it. Fill the pocket with the stuffing, packing it in close, then secure the entire leg with kitchen twine, using 2 or 3 lengthwise wraps and 4 or 5 crosswise laps to form a neat cylindrical package.

Cook in a roasting pan until rare at an internal temperature of 145°F, basting with the wine. Remove and allow to cool before carving. *Serves 8.*

# WILD TURKEY WITH RELISH

Adapted from: Amelia Simmons, *American Cookery*, 1796, p. 18

1 wild turkey, oven ready, 7-10 lb.
  (alt: domestic turkey—adjust for weight)
salt and freshly ground black pepper
1 onion
fresh parsley, thyme, and rosemary

## CRANBERRY RELISH

3 cups cranberries, fresh
½ cup sugar
½ cup each of white wine and chicken stock
2 tablespoons orange peel, grated
salt and freshly ground black pepper to taste
a pinch of cinnamon

In a letter home to his family from the Virginia Colonies in 1680 the colonist planter Mahon Stacey observed, "…cranberries make an excellent sauce for venison, turkeys and other great fowl." And so it was that the eager settlers waded through the New England bogs and swamps to pick the wild berries named after the great cranes that migrated overhead (*gru canadensis*). One hundred years later, the berry was propagated commercially and harvested with cranberry rakes and sold in stores. Here is roasted wild turkey, served with the original cranberry relish, which had passed into the canon of familiar recipes when it was first recorded by Amelia Simmons in the first American cookbook in 1796.

Rotate the wings behind the bird's back and interlock the first joints. Rub the skin with olive oil, then salt and pepper the bird, inside and out. Stuff the bird with a quartered onion and chopped parsley, thyme, and rosemary. Tie the drumsticks together. Place the bird right side down on a roasting rack in a 375°F oven with 1 cup of stock in the pan. Roast the bird for 1½ hours, then turn bird to back-side up and continue roasting for 45 minutes. Turn bird to breast side up and complete roasting. Throughout the roasting, baste the bird, using foil to prevent scorching during the last 10 minutes of each stage. Cook the bird for a total of 17 minutes per pound or until an internal temperature at the leg reads 165°F.

For the relish, combine the cranberries, sugar, stock, wine, and grated peel in a medium saucepan and bring to a slow simmer. Cook, stirring slowly, until the berries burst. Do not overcook. Adjust the seasonings with salt, pepper, and cinnamon. Allow the relish to cool, and set into a loose jelly. Serve with sliced turkey. *Serves 8-10.*

# "First Catch Your Hare"

Adapted from: Hannah Glasse, *The Art of Cookery, Made Plain and Easy*, 1805, p. 21

Winston Churchill was one of the first to get it wrong, and food writers ever since have mistakenly perpetuated the myth. Hannah Glasse, in giving instructions for roasting a Hare in her famous cookbook, advised that the first step was to skin the rabbit. The term used for skinning all manner of game in 1805 was "to case" the animal, or to peel off the hide and hair, and that is the instruction given by Mrs. Glasse. In the early fixed-type printing of the day, the letter "f" was often substituted for "s" which may have produced some confusion on reading, and led to early commentators suggesting that the instructions began with the very sensible instruction to "First caf'd ('catch') your hare…" before cooking it. Here is an adaptation of Hannah Glasse's true recipe for roast hare with her stuffing.

1 young hare, or rabbit, cut up into serving pieces (2 lbs.)

## Stuffing

½ cup fresh bacon, chopped
1 cup bread crumbs
⅓ cup fresh parsley, chopped
2 tablespoons bouquet garni
mixed herbs—basil, marjoram, savory, thyme
grated nutmeg to taste
2 eggs, beaten
3 tablespoons butter

 First inspect your hare or rabbit to see that it is free of skin, fat, or tissue. Wash and cut into serving-size pieces. Half fry out the bacon, then combine the bacon, the reserved fat, the parsley, sweet herbs, nutmeg, and the beaten eggs. Combine this well with the bread crumbs to make the "pudding."

In a small oval ovenproof terrine with sides at least 2" tall, arrange the pieces of rabbit, and spoon the stuffing, or pudding, all around the rabbit pieces. Dot the surface with the butter.

Roast in a 350°F oven for one hour, covering with a lid or foil to prevent scorching. The roast hare is ready when the internal temperature reaches 145°F. *Serves 4.*

# LITTLE FRIED BIRDS

Adapted from: Eliza Smith, *The Compleat Housewife*, 1742, p. 163

2 cups cooked, finely diced turkey dark meat,
    no skin or tendon
4 tablespoons chopped green onions
4 tablespoons butter
4 tablespoons dry sherry
2 teaspoons mixed herbs, dried
salt and pepper to taste

## PASTRY

3 cups all purpose flour
1½ tablespoons sugar
1½ teaspoons salt
3 sticks chilled unsalted butter
9 tablespoons ice water
peanut oil for deep-frying

There was a strong and growing confidence in America as a market for English books in the early 18th century. Williamsburg, Virginia, was home to one such publisher named William Parks who, without scruple or permission, reproduced a fifteen-year-old English book, *The Complete Housewife* by Eliza Smith, and successfully marketed it to the Virginia audience. This recipe originally called for lamb kidneys with suet fat, but it is lightened here with the rich turkey dark meat that is delicious but under utilized.

Sauté the onions in butter until soft. Add the turkey and turn to coat and cook slightly. Add the sherry and continue cooking until almost dry. Add the herbs, stir briefly to incorporate, and remove from the heat and reserve.

*To Make the Pastry*: Combine the flour, sugar, and salt in a food processor. Add the diced butter and pulse 10 seconds. Add the water and pulse just until the dough is formed. Wrap and chill for one hour. Roll out the dough to ½" thickness, fold in thirds like a business letter and repeat. Wrap and chill until needed.

Roll the chilled pastry to ¼" thickness, and cut into 6" squares. Put two tablespoons of filling in each square, moisten the inside edges with water, and fold to make a small parcel, sealing the edges.

Set the deep fryer with at least 3" of oil to 365°F and fry the pasties, 3 at a time, until the pastry is brown and appealing. Remove and drain. *Serves 6.*

# Dutch Pork and Apples

Adapted from: Molen-Willebrands, Ed., *De Verstandige Koch*, 1669

The Dutch immigrants around New York (once called New Amsterdam) loved to cook salty meat, geese, and pigs mixed with the fresh fruit of their new land. Fluffy Dumplings floated on top of these rich braises and the joy of time and place is reflected on the cover of the oldest Dutch cookbook to make the trip to the New World, which depicts a cheerful kitchen staff kneading dough and readying the meat. Geese and pigs were so much a part of the New Amsterdam street scene that numerous tourists reported the inconvenience to carriages, while still commenting on the heartiness of the vittles.

3 lbs. smoked pork butt
2 cups dried apples, sliced, cored
6 cups chicken broth
2 tablespoons brown sugar
1 onion, sliced

## Dumplings

2 cups flour
1 teaspoon baking soda
1/4 teaspoon salt
2 tablespoons butter, cut into small bits
1 1/2 cups milk
1 egg

 Put the pork in a Dutch oven with water to cover, bring to a boil on the top of the stove, and reduce the heat to a simmer. Continue the simmer for 2 hours, partly covered.

Drain and reserve the meat. Cut the meat into chunks, 2" square, discarding any fat. Return the meat chunks to the Dutch oven, add the apples, broth, brown sugar, and onion and simmer for 20 minutes.

To make eight dumplings combine the flour, salt, and soda. Add the butter and cut it into the flour. Add the eggs and milk and stir thoroughly to make a moist dough. Drop large spoonfuls of dough into the gently simmering Dutch oven. Cover and continue the simmer for 10 minutes. Serve in individual soup bowls. *Serves 4.*

# AMERICAN PORK PIE, CHESHIRE STYLE

Adapted from: Amelia Simmons, *American Cookery*, 1796, p. 116

2 recipes Shortcrust Pastry (see page 50)

1 lb. lean pork

1 lb. fat pork

1 cup onion, chopped

¼ teaspoon nutmeg, ground

salt and pepper to taste

1½ lbs. of pippin apples

1 tablespoon brown sugar (optional)

1 tablespoon fresh sage, chopped (optional)

4 tablespoons butter

½ cup cider

Amelia Simmons' "American Pork Pie" is very much like the English Cheshire Pie that Hannah Glasse offered fifty years earlier in *The Art of Cookery*. The combination of pippins and pork in a sturdy coffin or "pye" was traditional in the Old Country and Amelia simply made it available to "all grades of life."

 Preheat the oven to 375°F. Line a 10" ovenproof pie dish with the pastry and refrigerate.

Grind the pork, lean and fat. Add the onion, nutmeg, and salt and pepper and continue grinding until thoroughly blended.

Peel, core and slice the apples; season the slices with the brown sugar and sage.

Arrange a layer of pork on the bottom of the pastry-lined dish, then a layer of apples, then cover with the remaining pork. Dot the surface with the butter. Pour the cider around the edges. Cover the dish with pastry, and decorate if you wish.

Brush the pie lid with beaten egg and bake for about 1 hour, or until golden brown. May be eaten hot or cold. *Serves 6.*

# OXFORD KATE'S SAUSAGE

Adapted from: Martha Washington's *The Booke of Cookery*, 1749, p.62

The mixing of beef, suet, and pork in a homemade sausage patty, or in this case a finger sausage, was unique to Oxford homemade sausages, and adopted by Martha Washington in her collection of old family memorabilia called *The Booke of Cookery*. The name "Oxford Kate," as used by Martha, referred to the English origin of this recipe, a well-known tavern that was near the gates of the old academic city. American frontiersmen quickly found this "pan sausage" to be tasty and easy to make.

1 lb. lean beef or venison
1 lb. lean pork
½ lb. beef suet fat (alt: pork fatback)
2 tablespoons freshly ground black pepper
2 tablespoons kosher salt
½ teaspooon mace, ground
½ teaspoon cloves, ground
1 tablespoon sage, ground
4 eggs, slightly beaten

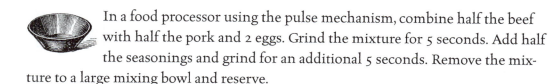

In a food processor using the pulse mechanism, combine half the beef with half the pork and 2 eggs. Grind the mixture for 5 seconds. Add half the seasonings and grind for an additional 5 seconds. Remove the mixture to a large mixing bowl and reserve.

Repeat with the remaining ingredients. Using your hands, combine the two batches to produce a uniform sausage mixture, and follow Martha's directions.

"...temper alltogether with yr hands. & ...roule ym out about ye length & biggness of yr finger. when yu fry ym ye butter must boil in ye pan before you put ym in. when they are pritty browne, take ym up. theyr sauce is mustard."

*Makes 12 finger sausages.*

# Scotched and Colloped Beef

Adapted from: Martha Washington's *The Booke of Cookery*, 1749, p. 45

4 beef steaks, 10 oz. each (alt: venison steaks)
1 cup vinegar
½ cup orange juice
2 cups beef stock
1 cup red wine
1 tablespoon honey
1 tablespoon bourbon whiskey
5 juniper berries, crushed
1 tablespoon fresh parsley, finely chopped
2 tablespoons white breadcrumbs
½ teaspoon nutmeg, ground
½ teaspoon cinnamon, ground
juice of one lemon and juice of one orange,
  strained
3 tablespoons butter

In the days before farm animals were fork tender, the finest taverns near Williamsburg went to great lengths to present palatable meat. In this case the rump or round steak was sliced thinly (*scotched*) and then beaten until tender (*colloped*) and quickly pan fried. The sauce came from the stale bread crumbs used to thicken the reduction in the skillet. This sauce was the specialty of Sir John Nott, in 1723, who wrote cookbooks for the use of roadhouse tavern keepers. If this dish is anything to go by, tavern fare reached a very high standard.

 Trim all the fat and silverside from the steaks. Using a kitchen mallet or the side of a cleaver, beat the steaks, reducing their thickness by half. In a large bowl, add the steaks to the vinegar and orange juice and marinate for one hour. Remove and pat the meat dry. Braise the steaks in a large, heavy skillet in the beef stock and wine at a bare simmer for 20 minutes or until medium rare. Remove and reserve the meat on a warm platter.

Make the sauce by reducing the skillet contents over high heat until one cup remains. Add the honey, whiskey, juniper berries, nutmeg, and cinnamon and simmer for 5 minutes. Add the fruit juices and whisk to combine. Add the bread crumbs.

Remove the pan from the heat, add the butter in small pieces, and whisk to form an emulsion. Add the parsley, salt and pepper to taste, and pour the warm sauce over the collops. *Serves 4.*

# Lobster Bisque

Adapted from: Eliza Smith, *The Compleat Housewife*, 1742, p. 48

Shortly before the American Revolution, lobster had not yet become a "trophy" meal. Instead, it was considered an abundant, reliable food resource, like the crawfish and eel that were everywhere to hand. The books under review here often lump both shellfish together. The fish and lobster stock that Eliza Smith describes is both the basis of the bisque, and the measure of its culinary success today. We use flounder meat and trimmings and other lean white fish to produce a light stock. Eliza also called for "grigs" in the stock, and if you can find these tiny freshwater eels, please add them.

## Fish and Lobster Stock

*4 cups white fish, chunks, using flounder, whiting, and grig*
*2 cups lobster/crayfish shells or shrimp peelings*
*8 cups water*
*¼ teaspoon each ground cloves and ground mace*
*½ teaspoon dried marjoram*
*½ cup onions, chopped*
*salt and pepper*

## Lobster Bisque

*2 cups lobster meat, cooked*
*2 cups fish meat strained from the stock, cleaned of bones or scales*
*6 cups fish and lobster stock*
*1 cup stale bread crumbs*
*8 tablespoons butter, divided*
*4 tablespoons flour*
*lemon slices, for garnish*

 *To make the stock*: Combine the fish meat, trimmings, and lobster shells in a large pot, add the water, spices, and onion and bring to a boil. Simmer for 30 minutes. Strain and reserve the stock. *Makes 6 cups.*

*To Make the Bisque*: Make a white roux from 4 tablespoons of the butter and all of the flour, stirring over very low heat for 10 minutes; remove and reserve. Set the stock to simmer, stirring in the reserved roux until the stock thickens.

Cut up the lobster meat in bite-sized chunks and in a small skillet brown it lightly in the remaining 4 tablespoons of butter, then reserve the meat. Add 1 cup of the stock to the skillet and deglaze the pan, allowing the stock to reduce until it reaches 1 cup. Add the stale bread crumbs and the reserved fish meat, and using the back of a fork, mix the ingredients thoroughly and form small dumplings from the fish mixture.

In a large tureen, place the reserved lobster meat and then pour the hot, thickened stock over. Float the dumplings and garnish with lemon slices. *Serves 4.*

# Merrimack Eel Pie

Adapted from: Hannah Glasse, *The Art of Cookery Made Plain & Easy*, 1805, p. 124

1 lb. fresh eel, sliced (alt: cod/haddock, skin
    removed, boned and cut in strips)
2 cups potatoes, peeled and diced in 1" cubes
3 eggs, hard-boiled
2 cups fresh spinach leaves, washed and
    trimmed
1 onion, finely chopped
olive oil
1 cup heavy cream
1 cup cheese, Gruyere or other, grated
1 lemon, juiced
1 tablespoon English mustard
2 tablespoons parsley, finely chopped
salt and freshly ground black pepper to taste
ground nutmeg to taste
2 tablespoons unsalted butter

In the very old days, when Manchester, New Hampshire, was known as "Derryfield," the month of October was given over to the business of getting and salting eels from the Merrimack River. An early Dutch cookbook of the day, *Der Verstandige Kock* (Amsterdam, 1683) recommends the split eel to be boiled in salted water with sorrel, chervil, and parsley, and then served with butter and vinegar. Hannah Glasse drew on all of this, and recommended a hearty "eel pie" that was the state of the art in 1805. Here is her best version, with an eel substitute of fresh fish, if necessary.

 Preheat the oven to 450°F. Boil the potatoes until tender, about 8 minutes; drain, mash lightly, and reserve. Hard-boil the eggs; peel, quarter and reserve. Steam the spinach for one minute; drain, chop, and dry on towels.

In a small sauté pan gently fry the onion in a little olive oil until soft. Add the cream and bring to a simmer. Remove from the heat, stir in the cheese, lemon juice, mustard and parsley.

In an oblong ovenproof dish, layer the spinach, eel slices, and eggs. Adjust the seasonings with salt, pepper, and nutmeg. Pour the cream over and layer the mashed potatoes on top. Dot the surface with 2 tablespoons of butter and bake for about 30 minutes, or until the surface is golden brown. Cover the dish after 10 minutes. *Serves 4.*

# Planked Shad

Adapted from: Amelia Simmons, *American Cookery*, 1796, p. 6

On the banks of the Schuylkill River, near Philadelphia, planked shad was cooked and eaten for centuries before the process was institutionalized. The taste is unique. General Washington and General Lafayette raved over the fish, but grumbled over the "impossibly fussy" shad bones. They were guests of the Schuylkill Club, named after the Dutch for "hidden river." The Generals owed more to the shad than they wanted to admit because bumper harvests of Connecticut shad are said to have carried their troops through several winters. Long after the Revolutionary War, shad is still a spectacular dish.

1 shad, 4-5 lbs. whole, filleted*, skin on, with interstitial bones removed (*see below)
1 wooden plank for each fillet (18" x 8" x 1" for outdoor barbecue or 13" x 7" x ¼" for oven)
water, as needed to soak the planks for 3 hours
1 slice of bacon for each filet
4 small stainless nails (for outdoor barbecue)
4 tablespoons butter for each fish
1 cup of parsley, chopped
1 lemon, cut in wedges
salt and freshly cracked black pepper over each raw fillet

 *Fillet the fish in the conventional manner, discarding head, spine, and tail. Remove the interstitial bones from each fillet by excising two ½"-wide ribbons of flesh that contain the tiny bones, cutting from nape to tail, twice on the flesh side of each fillet. These two "lines" of bones are located parallel to, and above or below, the midline by approximately 1". Locate the lines of bones on the flesh side of the fillet with your finger before excising with a sharp knife.

For an outdoor barbecue, prepare a fire that will burn as coals for at least one hour. The use of a trench is optional and mostly for large productions. A small fire with 10 lbs. of briquettes on the ground is satisfactory where appropriate. Position the fillets on the planks, one each, skin down, tail down, with four or more nails, and one slice of bacon hanging down. Arrange the planks at a 70° angle to the ground, approximately 18" from the fire. Brush with butter every 5 minutes.

For the kitchen preparation, preheat the oven to 400°F then revert to the broiler setting when the fillets are introduced. Place fillets, skin-side down, one each to a plank with a slice of bacon over. Brush with melted butter and place on the middle rack of the broiler, with a catch pan beneath, for 30 minutes, basting regularly.

Remove from the fire and serve the planks with parsley and lemons. *Serves 6.*

# CORN CHOWDER WITH CLAMS

Adapted from: Amelia Simmons, *American Cookery*, 1800

## CORN STOCK (MAKES 6 CUPS)

*8 corn cobs, kernels scrapped away and reserved*
*1 leek, washed and sliced*
*1 celery rib, sliced*
*3 cloves garlic, minced*
*1 ham hock, smoked (optional)*
*8 cups chicken stock*
*1 bay leaf*
*1 teaspoon dried thyme*
*salt and pepper to taste*

## CHOWDER WITH CLAMS

*½ cup diced bacon*
*1 tablespoon butter, unsalted*
*2 carrots, peeled and diced*
*2 celery ribs, diced*
*1 onion, chopped*
*2 dozen littleneck clams, scrubbed*
*2 cups new potatoes, boiled in skins, quartered*
*6 cups Corn Stock*
*½ cup cream*
*1 teaspoon salt*
*1 teaspoon fresh thyme and parsley, chopped*

The early chefs and cookbook writers were fascinated with corn. The nuance and flavor brought by that native plant led to indigenous polenta, flapjacks, and of course, the first major revision of chowder since an early French sailor put fish to boiling water. In this version, not published until the second edition in 1800, Amelia Simmons summons up a corn stock as the basis of her chowder and proves again that the best cooking is the simple application of fresh ingredients.

*To Make the Corn Stock:* Place all ingredients for the corn stock in a large stock pot. Bring the pot to a boil, stir once, and lower the heat to a simmer. Simmer for 1 hour. Strain the stock and reserve.

*To Make the Chowder:* Fry out the bacon in a Dutch oven, add the butter, and then the carrot, onion, and celery, and cook over moderate heat until soft. Add the clams, potatoes, corn stock, and the reserved corn kernels and bring to a boil. Cover and cook, stirring every 5 minutes until the clams have popped open. Add the cream and adjust the seasonings. Garnish with the thyme and parsley. *Serves 6.*

# ASPARAGUS DINNER ROLLS

Adapted from: Hannah Glasse, *The Art of Cookery Made Plain & Easy*, 1805, p. 35

The Delaware Valley was a center for commercial asparagus production toward the end of the 18th century. Thomas Jefferson grew it at Monticello, and the American Gardener's Calendar of 1806 extolled its use as a wholesome vegetable. From its first European cultivation 800 years earlier, the succulent tips were known as "sperage" or "sperach" which eventually became "asparagus officinalis" by the 16th century. It didn't take long after that for English users to invent the corruption of "sparrowgrass" and that was the name that stuck in the American colonies. This recipe is an advance on the "points of toast" etiquette that was a dining nightmare.

24 fresh asparagus spears
4 tablespoons butter
6 small brioche rolls, 2" x 4", lightly cooked
   (see recipe p. 44)
6 egg yolks
2 cups cream
1 teaspoon ground nutmeg
salt and pepper to taste

 Cut the tops off the rolls and remove most of the crumb. Melt the butter in a small saucepan and brush the rolls, inside and out. Place the rolls on a baking sheet and brown them carefully in a 400°F oven, being careful not to burn.

Trim the asparagus to equal lengths that will leave the spear over the edge of the roll. Lightly steam the asparagus for 5 minutes, not more. Set aside 12 of the best asparagus.

Chop all the extra asparagus bits lightly and reserve. In a saucepan, combine the cream, egg, salt, and nutmeg, and stir over moderate heat until the mixture thickens and begins to boil. Remove from the heat. Add the reserved asparagus.

Spoon the mixture into the bottom half of each roll, dividing the mixture evenly. Place 2 asparagus stalks on the long axis of each stuffed roll. Cover with the lids and serve hot. *Serves 6.*

# SHAKESPEARE'S BEST BREAD

Adapted from: Gervase Markham, *The English HusWife*, 1615, p. 209

6 cups all purpose flour
2 teaspoons salt
1 tablespoon instant rise yeast
   (alt: Nottingham Brewing Yeast—11g.)
2½ cups water, warm

"Your best and principal bread," Gervase Markham wrote in a sympathetic description of the small, tender loaf, leavened with yeast, and called a "manchet." This distinguished it from all the other contemporary breads in Shakespeare's time made from coarsely ground wheat or other grains, with only the roughest particles of bran extracted. The commoner's loaf was leavened with sour dough, if at all. The "goode English hus-wife," on the other hand, saved over a bit of yeast from the weekly brewing which gave her white bread a distinctive appeal that confirmed her family's status.

 In a food processor using the dough blade, combine the salt, 5 cups of flour, and the yeast and process for 5 seconds. With the machine running, slowly add the water, then stop and scrape down the sides of the bowl. Process for 5 seconds further.

The dough will be sticky and too wet to knead by hand. Scrape the dough onto a counter and work in the remaining flour. Place in a large, oiled bowl, cover with plastic wrap and allow the dough to rise for 2 to 3 hours, or overnight if refrigerated.

Turn the dough out on a floured work surface, and divide into 16 equal pieces. Knead and form each piece into a small plump loaf. Place on a peel or baking sheet sprinkled with cornmeal and allow to rise until doubled in size.

Pre-heat the oven to 500°F, including the baking stone, if used. Slide the rolls onto the hot stone. Slash the top of each loaf with a razor, spray the walls of the oven with water, close the oven door, and bake until the rolls are a deep, golden brown. Reverse the manchets once in the oven, to ensure even browning. Takes about 20 minutes.

Remove from the oven and spray again lightly to produce a shiny crust. Cool on wire racks before serving. *Makes 16 rolls.*

# SLAPJACKS FOR ICHABOD CRANE

Adapted from: Amelia Simmons, *American Cookery*, 1796, p. 34

The *Legend of Sleepy Hollow* was Washington Irving's review of the bucolic life along the Hudson River Valley of colonial New York. His hero, Ichabod, was bemused as "soft anticipations stole over his mind of dainty slapjacks, well buttered and garnished with honey or treacle by the dainty little hand of Katrina Van Tassel." Every reader was invited to dream about the nearly magical appeal of cornmeal, manifest in an Indian Slapjack.

*2 cups ground corn meal*
*½ cup flour*
*2 teaspoons baking soda*
*1 cup milk*
*2 tablespoons butter, melted*
*2 tablespoons honey*
*2 eggs, beaten*
*butter to fry*
*maple syrup (alt: honey and treacle)*

 Combine all the dry ingredients in a large bowl. Add the milk, melted butter, eggs, and honey, and beat to form a thick batter.

Heat the frying pan or griddle and add butter, and allow it to foam.

Using a ladle or large spoon, pour approximately ½ cup of batter in the center of the pan, allowing the batter to spread out with a resulting thickness of ¼".

Cook until bubbles appear across the top and the edges begin to take on color. With a large spatula, carefully loosen the slapjack, then in a single motion flip it to cook the other side.

When the second side is done, remove to a platter and keep warm. Serve with dribbled butter and syrup. Three pancakes make a meal. *Makes 6.*

# The Continental Brioche

Adapted from: Martha Washington's *The Booke of Cookery*, 1749, p. 113

3 cups white flour
1 cup whole wheat flour
⅓ cup bran flakes
1 teaspoon salt
1 packet instant yeast (alt: brewer's yeast)
1 teaspoon sugar
1 cup beer, flat
1 egg, slightly beaten
1 cup milk

The Colonials gave the term French bread to this light, enriched bread that we would call "brioche." The eponymous French crusty baguette was a different loaf of bread entirely and would not have found favor on American tables where genteel diners preferred a soft crust. There's another difference between French and American yeast baking. The Americans (and the English) were a nation of brewers and used brewer's yeast. The French were vintners and used sourdough, fermented from grapes. Use brewer's yeast for its distinct flavor, if you can get it, and add a cup of whole wheat flour and a shake of bran flakes to the white flour for this colonial French loaf.

 In a large bowl mix the flours, bran flakes, and salt. In a small bowl combine the yeast, sugar, and flat beer and allow to proof for 5 minutes. Add the egg and the milk to the yeast mixture, then pour into the flour and mix well. Do not knead.

Cover the mixed dough with a wet cloth and allow it to rise for 1½ hours, then gently deflate. Form the dough into 2 small loaves and allow to rise for another hour.

Bake in a 400°F oven for 45 minutes, or until golden brown. Remove the loaves, brush the tops with milk, and cool before eating. *Makes 2 small loaves.*

# MOLASSES GINGERBREAD

Adapted from: Amelia Simmons, *American Cookery*, 1796, p. 123

The history of gingerbread is as old as the Greeks (called *melitates*) and as recent as the corner bakery. The first *American Cookery* had five recipes for the bread, some of which did not contain ginger at all! This version uses a first boil molasses, the table grade, which was a Colonial substitute for the treacle that had become the English sweetener of choice. Significantly, it was just following this time that Colonial cooks last used pearl ash (made from wood fire ashes) as a leavening agent, and the new baking soda, used here, became the predominant choice.

½ teaspoon cinnamon, powdered
½ teaspoon nutmeg, ground
¼ teaspoon coriander, ground
½ teaspoon salt
2 teaspoons baking soda
2 cups all-purpose flour
1 cup molasses
½ cup butter
½ cup milk with 1 tablespoon of vinegar
1 egg, beaten

In a large bowl, combine the dry ingredients. In a small pan over moderate heat, warm the butter and the molasses until the butter is melted.

In a large measuring cup, combine the butter mixture, the sour milk, and the beaten egg, and pour over the dry ingredients. Mix well and pour the batter into a greased and floured cake tin and bake at 350°F for 25 minutes.

The gingerbread will rise and then sink again when removed from the oven. Cut into squares and cool completely before serving. *Serves 8.*

# Marzipan Tea Cakes

Adapted from: Martha Washington's *The Booke of Cookery*, 1749, p. 324

1½ pounds blanched almonds
3 large egg whites
¼ teaspoon salt
2 teaspoons vanilla extract
1 teaspoon almond extract
4 cups powdered sugar

In the time and place when afternoon tea was a reflective moment, marzipan, as a confectioner's triumph was everywhere on display. Sometimes called "marchpane," the confection achieved icon status in Martha Washington's mother's time. Hostesses formed the almond paste into small candy shapes such as triangles or hearts. Most commonly, marzipan paste is used to cover the traditional Christmas fruit cake, which is then slowly eaten during the following months.

 In a food processor grind the almonds to a powder and reserve. Whisk the egg whites to stiff peaks, then add the salt and extracts. With a spatula, stir the almond extract into the egg whites.

Transfer the mixture to a clean bowl and sift in 3 cups of the sugar, one cup at a time, stirring. Knead this paste with your hand, adding the additional one cup of sugar as necessary to form a smooth pliable dough. Turn the dough out onto a work surface, divide it into quarters, wrap in plastic, and chill overnight as the dough becomes a paste.

Allow the paste to reach room temperature. Then, using a sugar-dusted rolling pin, roll out the paste to a rectangle with a thickness of 1½". Cut into the desired shapes. Place the shapes on a foil-lined baking sheet and decorate as desired, with food coloring, cloves, or wooden toothpicks. Dry the "cakes" overnight. *Makes 8.*

# BRESCIA CHEESECAKE

Adapted from: Susannah Carter, *The Frugal Housewife*, 1772, pg. 164

One of the 18th century's gilded globetrotters, Lady Mary Montagu, was Britain's Ambassador at large. While her husband played at horses and international intrigue in old Constantinople, Lady Montague went on and on in her diaries and correspondence about many worthy causes, not the least of which was her reputation for creating the best cheesecake in all of northern Italy. "They are receiv'd with universal applause and I have reason to believe [they] will preserve my memory even to Future ages." That's a cheesecake to be proud of, and Susannah Carter trotted out the standard of that day, refined here for contemporary tastes.

1 prebaked graham cracker crumb shell
1 packet gelatin, unflavored
½ cup cold water
3 8-oz. packages full fat cream cheese
1¼ cups white sugar
1 5-oz. can evaporated milk
⅓ cup Amaretto (almond liqueur)
½ cup ground almonds
2 teaspoons almond extract
1 teaspoon lemon juice
1 teaspoon vanilla extract
1 cup whipping cream

Chill the cracker crumb shell. Dissolve the gelatin in the cold water, whisking well.

In a large bowl, beat the cream cheese and sugar until creamy. Gradually add the evaporated milk, the liqueur, the ground almond, the almond extract, the lemon juice, and the vanilla extract. Beat until light and fluffy. Trickle in the gelatin, mixing it until thoroughly blended.

In a separate bowl, whip the cream to the point of soft peaks, and then gently fold the whipped cream into the almond mixture.

Pour the almond batter into the shell and chill it overnight. Top with extra whipped cream, if desired, and decorate with almond slivers if desired. *Serves 12.*

# Getting Elected is a Piece of Cake

Adapted from: Amelia Simmons, *American Cookery*, 1796, p. 43

2 packages of instant yeast (alt: brewers' yeast)

½ cup warm water

3½ cups unbleached flour

½ cup warm milk

1 teaspoon salt

½ teaspoon each of nutmeg, cloves, and mace

1 cup raisins

½ cup walnuts, chopped

1 stick unsalted butter

¾ cup brown sugar

3 eggs

## Glaze

1 cup confectioner's sugar

¼ teaspoon vanilla extract

3 tablespoons milk, scalded

In the fervent atmosphere of newly independent America, elections were an event worth celebrating. No other nation in the world allowed its citizens such power, and a grand cake was an important part of the festivities. Amelia Simmons, the number one drum thumper for America in those days, was quick to see the need for a recipe for "Election Cake" so everyone could celebrate the winner. Amelia's great cake called for 30 quarts of flour and 10 pounds of butter, intended to serve all the town's celebrants. We have adjusted the calls for a family feast.

 Combine the warm water and milk in a small bowl and proof the yeast. In a large bowl combine 1 cup of flour with the yeast mixture and stir well. Cover this "sponge" and leave it to rise for about 45 minutes or longer.

In a large bowl, combine the rest of the flour, the salt, and spices. Reserve. Chop the raisins and mix with the nuts and add to the sponge. Cream the butter and brown sugar until blended; add the eggs and beat until thoroughly combined. Add the butter mixture to the sponge and stir once. Add the reserved flour and spices to the sponge.

Butter a bundt pan and pour the batter in. Cover and let rise in a warm place until the dough reaches the top, about one hour. Bake in 350°F oven for 45 to 50 minutes. Cool the cake for 15 minutes, then turn it out on a rack.

For the glaze, stir the confectioner's sugar, the vanilla, and 3 tablespoon of scalded milk until a uniform consistency is reached. Spread this on top of the cake and let it drizzle down the sides. *Makes 12 slices.*

# Raspberry Cream

Adapted from: Amelia Simmons, *American Cookery*, 1796, p. 32

This dish is the brightest in a long line of trifles or "fools," something light-hearted to eat after the serious business of an 18th century dinner. A simple combination of fruit and cream focused one's attention on the quality of the ingredients and left the hostess free to enjoy herself. Gooseberries and raspberries were the favorites, and trifles, in one form or another, appeared in all the cookbooks of this time. Modern pasteurized cream has little flavor or richness compared to the resources Amelia Simmons had at her disposal; use English clotted cream if available.

2 lbs. fresh raspberries
1 tablespoon Drambuie liqueur (optional)
2 pints fresh clotted cream
powdered sugar to taste

 Wash the raspberries and pat dry. With a metal spoon mash the raspberries against the side of bowl, causing them to spill their juice into the bowl.

Add the liqueur and stir to combine.

Over a bowl of ice, whip the cream until thick and unctuous.

With a spatula, blend the cream into the crushed fruit, sweeten with the sugar to taste, and refrigerate for an hour.

Pile the cream into tall glasses, garnish with whole berries and a sprig of mint.
*Serves 4.*

# CARROT PUDDING

Adapted from: Eliza Smith, *The Compleat Housewife*, 1742, p. 137

## SHORTCRUST PASTRY

1¼ cups flour

½ teaspoon salt

1 stick butter, cut into small pieces

6 tablespoons ice water

## CARROT "PUDDING"

1 cup grated carrots

¼ cup white bread crumbs, disced

1 egg white

½ cup whipping cream

4 tablespoons unsalted butter, melted

1½ tablespoons brandy

1 tablespoon rose water

4 tablespoons sugar

½ teaspoon nutmeg, grated

Writing for an English audience but selling the books in America before the Revolution, a lot of archaic terminology was passed about, and then forgotten. "Pudding" usually signified the course offered at the end of the meal, in the place of what we now recognize as dessert. And so pies, cakes, and tarts could all qualify as "pudding" in that sense. In this case, Eliza Smith baked her carrot filling in a shortcrust pastry and made a dessert pie.

 *To Make the Shortcrust Pastry*: Sift the flour and salt onto a work surface. Make a well in the center and add the butter pieces. Cut them into the flour and add the ice water gradually until a paste is formed. Hammer the dough with a rolling pin or until it is smooth, then cover and refrigerate for an hour or more.

*To Make the Carrot Pudding*: Line a 10" pie pan with the pastry. Mix all the filling ingredients together and spread in the pie pan. Bake in a 350°F oven until the filling is puffed and the top nicely colored. Serve warm or cold. *Serves 6.*

# Warden's Marmalet

Adapted from: Martha Washington's *The Booke of Cookery*, 1749 p. 99, p. 275

**M**armalade or *marmalet* was a culinary term generally used in a sense synonymous with jam in the Colonial period, and was made from every imaginable fruit from citrus to apples, worldwide. Martha Washington's keepsake recipe book had recipes for all of these, and in particular dwelt on the splendid Warden's pear, the sentimental favorite of a hundred pear varieties that were brought over and given a chance in the orchards of America. This marmalade, or jam, can be used as though it were a very thick honey, or spread, on toast or even slapjacks.

6 pounds of firm ripe pears, peeled and cut in half lengthwise
2 cups sugar
1 tablespoon cinnamon
4 teaspoons lemon peel, finely grated
3 cups pineapple juice, unsweetened

 Cut away and discard the stems, skins, and cores of the pears. Grate the pears on a four-sided kitchen grater; then combine the pear pulp, the sugar, cinnamon, and the pineapple juice in a large saucepan.

Bring to a boil, reduce the heat, and simmer uncovered for 45 minutes or until the mixture holds its own shape. Stir frequently and skim off any foam that rises to the surface.

Stir in the lemon peel and simmer 2 minutes longer. Remove from the heat and pour into sterilized, sealable jars. *Makes 2 cups.*

# CHERRY WINE

Adapted from: Martha Washington's *The Booke of Cookery*, 1749 p. 378

Take a good quantety of spring water
    and let it boy halfe an houre.
then beat 4 pound of raysons, clean pickt & washed,
    & beat them in a morter to pas .
then put them in an earthen pot, & pour on ym
    12 quarts of this water boyling hot,
& put to it 6 quarts of ye Juice of cheries,
    & put in the pulp & scins of ye cheries
after they are strayned. & let all these steep together,
    close covered, 3 days.
then strayn all out & let it stand 3 or 4 hours to settle.
    take of ye cleerest, & run
Ye rest thorough a Jelley bagg. then put ye Juice up
    into bottles & stop them up close,
& set them in the sand.

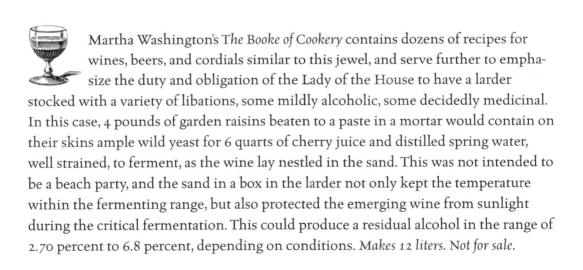 Martha Washington's *The Booke of Cookery* contains dozens of recipes for wines, beers, and cordials similar to this jewel, and serve further to emphasize the duty and obligation of the Lady of the House to have a larder stocked with a variety of libations, some mildly alcoholic, some decidedly medicinal. In this case, 4 pounds of garden raisins beaten to a paste in a mortar would contain on their skins ample wild yeast for 6 quarts of cherry juice and distilled spring water, well strained, to ferment, as the wine lay nestled in the sand. This was not intended to be a beach party, and the sand in a box in the larder not only kept the temperature within the fermenting range, but also protected the emerging wine from sunlight during the critical fermentation. This could produce a residual alcohol in the range of 2.70 percent to 6.8 percent, depending on conditions. *Makes 12 liters. Not for sale.*

# CRANBERRY KETCHUP

Adapted from: Amelia Simmons, *American Cookery*, 1796, p. 18

Only the old "foodies" know that "ketchup" is not an American invention, and in the early days of its development it was neither sweet nor red. When British sailors brought the recipe home from China it was brimming with anchovies and soy sauce, and the 18th century recipes for adaptations of ketchup in Great Britain used kidney beans, mushrooms, and even walnuts. It is only natural that the Colonists used their new fruit, the cranberry, for homemade sauce. It was, however, the American T.J. Heinz who sold a tomato version in a unique and stylish bottle that captured the world's attention in 1890, and sold 5 million bottles by 1905.

1 lb. fresh cranberries
½ cup onions, finely chopped
½ cup water
½ cup apple cider
1 cup sugar
¾ teaspoon cinnamon, ground
¾ teaspoon allspice, ground
¾ teaspoon salt
¾ teaspoon celery seed
½ teaspoon freshly ground black pepper

 Wash the cranberries. In a large saucepan combine the cranberries with the onion and water and bring to a boil. Reduce the heat to low, cover, and simmer for 10 minutes.

Purée the cranberry mixture, return to the saucepan and add the remaining ingredients. Bring to a boil and cook uncovered for 15 minutes until most of the liquid is evaporated. Continue stirring, and do not allow the mixture to scorch.

Adjust the seasoning with salt and black pepper. If not used immediately as an accompaniment to wild game or poultry, the ketchup may be canned in sterilized jars in an approved manner. *Makes 2 cups.*

# TO MAKE VINEGAR

Adapted from: Gervasse Markham, *The English Huswife*, 1615, p. 133

*11 gallons of beer, unpasteurized*
*4 tablespoons cream of tartar, for fining*
*2 gallon crock pot with spigot*

The good housewife not only brewed the beer for the household in Markham's day, but also made the potions for the sick and the vinegar for all purposes. Vinegar was an essential ingredient in pickling, but was also valued for sickroom cleanliness. The basic idea is that a quantity of brewed beer, or for that matter wine, left in the sunlight will go sour, and with or without the vast quantity of 500 damask roses, as called for in this original, the sugars and oils will precipitate out, leaving pure vinegar.

Add the beer to the crock pot with a secure fitting lid or garden stone to cover. Place the crock pot in a refrigerator, or in winter weather in a corner of the garden with temperatures always below 50°F.

Allow the beer to lose its carbonation yet be protected from wild yeasts and insects for thirty days. Add the cream of tartar or other fining agent to the beer and stir to combine, then continue the conversion for thirty more days.

Strain the vinegar and store in clean, corked or capped bottles. This makes about two pints of country vinegar with a shelf life of 60 days, depending on conditions. *Makes 2 bottles.*

## Chapter Two

# Domestic Goddesses
## of the New Century

Mary Randolph, *The Virginia Housewife*, 1824

Eliza Leslie, *Seventy Five Receipts for Pastry, Cakes and Sweetmeats*, 1828

Eliza Leslie, *Directions for Cookery*, 1837

Two talented women wrote important American cookbooks in the early years of the nineteenth century. The first was Mary Randolph. She was the daughter of a great house, a cousin to Thomas Jefferson, and moved amongst the leading families of Virginia. Her talent as a cook was recognized early but it was only toward the end of a tumultuous life that she was persuaded to record her recipes in *The Virginia Housewife*, the first Southern cookbook, published in 1824.

The second, Eliza Leslie, lived in Philadelphia and, like Mary Randolph, was a reluctant cookbook author. Although it was cookbooks that made her living, Miss Leslie would rather have been writing fiction. She was inclined to stoutness that was understandable given her profession and also apparently ascerbic, yet Miss Leslie wrote in elegant prose. Her *Directions for Cookery*, published 1837, sold at least 150,000 copies in its publishing history.

Mary Randolph came from a tradition of gracious living. After her death it was said that she had spent three fortunes in cooking. She had married a first cousin, David, and the couple set up house in a fine tobacco plantation home where they wined and dined the best of society, including Thomas Jefferson, whose daughter married Mary's brother.

Mary had learned the art of housekeeping from her mother and her early influences came from English authors such as Hannah Glasse and Maria Rundell. She had a fine palate and was careful to follow Hannah Glasse's advice not to overcook vegetables. She offered Southern specialties too: "Barbecued Shoate" or "Pig, Ochra and Tomatoes," "Gumbo," a beaten biscuit called "Apoquinimic cakes," catfish and a dish of field peas were given a place in the pages of *The Virginia Housewife*. She was aware also of the latest fashions; she had a recipe for "maccaroni" (one of Thomas Jefferson's favorites), a very early Italian polenta, and her book contained 12 uses for the tomato. The tomato had not yet won widespread acceptance by the American public, but Thomas Jefferson was a big fan and perhaps it was from him that Mary learned to enjoy tomato ketchup, tomato soy, and tomato marmalade.

She went French with *a la modes* and *en daubes* and acknowledged the English influence with receipts for an English plum pudding, crumpets, and custards. She even gave directions for cooking curry and a Spanish recipe for the chilled tomato and garlic soup called "Gazpacho."

Although she made extravagant use of costly ingredients, Mary Randolph never gave way to excess. Good taste was, in fact, apparent in her presentations.

> "A dinner justly calculated for the company and
> consisting for the greater part of small articles, cor-
> rectly prepared and neatly served up, will make a
> much more pleasing appearance to the sight and
> give a far greater gratification to the appetite, than

a table loaded with food and from the multiplicity of dishes, unavoidably neglected in the preparation and served up cold." From the introduction to *The Virginia Housewife*, 1824.

Life did not always smile on the Randolphs. When David was removed from office in 1808, impoverishment followed. The couple gave up the mansion and Mary, undaunted, decided to open a boarding house. It was a bold step for someone in her position, but an obvious one for a talented cook who was not afraid of hard work and who was determined to take care of her family.

*The Virginia Housewife* was an immediate success when it appeared in 1824. A second edition of the book came out in 1825, and she was working on a third when she died in January 1828.

Miss Eliza Leslie covered very different ground in her home market of Philadelphia. She knew early on that she wanted to write, but the early death of her father obliged the Leslie women to take in boarders. Perhaps it was in an attempt to improve her cooking that she attended Mrs. Goodfellow's cooking school in Philadelphia, which was the first in the country. *Seventy Five Receipts for Pastry, Cakes and Sweetmeats* was a collection of recipes from the school and appeared not long after.

In her preface to the book, Eliza waved a patriotic flag that made it clear hers was an American cookbook.

> "There is frequently much difficulty in following directions in English and French cookery books, not only from their want of explicitness, but from the difference in the fuel, fireplaces and cooking utensils… many of the European receipts are so complicated and laborious that our female cooks are afraid to undertake the arduous task of making anything from them."

Her own recipes were a model of clarity; each was separately titled and listed ingredients at the beginning. At the time, this was an innovation.

The American market was flooded with French chefs fleeing the revolution in France. Thomas Jefferson had managed to capture one of the finest, Julien Honore, to work for him at the newly constructed White House, but this embrace of French culture was seen by some as unpatriotic for the young country that had been founded on anti-royalist sympathies.

Eliza herself seemed to turn coat in 1832 when she published a translation of a French cookbook, and it was not until 1837 that she produced a volume of original recipes. *Directions for Cookery* was her most famous cookbook, although even here she flirted with French touches to otherwise good American cookery. Fanciful floral decorations on a jellied beef a la mode were conspicuously out of place. Still, apart from occasional lapses into excess, her recipes worked and were a definite step forward from the terseness of Amelia Simmons and the breezy assurance of Susannah Carter. Eliza Leslie was writing for a market of young women who were setting up house for the first time and she did not assume prior knowledge; a novice could follow her recipes successfully. Cookbooks in the future followed this lead.

In later years, Eliza Leslie's works were reprinted in combined and retitled formats as her publishers capitalized on her success. She became a well-known figure and started to write for an increasingly middle class and genteel audience, who did not want to learn the ground rules of basic cookery. Instead, they needed help in selecting a dinner party menu or how to preserve an oil painting or launder a satin ribbon. Even though Miss Leslie's cookbooks expanded to write about such matters, her recipes continued to be popular and increasingly celebrated the diversity of American cookery with recipes for "Kentucky Sweet Cake," "Carolina Grits," "Backwoods Pot Pie" and other regional specialties. With the works of these two fine writers, American cookbook writing had come of age.

# Old Dominion Glazed Ham

Adapted from: Mary Randolph, *The Virginia Housewife*, 1824, p. 49

When the Ambassadors of France and Belgium sat down for dinner at Monticello in 1802, President Thomas Jefferson assured them that this smoked ham was the pride of Virginia, and easily the best companion to the Chateau Lafitte, 1785 Grand Cru, that he intended to serve. We have added the sweet/hot glazing of the chipotle pepper, quenched by the bread crumbs that Jefferson's cousin Mary Randolph always called for. If your Grand Cru cellar has run dry, serve with champagne.

1 Smithfield ham, smoked (12 lbs. or more)

## Old Dominion Glaze

1 cup raspberry preserves

2 tablespoons butter, melted

2 tablespoons white wine vinegar

2 chipotle peppers in adobo sauce (alt: 2 tbsp. minced ginger)

3 garlic cloves, minced

1 tablespoon black pepper

4 cups browned bread crumbs

Scrap away any excess mold from the hard skin of the ham, then soak the ham for 3 days, changing water daily to reduce the salt. Boil the ham for 1 hour, then remove, drain and pat dry.

With a sharp knife remove the skin, and beneath it slice away all but ¼" of the subcutaneous fat over the meaty part of the ham. Mix all of the glaze ingredients, then spread evenly over the superior aspect of the ham. Sprinkle the bread crumbs evenly over the ham, add the stock and Madeira and bake in a 375°F oven for 3 to 4 hours, at 30 minutes per pound, or until you reach an internal temperature of 150°F.

Remove the ham and arrange on a carving platter. Allow 30 minutes for the ham to cool, then carve into thin slices and serve on warmed plates with vegetables. *Serves 10.*

# PAN ROASTED DUCK BREASTS WITH HUCKLEBERRY

Adapted from: Eliza Leslie, *Directions for Cookery*, 1837, p. 149

*4 duck breasts, oven ready, bone out*
*2 tablespoons fresh thyme, chopped*
*4 tablespoons unsalted butter*
*2 tablespoons peanut oil*
*salt and pepper to taste*
*2 shallots, diced*
*1 cup port wine*
*1 cup beef stock (alt: duck stock)*
*1 cup huckleberries (alt: blueberries)*

The annual wild duck migration in the fall was an occasion for unrestrained harvesting, bringing millions of birds to the Atlantic shoreline. In the earliest days the birds were netted or stunned with cannon like weapons known as punt guns. With the development of better firearms, the taking of wildfowl and shorebirds for sale became a full-blown industry and eventually a national disgrace. By the time of Eliza Leslie's book, the development of the percussion cap had made shotgunning for ducks a gentleman's pastime, and produced many happy opportunities for family repasts employing the abundant and savory wild ducks as entrée. Today's wild duck populations are quite volatile, and domestic ducks are recommended here.

 Score the duck skin, salt and pepper the breasts, scatter the thyme leaves over the meat, then wrap each breast in plastic wrap and refrigerate at least one hour or overnight.

Preheat the broiler with a rack in the top third of the oven. Using a large sauté pan, add the peanut oil and ½ the butter over medium-high heat. When the foam subsides, over moderate heat, brown all four duck breasts skin-side down at the same time, until golden. Do not turn. Reserve the sauté pan and its oils. Remove the breasts to an oven dish, and place skin side up under the broiler for another 7 to 10 minutes, or until the flesh is opaque. When done, remove and reserve the duck breasts in a warm place, covered.

Using the same sauté pan, add the shallots, port wine, and beef stock and deglaze the pan over high heat, allowing the stock and wine to reduce to 2 tablespoons. Add the huckleberries, and simmer over low heat for 15 minutes. Remove from the heat, and serve the sauce over the duck breasts. *Serves 4.*

# LONDON'S BEST CURRY POWDER

Adapted from: Eliza Leslie, *Directions for Cookery*, 1837, p. 146

During the reign of Queen Victoria, all English subjects became quite accustomed to the exotic foods of India, particularly curry, and London merchants were quick to fill the American orders when supplies were available. Colonists, on the other hand, were a self-reliant lot and rather than pay the top price, they developed the custom of grinding their own curry powder. When a packet of London's Best was not on hand, here is the way Eliza Leslie ground her own curry powder and served up chicken curry, two generations after American Independence.

## CURRY POWDER

2 tablespoons powdered ginger

1 tablespoon ground turmeric

1 teaspoon freshly ground black pepper

½ teaspoon mace

½ teaspoon cloves, ground

6 cardamom seeds

¼ teaspoon cayenne pepper (or to taste)

1 teaspoon salt

## ELIZA'S BEST EAST INDIAN CURRY

2 chickens, skinned, boned, and cut into
    spoon-sized pieces

4 tablespoons curry powder, London's Best
    if available

1 cup onions, chopped

1 garlic clove

4 tablespoons peanut oil

2 tablespoons flour

1 cup unsweetened yogurt or sour cream

1 cup chicken stock

4 tablespoons lemon juice

garnish with fresh cilantro, chutney and
    fried bananas

 To *Make Curry Powder*: Combine all the ingredients in a mortar or spice mill and grind to a powder. *Makes 4 tablespoons.*

To *Make Indian Curry*: In a large sauté pan soften the onions and garlic in the oil, then add the curry powder and stir until it forms a thick purée or paste. Reserve.

Dust the chicken pieces with flour and in a separate skillet brown them lightly in oil until golden, about 10 minutes. To the skillet add the stock, yogurt, and the curry paste; stir well until blended. Cover and simmer slowly until the chicken is cooked.

Add the lemon juice and cilantro, adjust the seasonings and serve over hot rice with the garnish. *Serves 8.*

# SALMAGUNDI

Adapted from: Mary Randolph, *The Virginia Housewife*, 1824, p. 153

### SALMAGUNDI CHICKEN SALAD

2 cups of lettuce leaves, torn in bits

⅓ cup green beans, cooked

8 cherry tomatoes

2 cups chicken breast meat, cooked, skin
    removed, cut in bite-sized pieces

½ cup fresh grapes, green

1 orange, peeled and cut into sections

3 eggs, hard-boiled

3 tablespoons toasted almonds

3 tablespoons raisins

1 can anchovy fillets

4 radishes, sliced

12 spring onions

3 gherkin pickles, sliced

### DRESSING

1 cup orange juice

3 tablespoons orange zest, diced

6 oz. olive oil

2 oz. red wine vinegar

1 tablespoon prepared mustard

salt and pepper to taste

The measure of Mary Randolph's sense of style and vision is difficult to exaggerate. This "chicken salad" has all the characteristics of the "light and modern" food so loudly demanded of today's cuisine, and it obtained popular success and notoriety in its day while lugging around a name like an unhappy lizard.

In a large glass serving bowl, layer the ingredients beginning with the lettuce, green beans, tomatoes, and chicken. Follow with the fruit and wedges of hard-boiled eggs. Arrange the onions, radishes, gherkins, and anchovies on top, and scatter with raisins and almonds.

Combine all dressing ingredients. Pour the dressing over the salad, but do not toss. Serve at once. *Serves 6.*

# CHRISTMAS GOOSE PYE

Adapted from: Eliza Leslie, *Directions for Cookery*, 1837 p. 153

One hundred and fifty years ago the kitchen process of boning a goose or chicken was the best way to bring all the meat and flavors to the table whether in a galatine or ballotine, or in this most spectacular three-in-one combination, the "Christmas Pye." The boning is done with an initial incision down the spine of each bird, and then free-form whittling with a small knife around the inside pieces. Cut off and discard all wings at the shoulder. In the end you have a collection of bones on one side, to discard, and two meat fat and skin pillow cases on the other ready for stuffing. This presentation has one added attraction in the form of a gorgeous pastry shell. It is served by carving straight across, like a loin of beef, only more glamorous!

## THE PASTRY

9 cups flour

3 tablespoons salt

8 oz. butter, cut into bits and refrigerated

8 egg yolks plus ice water to fill to 2 cups

1 egg white

1½ cups lard, softened (alt: vegetable shortening)

## THE PYE FILLING

1 small goose, boned and open down the back

1 small chicken, boned and open down the back

1 small pork loin, 1½ lbs. (optional: marinated)

2 cups smoked ham chunks and slices

6 tablespoons melted butter

1 teaspoon each of mace, nutmeg, sage, salt and pepper

*To Make the Pastry:* Chill a food processor bowl, then using the dough hook process 4 cups of flour and the salt. With the machine running, add the chilled butter, one bit at a time. Then continue with the machine running and add the egg yolks in water and the softened lard, stopping as necessary to scrap down the sides. Work in batches if necessary. Gradually add the remaining flour to form a dough, then wrap and refrigerate the dough 2 hours to overnight.

*To Make the Pye:* Select a large hinged adjustable tart ring with 2" sides, set to approximately 12" diameter. Place the ring on an oiled baking sheet, and oil the interior of the ring. Line the bottom and sides of the ring with buttered wax paper. Roll out the pastry to ⅜" thickness and cut and affix one circle for the bottom, and one or more panels for the sides with at least 1" overlap on the edges. Brush the edges with the beaten egg white and pinch to seal. Roll out and reserve the remaining pastry for the lid.

Salt and pepper the three meats, both inside and out, and rub the spices onto both sides of the chicken. Place the loin inside the chicken and fold over the loose ends. Place the folded chicken inside the goose and fold as before. Place the stuffed goose inside the pastry, fill the gaps with the smoked ham, pour the butter over all, and secure with a pastry lid. Cut two steam holes in the lid, and decorate with pastry shapes.

Cover with foil and bake in a pre-heated 375°F oven for 2½ to 3 hours until the internal temperature is 160°F. Remove and cool, then decant before carving. *Serves 8.*

# GUMBO

Adapted from: Mary Randolph, *The Virginia Housewife*, 1824, p. 81

The modern dish "gumbo" is named after its principal and necessary ingredient "akimgumbo," a West African word for the flavorful green seedpods that lend their distinctive texture and flavor to the dish. After that, there are almost no limits as to the contents of great gumbo, although the modern dish always begins with a rich, mahogany brown roux, traditionally made from flour and lard. Mary Randolph said it all in three recipes on the same page "Okra and Tomatoes," "Gumbo—A West India Dish" and "Pepper Pot."

## THE ROUX

3 tablespoons flour
1 tablespoon peanut oil

## THE GUMBO

3 cups okra, washed, trimmed and chopped
3 cups onions, chopped
3 cups, celery, chopped
3 peppers: 1 green, 1 red, and 1 yellow, chopped
2 jalapeno peppers, seeded and chopped
2 cups chicken, cut into bite-sized pieces,
    fat discarded
2 cups link sausage, cut into 1" sections
2 cups shrimp, deveined and peeled
8 cups chicken stock (alt: add cups white wine)
2 cups tomatoes, peeled and chopped
¼ cup Tabasco Sauce
2 bay leaves
½ teaspoon cayenne pepper
1 lemon sliced
filé powder served individually

 In a large heavy Dutch oven over low heat, make the roux by heating the oil over low heat and mixing in the flour, stirring constantly until the flour takes on a dark brown color and the roux smells like popcorn. Add the onions, peppers, and celery and let them sweat in the roux. Add chicken and chilies and cook for about 5 minutes. Add the sausages, the tomatoes, the Tabasco, bay leaves, and cayenne. Add the stock and incorporate with the roux.

Simmer over gentle heat for one hour, stirring from time to time. Add the shrimp and lemons about 15 minutes before dinner. Adjust the seasonings and serve over rice, with the filé powder sprinkled over each bowl. *Serves 8.*

# Redsnapper Caveach

Adapted from: Mary Randolph, *The Virginia Housewife*, 1824 p. 64

6 red snapper fillet portions, skin on, cut in
    slivers "as thick as your hand"
½ cup olive oil
3 onions, sliced
1 teaspoon coriander seeds
1 tablespoon peppercorns, green
¼ cup orange zest
1 garlic clove, minced
2 red peppers, cored, seeded, and sliced
¾ cup dry white wine
½ cup orange and lemon juice mixed
6 Roma tomatoes, drained and cubed
salt and pepper to taste
2 tablespoons chopped cilantro

Pickled herring, salmon gravlax, and soused bluefish were all familiar methods of bringing the bright taste of fresh fish and subtle seasonings to the table as an appetizer in the days before modern refrigeration techniques were available. "To caveach fish" as described by Mary Randolph is to have the benefits of both a pan-fried fillet and the savory flavor notes of onions and vinegar. In this adaptation, the peppers and tomatoes that were becoming part of the standard repertoire are added for contrast, and the splendid firm white-fleshed red snapper, although not available in those early markets, is brought in for its texture.

Heat 3 tablespoons of the oil in a large skillet and cook the fish, skin side down, for about 3 minutes or until the skin is crisp. Remove and reserve the fish slices. Add the remaining oil and cook the onions until soft. Add the coriander seed, peppercorns, zest, garlic, and peppers, and cook gently for 5 minutes, stirring. Add the wine, fruit juices, and tomatoes and simmer, stirring for 10 minutes, and cool.

Transfer the fish to a shallow glass or ceramic bowl, cover with the wine and seasonings mixture, and chill overnight, covered. Drain and serve the fish at room temperature scattered with chopped cilantro, as an appetizer. *Serves 6.*

# Salmon Papillon

Adapted from: Eliza Leslie, *Directions For Cookery*, 1837, p. 45

Eliza Leslie did as much to advance the standard of cookbooks as anyone in 19th century America. As her style matured she insisted on listing the ingredients first, and then brought imagination and dedication to publicizing the brilliant curriculum she had learned as a student at Mrs. Goodfellow's exclusive cooking school in Philadelphia. At this stage, cooking was in vogue in the big cities, and you will notice here the "en papillon" treatment, together with a sensitivity to the epicurean adventure that animates her second book, *Directions for Cookery*.

## Mrs. Goodfellow's Fish Sauce

1 can anchovies with oil
¼ cup shallots, chopped fine
2 tablespoons prepared horseradish
½ teaspoon ground cloves
½ lemon cut in thin slices
12 black peppercorns
2 cups Madeira wine

## Salmon en Papillon

4 sheets of oven parchment, 12" x 12" cut into heart-shaped rounds
2 tablespoons butter for treating the paper (alt: non-stick spray)
4 salmon steaks 1½" thick (alt: similar fillet sections)
2 tablespoons melted butter
salt and freshly cracked black pepper

*To Make the Fish Sauce:*
Combine all ingredients in a saucepan, and simmer over medium heat, stirring regularly, until the liquid is reduced to the desired consistency. Strain and serve over the salmon. Makes ⅔ cup.

*To Make the Salmon:* Lay out the paper on a working surface, and butter the paper on both sides. Season the steaks with salt and pepper, and put a pat of butter in the middle of each steak. Lay a steak on each paper. Begin at the bottom of the heart and crimp the paper carefully around the edges until the final crimp at the "V" of the heart. Arrange the papillotes on a rack on a broiler pan and send to the broiler of an oven; high broil for 12 to 15 minutes. The paper will puff up, but should be slashed open to reveal its bouquet only to the diner. Spoon a dash of "Anchovy Fish Sauce" on the opened steak. *Serves 4.*

# GASPACHO

Adapted from: Mary Randolph, *The Virginia Housewife*, 1824 p. 89

9 tomatoes, peeled, seeded, and chopped

1 onion, peeled and chopped

3 garlic cloves, finely minced

1 cucumber, peeled, seeded, and chopped

1 green pepper, stemmed, seeded, and
   chopped fine

6 tablespoons red wine vinegar

6 tablespoons olive oil

2 tablespoons prepared mustard

1 cup breadcrumbs, whole wheat

2 teaspoons salt

black pepper to taste

It has been established that Mary Randolph was in regular contact with her sister living in Spain during the early years of the 19th century, and they traded recipes. The Iberian recipes for tasty leftovers (*ropa vieja*) and for a beef and pork stew (*ollo*) certainly made it into print in this book. Mary returned the favor with "Gaspacho," [sic] an advance on a traditional Arab/Spanish recipe for a bread, olive oil, and garlic soup. The spelling of the word may have changed, but since Mary's time this elegant appetizer always contains tomatoes.

In a food processor, purée the tomatoes, onion, and garlic, working in batches if necessary, and reserve the mixture in a large serving bowl.

In the food processor, mince the cucumber and green pepper, add the vinegar, oil, prepared mustard, and bread crumbs and continue processing until mixed well.

Add the bread crumb mixture to the serving bowl, and adjust the seasonings with salt and pepper. Refrigerate for two hours.

Serve in chilled bowls garnished with croutons, minced red onion, and peppers. *Serves 4.*

# FRENCH GREEN PEA SOUP

Adapted from: Eliza Leslie, *Directions for Cookery*, 1837 p. 438

Eliza Leslie's writing and instructions were addressed to an audience that she assumed had little experience. To encourage success in the kitchen, she included helpful comments such as how to strengthen the color of this soup by adding a cupful of the juice of spinach. Her cooking instructions were specific: "Boil it till the last peas are quite soft, but not till they go to pieces."

5 cups fresh-shelled green peas, 1 cup reserved
2 onions, sliced
4 cups chicken stock
½ cup fresh basil leaves
2 tablespoons butter
salt and pepper
2 cups spinach leaves (optional)

 Put 4 cups of the peas in a stock pot with the onions and the stock. Season with salt and pepper, and simmer for 1 hour, until the peas are soft. Off the heat, mash the peas or purée in a food processor.

While the soup is cooking, cook the washed spinach in the smallest amount of water possible until it is tender, then pound it smooth and extract as much of the juice as possible by pressing the spinach in a sieve. Stir the spinach juice into the reserved puréed soup. Bring the soup to a simmer and add the remaining uncooked whole peas. Cook until the whole peas are "quite soft but not till they go to pieces." Stir in the chopped basil leaves and the butter. Season with salt and pepper and serve hot, garnished with croutons. *Serves 4.*

# POLENTA MODERNA

Adapted from: Mary Randolph, *The Virginia Housewife*, 1824, p. 84

*6 cups water*
*1½ cups cornmeal*
*3 tablespoons butter, divided*
*6 tablespoons grated cheese*
*2 teaspoons salt*
*freshly ground black pepper*

Caesar's legions marched across Europe on a daily ration of "polenta." Since then both the name and the ingredients have changed, but all modern Italian kitchens from Lombardy to Tuscany have their own specialized version. For Imperial Roman soldiers the dish was made from chestnut flour, or even barley flour. In spite of the New World's offer of cornmeal, Italian cooks didn't make the switch in their polenta until around the middle of the 18th century. Since then, the dish—whether golden or white—is made exclusively from cornmeal, and Mary Randolph was the first American to write it down.

In a mixing bowl combine the cornmeal with one tablespoon of butter and 2 cups of water.

In a heavy saucepan over medium heat, bring 4 cups of the water to a boil. Add the remaining butter and salt. Slowly pour the cornmeal mixture into the boiling water in a slow stream, stirring and scraping the sides constantly with a wooden spoon.

Reduce the heat until the mush is barely moving and cover. Cook for 45 minutes, stirring every 5 minutes, scraping the pan bottom to avoid scorching and abject ruin.

Stir in the cheese, add more butter and freshly ground black pepper, and serve.
*Serves 6.*

# TURNIP GREENS WITH BACON AND VINEGAR

Adapted from: Mary Randolph, *The Virginia Housewife*, 1824 p. 103

There are some dishes in this world whose provenance is so inherently manifest, so unmistakably marked with the soil and "terroire" of their origin that their fitness in history and geography is beyond dispute. I submit that for the denizens of the South, such a dish is turnip greens in full battle dress. "De gustibus non disputatem," as we often say, so rather than attempt to persuade, let me defer to Mary Randolph, writing in 1824 as the doyen of the old South, about this stalwart vegetable.

*24 large turnip leaves, trimmed of broken bits*
*4 slices of bacon*
*1 cup small turnips, washed and peeled*
*¼ cup vinegar, for dressing*

 Peel off half an inch of the stringy outside. Wash and allow the leaves to stand. Break away the leaves from the stalk and reserve each. Chop the stalks into dice, about ¼" inch.

Trim the turnips into slightly larger dice.

Fry out the bacon, then add the chopped stems and the turnip dice over low heat, allowing the bits to cook slowly rather than brown. Remove from the heat and strain off most of the bacon grease. Add 1 cup of water and all the turnip leaves to the pot. Cook over moderate heat for 20 minutes or until the dice are tender to the fork. Drain and serve with vinegar. *Serves 4.*

# Stilton Rarebit

Adapted from: Eliza Leslie, *Directions for Cookery*, 1837 p. 387

4 slices rich white yeast bread
6 tablespoons butter
1 tablespoon flour
½ cup porter (alt: stout beer)
¼ cup milk
1 teaspoon dry mustard
¼ teaspoon cayenne pepper
1 egg yolk, large
6 oz. Stilton cheese, grated (alt: sharp cheddar)
salt and freshly ground black pepper

Stilton is a famous English village that in the early 18th century lent its name to a blue veined creamy cheese still made in the village today. The cheese has long since become an icon, protected by copyright and glorified by gourmands worldwide. So much so, that Eliza Leslie not only gave advice for making your own cheese after the Stilton fashion, but here she also offers a complete "knock-off" known originally as "Welsh Rabbit." The name is a play on the scurrilous denigration of persons "welshing" on their bet. In the end we have a poor ploughman's hearty lunch and a generous cheese and bread substitute until the real rabbit comes along.

Spread the bread with half the butter. Arrange the bread slices in a large roasting pan, toast under a broiler, and set aside.

In a small saucepan, melt the reserved butter; add the flour, stirring until a roux is formed. Add the porter and milk, and the mustard and cayenne. Stir until smooth. Remove from the heat and beat in the egg yolk, then stir in the cheese. Add salt and pepper to taste.

Pour the cheese and milk mixture over the toast and return to the broiler until the cheese bubbles and is golden. *Serves 4 as an appetizer.*

# PUMPKIN BREAD

Adapted from: Eliza Leslie, *New Receipts for Cooking*, 1854, p. 378

Before cast iron ovens were common, families made their bread in cozy, fireside oven compartments or in the unique "Cloam oven" imported from Cornwall, England. This small device was nestled in the corner of the farmhouse fireplace like a miniature clay igloo with a lid freshly sealed in place with clay, tightly securing the cooking compartment after the dough was introduced. Pumpkin dough was popular in the early days because its rich, yeast-feeding sugars encourage the dough to rise before baking, and a well risen dough was essential to good hearth breads.

*1 small pumpkin, cleaned, skinned and*
*chunked, to make 4 cups of pulp*
*water to cover*
*1 package instant yeast*
*1 tablespoon honey*
*2 cups warm water*
*1 tablespoon salt*
*½ cup cornmeal, stone ground*
*3 cups whole wheat flour*
*3 cups flour*

Place the cut-up pumpkin parts in a saucepan and barely cover with water. Boil until tender, then drain and mash the pumpkin, sprinkling the yeast over the raw vegetable and incorporating well. Place the mashed pumpkin in a glass or ceramic bowl, cover with a damp towel, and refrigerate for a day.

In a large mixing bowl, dissolve the honey in the warm water and let it stand for 5 minutes. Add all the remaining ingredients and beat well. Gradually stir in 2 cups of the pumpkin yeast until the dough becomes quite stiff. Turn out on a working surface and rest for 5 minutes. Knead or use a pastry shovel to work the dough until it is smooth. Then allow it to rise in an oiled bowl for 2 hours.

Punch down the dough, shape it into a loaf, and place it on an oiled baking sheet. Cover the dough and let it rise for 1 hour. Slash the top, and bake in a preheated 425°F oven for 45 minutes. Remove and let cool.

Pumpkin yeast will keep for a week refrigerated. The bread freezes well. *Serves 8.*

# Apoquinimic Cakes

Adapted from: Mary Randolph, *The Virginia Housewife*, 1824, p. 139

2 cups flour
½ teaspoon sugar
½ teaspoon salt
2 tablespoons lard (alt: peanut oil)
2 tablespoons unsalted butter
½ cup milk

These biscuits were first made in the days before commercial baking powder. The pounding of the dough is a way of kneading, but its colorful aspect has drawn a lot of attention, and the product is generally known as "beaten biscuits." The taste and texture are quite unique, and the popular biscuit once prompted several inventors to produce "biscuit beaters" which are sadly now found only in antique stores.

Combine the flour, sugar, and salt. Rub the lard and the butter into the dry ingredients until the mixture resembles bread crumbs. Work the milk into the mixture and gather the dough together. Place the dough on a sturdy work surface and pound it for 20 minutes with a heavy rolling pin.

Pinch off a piece of dough the size of a golf ball, then pat it smooth and prick the exterior with the tines of a fork. Repeat with the remaining dough.

Bake the biscuits on a sheet in a preheated 400°F oven until golden brown. *Makes 24 biscuits.*

# Philadelphia Dutch A.P.'s

Adapted from: Eliza Leslie, *Directions for Cookery*, 1837, p. 354

If you can agree that the Pennsylvania Dutch are as much about Germany as about Holland, then you won't have much trouble unscrambling the name of a favorite childhood cookie "Anisplaetzchen." The street vendors in old Philadelphia sold two types of cookie: one laced with anise and the other with caraway seeds. To distinguish the cookies the initials "A.P." were inscribed on the former, while the latter were generally known as "seedcakes." Urban myth has since applied the initials to a variety of individual bakers and vendors from Anne Parmer to Ann Page and others, but we give the recipe here as Eliza Leslie did, naming them after the "anise" heritage, but calling for plenty of caraway seed instead. They are splendid with ice cream, as suggested by Eliza Leslie in her chapter on cakes.

2 cups all purpose flour
½ cup butter
½ cup white sugar
½ teaspoon cinnamon
¼ teaspoon nutmeg
1½ teaspoons caraway seeds, bruised
¼ cup dry sherry

Preheat the oven to 350°F. Cut the butter into the flour on a working surface, then add in the sugar and spices and blend carefully.

Add the sherry to the pastry, and combine to form a dough. Roll out the dough on a lightly floured surface to a thickness of ¼". Cut the cookies into 3" rounds, and place on an oiled baking sheet. Bake 12 minutes until firm, but not colored. *Makes 15 cookies.*

# Strawberry Shortcake

Adapted from: Eliza Leslie, *New Receipts for Cooking*, 1837, p. 000

## Shortcake Biscuits

*4 cups flour*
*1/3 cup white sugar*
*1 teaspoon salt*
*4 teaspoons baking powder*
*1½ sticks unsalted butter, divided*

## Strawberry Shortcake

*2 cups whole fresh strawberries*
*sugar to taste*
*3 tablespoons butter, melted*
*1 cup whipping cream*

"The strawberries, not being cooked, will retain all their natural flavor," announced Eliza Leslie as she rattled off her landmark departure from the accepted cuisine of her day and mixed fresh American strawberries, not at all the same flavor as their English cousins *fraises de bois*, with whipped cream and butter, and sent the whole thing off to the table in a revolutionary presentation of a dozen tiny strawberry biscuits.

*To Make the Biscuits:* Mix the dry ingredients then cut in 1 stick of the butter as though for a pastry. Roll the dough out to a thickness of ½". Cut into 12 rounds and place them on an oiled baking sheet. Brush with the remaining ½ stick of melted butter and bake at 450°F for 10 minutes or until golden. Cool. *Makes 12 biscuits.*

*To Make the Shortcake:* Wash and stem the strawberries, then set aside 4 of the best for decoration. Mash the remaining strawberries with the desired amount of sugar and reserve.

Tear or cut the biscuits in half on the horizontal axis, and set the two halves, inside up, side by side on a serving platter. Place an equal amount of the butter on each open biscuit portion. Spoon an equal amount of the mashed strawberry mixture onto six of the biscuit portions. Spoon an equal amount of whipping cream on each strawberry biscuit. Place the remaining biscuit over its pair and serve at once. *Serves 6.*

# CRÈME BRÛLÉE

Adapted from: Mary Randolph, *The Virginia Housewife*, 1824, p. 119

Food fashion is such that while many today recognize "crème brûlée" as a subtle blend of cream and sugar and fire, whose origin is claimed by every nation from France to Spain, few would have inquired after the name given in this book, "burnt custard." Mary Randolph was a lady ahead of her time, however, and sought out adventurous treatment of this version of the English standard. This recipe includes slices of sponge cake laid in the bowl as foundation for the custard, all of which is topped with a meringue, and then brought to a brilliant fire tinged pinnacle at the moment of service.

*4 round slices of a small savoy cake,*
*    3" diameter, ½" high (alt: sponge cake)*
*2 cups heavy cream*
*6 eggs, separated*
*2 tablespoons sugar*
*3 tablespoons brown sugar*
*    (alt: Demerara sugar)*

 Arrange a slice of the cake in the bottom of each of 4 separate, ovenproof serving bowls intended for the custard.

In a medium saucepan, or double boiler, heat the cream until it is scalded. This has occurred when tiny bubbles are apparent around the edges of the pan. Do not boil. Remove from the heat. Add the warm cream to the egg yolks in a clean bowl, stir well, and return the custard to the low heat. Add the sugar and stir until the custard thickens.

Pour the custard over the cake slices in each individual serving dish, arrange on a baking sheet, and refrigerate for an hour. Sprinkle the brown sugar evenly over the custards.

Under a high broiler setting (or using the salamander in a professional kitchen) place the baking sheet and 4 custards on the top rack of the oven for just long enough for the sugar to caramelize and form a crust. Whip egg whites to stiff peaks and cover each custard. Return to the fire for 5 minutes to set meringue. Remove and serve immediately. *Serves 4.*

# FIRST FAMILY STRAWBERRY ICE CREAM

Adapted from: Mary Randolph, *The Virginia Housewife*, 1824 p. 144

3 cups strawberries
2 cups sugar
2½ quarts heavy whipping cream
1 vanilla bean

First families were early enthusiastic ice cream eaters. George Washington bought an ice cream freezer in 1784 and Thomas Jefferson had a recipe for vanilla ice cream that, years later, was found in his papers. The ingredients needed—sugar, cream, and the labor to stir the ice cream continuously as it set—were hard to come by. Mary Randolph chided those who cheated by not attending to the chore of stirring and ended up with a solid ice mass rather than a smooth cream.

Hull the strawberries, slice and put them in a deep dish. Strew with ½ cup sugar and let stand for an hour. Mix 1 quart of the cream with the rest of the sugar and the vanilla bean and heat slowly to dissolve the sugar, but do not boil. Cool. Remove the vanilla bean. Stir in the rest of the sugar and chill the mixture for an hour. Pack the freezer according to directions with salt and ice, ladle in the chilled cream mixture, and crank. When the ice cream is frozen but still soft, stir in the berries and sugar and continue to freeze. Serve in tall glasses with handles. *Makes one quart ice cream.*

# TOMATO CATSUP: THE OLD FASHIONED WAY

Adapted from: Mary Randolph, *The Virginia Housewife*, 1824 p. 162

By the time Mary Randolph was writing her very successful review of the recipes of her day, tomatoes were familiar items on restaurant menus. A number of early food writers had already suggested tomatoes as likely candidates for the well established table sauce known as "catsup," and it was only a matter of time until the commercial side of food service elbowed its way into the family kitchen. But back then, when the nation was young, it was still considered a matter of honor to make your own sauces, and here is how Mary Randolph did it.

9–10 lbs. tomatoes, fresh picked
3 onions, large
⅓ cup kosher salt
2 tablespoons cloves, ground
2 tablespoons allspice, ground
2 tablespoons black pepper
1 tablespoon cayenne pepper

Gather a peck of tomatoes, or ten pounds worth, wash and stem them, and then cut them roughly into quarters. Peel and slice the onions and place both tomatoes and onions, in layers, in a large stockpot.

Sprinkle 3 tablespoons of the salt over the tomatoes, and over low heat, without any water whatsoever, stir frequently while gradually increasing the heat to low-medium as the tomatoes sweat out their juices for an hour.

Remove from the heat and allow the tomatoes to cool enough to handle. Strain the tomatoes into a clean pan and return to the stove top. Add the cloves, allspice, black pepper, and cayenne and bring to a simmer.

Stir regularly for an hour. Remove and allow to cool. Adjust the seasonings to taste, then bottle in jars with sealable lids, and refrigerate until needed. *Makes 2 quarts.*

# PINEAPPLE MARMALADE

Adapted from: Eliza Leslie, *Directions for Cookery*, 1837 p. 476

*4 large sweet pineapples*
*4 cups sugar (approximately)*
*½ cup lemon juice*

In colonial America, the pineapple held a special place. Its rarity and its unusual and attractive shape made it an exotic fruit. It was displayed on the table of a proud hostess, at once a symbol of her status and of how she valued the company of her guests. So sought after was the fruit that they were sometimes rented out for the evening by confectioners. The pineapple was often carved on gateposts or woven into tablecloths and became synonymous with good cheer and welcome. Eliza Leslie's marmalade was a luxury item in 1828, a one-of-a-kind pie filling and certainly a recipe of which to be proud. The addition of lemon juice to the pineapple is a modern one and improves the flavor.

Pare the pineapples and cut out the fruit. To each cup of fruit pulp, measure ¾ cup white sugar. Chop the pineapple, being careful to catch the juices. Put the fruit and sugar into a heavy-bottomed pan and bring it slowly to a boil, stirring often. Skim the scum that rises to the top. The marmalade should simmer for half an hour and appear clear, bright, and smooth. Stir in the strained lemon juice. Allow the pan to stand, covered, until the marmalade is cool, then remove to clean, sterilized jars. Seal and store. *Makes four 1-lb. pots marmalade.*

# MARY'S UNCLE'S PO' BOY SANDWICH

Adapted from: Mary Randolph, *The Virginia Housewife*, 1824 p. 69

The poor boy sandwich hit the streets of New Orleans in the 1920s, a full one hundred years after the idea appeared in *The Virginia Housewife*. Thomas Jefferson was fond of a late night snack; he even designed a dumb waiter so that he could serve himself with minimum inconvenience to the staff, who simply sent up small delicacies for the future president when he was working late. This oyster stuffed loaf from his kinswoman's recipe book was an ideal supper snack. Use a loaf made from the manchet loaf baked in chapter one.

4 manchet loaves (see p. 42)
1 pint oysters
1 tablespoon butter
1 cup béchamel sauce

## Béchamel Sauce

2 tablespoons unsalted butter
2 tablespoons flour
1 cup heavy cream
salt and pepper

Stew the oysters in a little butter for 5 minutes. Cut off the tops of the rolls, remove the crumbs, and reserve. Brush the rolls inside and out with melted butter and crisp in a 375°F oven for 5 minutes.

For the sauce, melt the butter, stir in the flour, and cook for 5 minutes, stirring constantly. Gradually add the cream and whisk to make a smooth sauce. Season with salt and pepper.

Combine the stewed oysters with the reserved bread crumbs and bind them with the sauce. Turn this into the crisped rolls and reheat in the oven. Top with the removed lids if you wish. Serve hot. *Makes 4 servings.*

# Epicure's Wow Wow Sauce

Adapted from: Eliza Leslie, *Directions for Cookery*, 1837, p. 172

## Mushroom Ketchup

1 lb. mushrooms

## Wow Wow Sauce

1 cup of claret or good dry red wine
1 cup of Mushroom Ketchup
2 flat tins of anchovies, mashed
grated rind of 2 lemons
2 grated shallots
2 tablespoons horseradish
2 teaspoons pepper
2 teaspoons cayenne
1 teaspoon celery seed

Dr. Kitchiner was an eccentric Londoner, a gourmand and keen clubber, whose cookbooks were in continuous print through the 19th century, both in his native England and in America. His recipes were convoluted and wordy and he freely admitted to a fondness for experiments in the kitchen, which did not encourage confidence amongst his more timid readers. It required Eliza Leslie's endorsement of this fiery sauce (better named Wow Wow) to ensure the success of his recipe. This recipe is adapted to modern kitchens.

 *To Make Mushroom Ketchup*: Spread 1 lb. cleaned mushrooms on a tray, sprinkle with 2 tablespoons salt and cover with foil. Let the mushrooms stand overnight. Next day, tip the contents of the pan into a food processor and purée until smooth.

*To Make Wow Wow*: Combine the mushroom ketchup and all the remaining ingredients in a couple of sauce bottles saved for the purpose; cover and infuse for 2 weeks. Store in the refrigerator. Shake the bottles every day. Use as a sauce over grilled fish or mashed potatoes. *Makes two 16 oz. bottles of sauce.*

# Nouilly à la Maccaroni

Adapted from: Eliza Leslie, *Directions for Cookery*, 1837, p. 210

*Yankee Doodle came to town,*
*riding on a pony*
*he stuck a feather in his cap*
*and called it macaroni.*

Pasta, in one way or another, had been an American fascination since before the revolution. When Thomas Jefferson toured Italy in 1787, he compared notes on macaroni machines, bought one, and eventually, being Thomas Jefferson, designed his own. His design looked like a vertical sausage grinder, with dough going in at the top, and strands of macaroni, later to be chopped, extruded at the bottom. This is the way Eliza Leslie, America's consummate gourmet, wished to "dress maccaroni" [sic].

1½ cups all-purpose flour
1 teaspoon salt
2 eggs
⅓ cup milk
½ lb. Parmesan cheese, grated
4 tablespoons butter

Sift the flour and salt onto the counter, make a well in the middle and add the eggs and milk. Gradually incorporate this with a fork to form a stiff dough. Knead until smooth, adding a few drops of olive oil if necessary.

Divide the dough into 4 sections; knead and allow to rest. Repeat until you have a resilient dough. If your food processor has an extruder you may make hollow macaroni; otherwise roll out into lengths and cut thin strips. Lay the strips on a clean, floured cloth or over a pasta rack to dry for half an hour.

Have ready a pot of boiling water. Add the macaroni, and continue a vigorous boil. At 5 minutes it should be "al dente." Add cold water to the pot to hold the temperature.

Sprinkle a quarter of the Parmesan in a buttered dish, add a layer of drained macaroni, and repeat the layers until used. Put butter bits on top of the dish and set in a 350°F oven for 15 to 20 minutes, until the top is slightly browned. Remove and serve. *Serves 4.*

# CHEESE CORN SOUFFLE PUFFS

Adapted from: Mary Randolph, *The Virginia Housewife*, 1824 p. 86

2 cups corn meal
2 cups water
3 tablespoons butter
¾ lb. grated cheese
6 eggs

Brillat Savarin, the French philosopher and gourmand, was a figure well known to ambitious chefs in Mary Randolph's day. His many published aphorisms and lofty disquisitions on food matters made him an international celebrity. Eventually his debonair manner landed him in trouble with Swiss chefs when he casually referred to a "fondue" as a "soufflé." Mary Randolph went with the Swiss when she gave her charming recipes for "fondues," which are really miniature cheese soufflés. Terminology aside, they make delicious mouthfuls on their own or as an accompaniment to a green salad.

 In a medium saucepan combine the corn meal, water, and butter and stir over medium heat until it forms a thick batter that begins to hold its shape. Remove from the fire.

In a large mixing bowl, combine the cornmeal with the cheese and mix it well. With a spatula incorporate 2 of the eggs, beaten, and then 2 more, and finally the last 2 until the batter is light.

Heat the oven to 350°F. Oil a baking sheet and drop the batter in small lumps and bake until they turn a "delicate brown." *Makes 24 puffs.*

## Chapter Three

# Voices of Conscience
# From the Kitchen

Lydia Maria Child, *The Frugal Housewife*, 1832
Sarah Josepha Hale, *The Good Housekeeper*, 1841
Catharine Beecher, A *Treatise on Domestic Economy*, 1841
*Miss Beecher's Domestic Receipt Book*, 1846

Three remarkable women carried the tradition of American cookbook writing into the middle of the 19th century. It was a pivotal moment in the story of cookbook writing. In previous generations, young women learned the art and practice of cooking from their mothers and few bought or read cookbooks. But as literacy amongst women spread and as families moved across America to make new lives far away from home, they turned to books for guidance. At the time of the Revolution, about 50 percent of New England women could read; by 1840, the figure approached 100 percent. Lydia Maria Child, Sarah Josepha Hale, and Catharine Beecher wrote with this growing readership in mind. The resulting cookbooks became great kitchen classics, and their authors respected and beloved literary figures.

Lydia Maria Child was a literary star at the young age of 22, when her sensational novel *Hobomok* came out. *Hobomok* was the romantic—and for the time scandalous—story of an Indian warrior who fell in love with a white woman. The success of the book earned an invitation for the young Lydia Maria to attend a reception in honor of the French war hero, Lafayette, who was touring America's cities and sampling the finest in American cuisine. In 1829, Lydia Maria married David Child and the couple championed the abolitionist cause, which was to become a lifelong mission. Respect for Mrs. Child's work came quickly, but unfortunately was not followed by the income necessary to support the family. Lydia Maria soon found herself cast in the role of breadwinner and turned to her pen.

*The Frugal Housewife* by the author of *Hobomok* was written to help pay the Child's bills. Mrs. Child knew her audience exactly; she was a struggling young housewife who had just set up house for the first time and needed advice on planning menus and balancing her budget. The message was one that really hit home in the hard times that followed the recession of the 1820s. She wrote, "I have attempted to teach how money can be saved, not how it can be enjoyed."

Frugality notwithstanding, Mrs. Child's recipes clearly showed both her enjoyment of cooking and her thriftiness when it came to the clever use of leftovers. A joint of beef morphed into meat pie and meat hash on the second and third days. Salt cod and salt pork both turned up for dinner, followed by a pudding selection in which desserts were divided into "common" or "company," a distinction still observed in households today. *The Frugal Housewife* won a place on the kitchen shelves of many newly married couples and Mrs. Child's name became a household fixture. The book stayed in print until the 1850s and even appeared to great success in England.

Equally as celebrated was Sarah Josepha Hale, the highly influential magazine editor of *Godey's Lady's Book*, the arbiter in matters of good taste. *Godey's* began publication in 1830 and was read all across America; by 1860, the readership was said to number 150,000. When Mrs. Hale wrote her first cookbook, *The Good*

*Housekeeper*, she wrote for a ready-made audience. She had read the work of Mrs. Child and of Mrs. Mary Randolph, and decided to write a book that steered a middle course between cheap living and good living. Her recipes for "Manhattan Clam Chowder," "Pan Fried Trout," "Rhubarb Cream Cake," and "Molasses Ginger Pound-cake" were instant American classics.

Mrs. Hale is often, and rightly, credited with turning the Thanksgiving holiday into the institution it has become today. It was her tireless campaigning in the pages of *Godey's* that helped persuade Abraham Lincoln to mandate the national holiday in 1862. Her menu for the day included the roast goose and the celebrated pumpkin pie that were, in her words, "an indispensable part of a good and true Yankee Thanksgiving." Recipes for the dishes appeared in *The Good Housekeeper*.

Pride of place in her cookbook was given to bread, and Mrs. Hale wrote about it in almost poetic language. Modern consumers will marvel at the trials and tribulations that their 19th century equivalents encountered trying to buy decent, unadulterated flour. Mrs. Hale was sympathetic to the cause and gave short shrift to those merchants who added plaster of Paris, ground stones, and even bones to their flour for sale.

Nowadays, we all but take for granted the purity of our food, but it only came about thanks to the vigilance of advocates such as Sylvester Graham, who found a worthy champion in Mrs. Hale. Sylvester Graham's crusade on behalf of whole wheat bread was impassioned, to the extent that he was sometimes on the receiving end of assault from a hostile crowd. Mrs. Hale included a recipe for "Graham Bread" in her chapter on bread.

Catharine Beecher came from a family of successful women. At a time when the cult of womanhood emphasized the married woman's role in the home and family, she herself never married. Her life was in fact an early example of the independent single woman working professionally to improve the lot of others. She achieved this partly through her pioneering work in women's education (which lagged shockingly behind that of men) and her writing about food. *Miss Beecher's Domestic Receipt Book* (1846) emphasized basic traditional cooking and included many regional receipts, gathered perhaps on her lecture circuit. "Kentucky Corn Dodgers," "Pennsylvania Flannel Cakes," "Maine Puffs," "Sachem's Head Corn Cake" were just a few of the examples in the chapter on "Breakfast and Tea Cakes." But Miss Beecher was even more interested in simplifying and improving work in the kitchen and she promoted the use of labor-saving devices such as the ice cream machine, the new iron stove, and cream of tartar in baking recipes.

With her sister Harriet, Miss Beecher went on to write a book called *The American Woman's Home* in 1869, which guaranteed her place at the head of a growing field of domestic science writers. She became a reluctant celebrity. For these writers, cooking was a serious business, healthy eating a priority in the nation's well-being, and the preserving of fine recipes a worthy task for a dedicated cookbook author.

# FASHIONABLE FLANK STEAK ROLL

Adapted from: Lydia Maria Child, *The Frugal Housewife*, 1832, pg. 45

The *Frugal Housewife* goes on—and on—in the vein of kitchen economy at every opportunity. Child endorses "flank [steak] as the most profitable part of the whole ox to buy," and then goes on to admit that even though "flank" is not so pretty as the more fashionable pieces, it does have certain uses. She wanted her readers to know that butchers tended to keep back the best cuts for their better clientele, but that even the "other" cuts could work well. Surely among the uses she imagined, the rolled, stuffed, and braised presentation of "flank" brings a hearty gravy and flavorful *mirepoix* that will match any sturdy appetite.

2½ lb. flank steak, with a slit pocket for the stuffing sliced on the long axis

## STUFFING

1 cup finely chopped onion
1 cup finely chopped celery
2 cups diced stale white bread, toasted
1 garlic clove
1 egg, beaten
2 tablespoons mixed dried herbs
salt and pepper

## BRAISING

2 tablespoons butter
1 cup beef stock
½ cup each of vegetables for braising: celery, onion, and carrot roughly diced

 Make the stuffing by frying the finely chopped vegetables in the melted butter, add the bread cubes and herbs and toss with the beaten egg. Fill the pocket in the flank steak, but not too full. Lay the flank flat and roll loosely. Tie with kitchen string.

Brown the flank in butter in a heavy casserole so that the meat browns richly. Add chopped vegetables and pour around the stock. Cover the casserole and braise at 350°F for 1 hour, until the steak shows no signs of resistance when pierced with a sharp knife and the juices run clear. Make gravy by mashing the vegetables in the pan and thickening with a little flour and butter. Check the seasoning and serve the steak sliced, very hot, with the gravy poured over. *Serves 6.*

# CHICKEN WITH PARSLEY DUMPLINGS

Adapted from: Sarah J. Hale, *The Good Housekeeper*, 1841, pg. 58

4 leg-thigh chicken joints, separated
3 tablespoons olive oil
1 cup each of diced onion, celery, and carrot
½ cup dry white wine
4 cups chicken stock

## DUMPLINGS

2 cups unsifted all-purpose flour
1 teaspoon baking soda
2 tablespoons butter
¼ teaspoon salt
1½ cups milk
1 egg
2 tablespoons chopped fresh parsley

Mrs. Sarah J. Hale had many opinions, and she expressed them directly and often in her editorial columns in *Godey's Lady's Book*. But perhaps her favorite and most intense peeve was a poorly constructed dumpling, which she described as a libel on civilized cookery. "One might about as well eat, with the hope of digesting, a brick from the ruins of Babylon as one of the hard, heavy masses of boiled dough which usually pass under this name." Mrs. Hale's casserole, and its dumplings, however, were something special. Quite rightly, she insisted that they should be cooked "only" until they float on top of the braise.

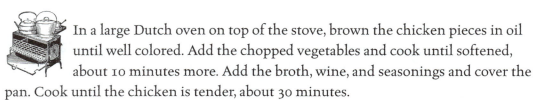 In a large Dutch oven on top of the stove, brown the chicken pieces in oil until well colored. Add the chopped vegetables and cook until softened, about 10 minutes more. Add the broth, wine, and seasonings and cover the pan. Cook until the chicken is tender, about 30 minutes.

When the chicken is 10 minutes away from being cooked, make the dumplings. Combine the flour, salt, and baking powder and rub the butter into the flour. Pour in the milk and egg, and gently combine to form a soft dough. Use 2 large wet spoons to mold the dough into balls and drop them into the pan, pushing them down beneath the liquid. Simmer for only 5 minutes more until the dumplings are soft and plump. Thicken and season the sauce if desired. *Serves 4.*

# PEASANT SMOKED PORK AND LENTILS

Adapted from: Lydia Maria Child, *The Frugal Housewife*, 1829, pg. 51

That old Yankee standby pork and beans had been a classic peasant dish in France from time immemorial. The casserole could simmer happily for hours over a fire with only an occasional stir with a long-handled spoon. The same dish that Mrs. Child described in some detail for her American readers appeared in only slightly different form on tables in French villages in Provence. Lentils and smoked sausage were chosen over pork and white beans, but the crowning touch was a braising liquid fragrant with tomatoes and cinnamon. In this guise, the dish transcends the peasant table and could be served at any sophisticated supper.

1 large smoked sausage

2 pounds ham hocks

2 large onions, sliced and divided in 2

1 stalk celery, sliced

1 carrot, sliced

4 smoked pork chops

freshly ground black pepper and kosher salt
    to taste

1 pound lentils, soaked and picked over

2 cloves garlic

2 large tomatoes, skinned, peeled, and chopped

¼ teaspoon cinnamon

½ cup dry white wine

chopped fresh parsley

Put the sausages to boil in about 3 quarts water or chicken stock along with half the onion, the celery, and carrot. Add the ham hocks. Simmer for 1 hour. Add the pork chops and cook for 30 minutes more. Keep warm.

Ladle out 1 quart of the broth and use to cook the lentils. Brown the rest of the vegetables and garlic in olive oil and add the rinsed and sorted lentils. Stir until coated with oil, then stir in the tomato purée, the wine, and seasonings. Add the reserved broth. Cover the pan and simmer for an hour until the lentils can be mashed.

Serve the lentils in a bowl, covered with chunks of sausage and chops with the broth poured over. Sprinkle heavily with chopped parsley. *Serves 8.*

# PIGEONS IN THE SUN

Adapted from: Sarah J. Hale, *The Good Housekeeper*, 1841, pg. 53

½ cup all-purpose flour
¼ teaspoon salt
½ bottle beer
4 pigeons (squab may be substituted)
½ piece of fat bacon cut into 2" strips, chilled,
    for larding
1 onion, chopped
1 carrot, sliced
1 tablespoon olive oil
bouquet garni
3 cups chicken stock
1 large egg white
salt and pepper to taste
lemon and parsley for garnish

Wild pigeons, including passenger pigeons, common pigeons, and even doves were seen as manna from heaven in 19th century America. They were harvested with nets and guns, and shipped in barrels of ice to Boston and later to the Fulton Market in New York. This picturesque presentation snatches the birds as they blaze across the sky and presents the lean, tasty meat fried in a mantle of rich, golden batter. Because the birds, or squab, are first browned and braised, the meat remains succulent.

Make the batter by combining the flour, salt, and beer and beat well. Set aside in a cool place.

Lard the pigeons with the bacon strips. Brown the birds and the vegetables lightly in olive oil and transfer them to a casserole. Add the bouquet garni and stock to cover. Simmer for 1 hour until the birds are cooked. When cool enough to handle, remove the breast filets. (Keep the scraps and bones for soup and feel you are doing your bit for economy just as Mrs. Hale would approve.)

Beat the egg white until stiff and fold into the batter. Dip the pigeon filets in the batter to coat. Fry them in hot vegetable oil until golden brown and crisp. Serve immediately, garnished with fried parsley and lemon wedges. *Serves 4.*

# Turkey Hash Ovals

Adapted from: Sarah J. Hale, *The Good Housekeeper*, 1841, pg. 108

Hash has a warm place in the heart of every cookbook. Sarah J. Hale had specific advice; chop the meat very fine (gristles and gelatinous matter may be included); boiling hardens the meat; and gravy can be made from broth and a little catsup! She didn't identify the type of catsup but readers of this book should consider "Cranberry Ketchup," page 53.

*2 cups cooked turkey, chopped*
*1 large potato, boiled*
*8 tablespoons butter, cut into bits*
*½ cup onion, chopped*
*½ cup celery, chopped*
*1 whole egg and 2 lightly beaten eggs*
*⅓ cup cream*
*1½ teaspoons salt and black pepper*
*½ cup flour*
*soft fresh white breadcrumbs—about 1½ cups*
*vegetable oil*

Mash the potato with 4 tablespoons of the butter. Grind the turkey and vegetables in a food processor. Beat in one egg. Add the potatoes, the cream, salt, and pepper, and beat until smooth. Chill this mixture for about 30 minutes.

Divide the mixture into 8 pieces and pat each into an oval cake. Dip each cake in flour, shake off the excess and then immerse in beaten egg and roll in the breadcrumbs. Chill again for 30 minutes.

Melt the rest of the butter with some vegetable oil and use to fry the turkey hash cakes until golden brown. Serve with a pickle or catsup, if you like, with a poached egg on top. *Serves 4.*

# Many Hands Make Light Work~Mince Pie

Adapted from: Lydia Maria Child, *The Frugal Housewife*, pg. 66

2 pounds beef round, cooked, cooled and minced

¼ pound suet

6 large apples, peeled

2 cups raisins and currants

½ cup white sugar

½ cup dark brown sugar

¼ teaspoon pepper

½ teaspoon salt

2 teaspoons cinnamon

1 teaspoon cloves

2 teaspoons nutmeg

½ cup brandy

1 cup apple cider

2 recipes "Shortcrust Pastry" (see p. 50)

1 tablespoon butter

The diary of Mary White of West Boylston, Massachusetts, records on a November day in 1838 that her husband and son had returned from a shopping trip with over four gallons of molasses, 30 pounds of sugar, 12 pounds of raisins, and three pounds of currants. She set the son to stoning the raisins while she pounded the loaf sugar, and the husband was left to mince the beef and suet. Mrs. White was set to make "the festive pie of the season" and here is Lydia Maria Child's recipe.

In a large bowl, combine the beef and suet. Add the peeled and chopped apples. Stone the raisins, add them with the sugars, spices, brandy, and cider and mix well. Cover and chill for 1 hour. Line 2 pie plates with the pastry, fill with the mince filling, cover with lid of pastry and brush the tops with the tablespoon butter. Bake for 45 minutes in a 400°F oven. Serve at room temperature. *Makes 2 pies.*

# RAZOR CLAM CAKES

Adapted from: Catharine Beecher, *Miss Beecher's Domestic Receipt Book*, 1846, pg. 62

The Eastern razor clam is generally used in fritters or cakes, rather than taken to clambake beach parties like its cousins the littleneck or the soft-shell. In this case, the redoubtable razor, which has its own following, is the clam most suited to chopping, saucing, and baking.

2 cups finely chopped razor clams
2 eggs
1 teaspoon dry English mustard
1 teaspoon thyme
3 drops Tabasco sauce
½ teaspoon salt
freshly ground black pepper
½ yellow onion, chopped
¼ cup fresh parsley, chopped
3 cups soft white breadcrumbs
6 tablespoons butter
2 tablespoons oil
lemon wedges

The clams should be washed and drained. Mix the eggs, mustard, thyme, Tabasco, salt and pepper. Stir in the clams, onions, parsley, and half the breadcrumbs.

Divide the mixture into 8 cakes. Chill. Toast the remaining breadcrumbs and when cool, coat the cakes evenly. Chill again for 30 minutes to firm up the breadcrumb coating.

Melt the butter and oil over moderate heat and fry the clam cakes for 10 minutes, turning once with a slotted spoon, until they are golden brown. As they brown, transfer the cakes to a warm plate in the oven to keep warm. Serve garnished with the lemon wedges. *Makes 8 cakes.*

# FROM THE EDITOR'S TABLE~PAN FRIED TROUT

Adapted from: Sarah J. Hale, *The Good Housekeeper*, 1841, pg. 66

4 rainbow trout, *cleaned but with heads and
tails on if possible*
2 teaspoons salt
*freshly ground black pepper*
½ cup flour
*unsalted butter, about 8 tablespoons*
*lemon wedges*

There is a tale, perhaps apocryphal, about the naming of "*Truite a la Meuniére*," the French name for this dish. It seems that on a surprise visit, Napoleon Bonaparte stopped at an old mill inn in the Auvergne valley. To the amazement of the miller and his wife, the Emperor ordered a fresh trout. After much red-faced stammering and shouted orders in the kitchen, a trout was quickly pulled from the old mill pond, heavily dusted in flour and quickly pan fried in an enormous portion of butter. The fish was served by the miller's wife whose appearance, completely dusted in flour herself, matched that of the fish. With a knowing smile Napoleon congratulated the chef, and suggested that henceforward the dish should be named "in the style of the miller's wife," and it has been "*truite meuniére*" ever since.

 Clarify the butter by melting it in a small pan over low heat; skim off the foam as it rises to the top, or strain the butter through a muslin cloth. Wash and dry the trout fillets and season with salt and pepper. Heat half the butter in a frying pan until it starts to hiss. Dredge each fillet lightly in the flour and put into the pan to cook for 3 to 5 minutes per side. The skin should be brown and crisp. Turn only once. Remove to a large platter in a warm oven.

To make the sauce, heat the rest of the butter and cook until it is golden brown. Pour the butter sauce over the trout, garnish with lemon wedges, and serve at once. *Serves 4.*

# SALMON POACHED IN CIDER

Adapted from: Sarah J. Hale, *The Good Housekeeper*, 1841, pg. 65

Salmon was indeed a bountiful resource during the Colonial times and through the American Revolution. The fish was eaten so regularly that indentured servants bound for the New World often adjusted their contracts of indenture to limit the number of days a week they could be fed salmon. All that changed with the loss of the salmon fisheries in the first half of the 19th century due to habitat despoliation. But the salmon are back, and the orchards are in bloom, and Sarah J. Hale shows the joy of poached salmon the old fashioned way, in tart apple cider.

*4 fat salmon steaks*
*3 tablespoons unsalted butter*
*2 tablespoons finely chopped onions and parsley mixed*
*8 mushrooms, washed and thinly sliced*
*3 tomatoes, skinned and sliced*
*1 bay leaf*
*salt and pepper*
*1½ cups dry apple cider*
*1 egg yolk*
*½ cup cream*
*2 teaspoons fresh lemon juice*

 Butter a shallow baking dish just big enough to hold the salmon steaks without touching. Sprinkle the onions and parsley in the dish, place the salmon steaks on top, and scatter the mushrooms and tomatoes over top. Season with salt and pepper. Pour in the cider and add the bay leaf. Bring to a simmer on top of the stove, then cover with foil and poach the salmon for 20 minutes, or until the fish flakes when prodded with a fork. Remove the fish with a slotted spoon and keep it warm while you prepare the sauce.

Strain the contents of the pan into a saucepan and reduce it over high heat until you have ½ cup left. Reduce the heat. Beat the egg yolk and cream together, and then beat it into the reduced liquor, until it thickens. Off heat, stir in the lemon, season, and pour over the salmon. *Serves 4.*

# AMERICAN CLAM CHOWDER

Adapted from: Lydia Maria Child, *The Frugal Housewife*, 1829, pg. 59

4 dozen clams
5 cups fish broth
4 medium potatoes, scrubbed and diced
½ cup parsley
1 large onion, diced
diced salt pork, about ½ cup
2 cups hot milk
1½ cups cream
salt and pepper

variation: *1 cup beer and 1 cup tomato
ketchup to replace the milk*

Chowder has been a mainstay in every cookbook since the first French sailor threw the first fish into his "chauderie pot." In this book we've seen Hannah Glasse, Amelia Simmons, and Fannie Farmer all rave about the dish. Fannie Farmer has three versions! But pride of place here goes to Lydia Maria Child whose version is not only the most complex, but also suggests the use of beer and ketchup.

Stew the onions in butter for 5 minutes, add the potatoes and parsley, stir to coat, cover the pan and cook until the potatoes are just tender. Meanwhile, fry the salt pork in hot butter until crisp. Add this to the pan along with the fish broth. Simmer for 5 minutes.

Cook the clams in water just until the shells open; remove the clams and dice. Add to the pan. Stir in the milk and cream, season to taste with salt and pepper, and serve with crackers. Variations can be added along with the clams. Top with crackers if desired. *Makes 12 servings.*

# Old Pease Soup

Adapted from: Sarah J. Hale, *The Good Housekeeper*, 1841, pg. 61

Pea soup has an ancient lineage. In 16th century English cookbooks like Robert May's *The Accomplish'd Cook*, there are four versions of what he calls "Pease Pottage." Perhaps that is why Mrs. Hale's receipt is for "Old Pease Soup." Her suggestion to add spinach is a good one. It boosts the green color and freshens the flavor, but it isn't original. Lovage was a common addition in older recipes. This is a stick-to-your-ribs soup, cooked year round and a larder staple.

1½ lbs. split peas, soaked for one hour in cold water
4 quarts chicken broth or water
2 ham hocks
4 stalks celery, chopped
2 large onions, chopped
salt and pepper
1 bunch spinach, washed and chopped roughly
2 tablespoons fresh mint, washed and chopped
4 tablespoons sour cream

Fry the chopped vegetables in some oil until they are wilted but not colored. Sort through the peas and put them in a soup kettle with the broth, the ham hocks, and the vegetables. Cover the pot and bring the soup to a boil. Stir once, lower the heat and simmer for about 1 hour until the peas are tender and soft enough to pulp through a sieve. Remove the meat from the ham hocks, shred it, and return it to the pan.

Once the soup is mashed, return it to the pan, add the spinach, season the soup well and let it come back to a simmer for 5 minutes. Add the fresh mint and sour cream as garnish. *Serves 8.*

# Dutch Era Slaw with Mint Dressing

Adapted from: Catharine Beecher, *Miss Beecher's Domestic Receipt Book*, 1841, pg. 80

3 cups green cabbage, thinly sliced
3 cups red cabbage, thinly sliced
⅓ cup red wine vinegar
¼ cup melted butter, cooled
salt and pepper
¼ cup fresh mint, finely chopped

Truth be told, vegetables were not very fashionable back in the 1830s. Mrs. Hale admitted they were an essential element in the well-balanced diet, but only if boiled to death. Mrs. Child was of the same school and recommended boiling times of 30 minutes for asparagus and 40 minutes for corn. Neither lady admitted the safe consumption of raw vegetables, so salad recipes were nonexistent. Catharine Beecher was more radical. This Dutch "koolsla," or coleslaw, is an adaptation of her simple recipe. Note the mayonnaise-less dressing, which was a much later addition.

 Mix the cabbage in a large salad bowl. Add the vinegar and the cooled melted butter and combine. Sprinkle over the mint and seasonings, and toss to combine. Cover and let stand for at least one hour before eating. Eat at room temperature. *Serves 4.*

# SLIPPERDOWNS

Adapted from: Catharine Beecher, *Miss Beecher's Domestic Receipt Book*, 1846, pg. 96

Slipperdowns are Catharine Beecher's answer to the English muffin. Cornmeal mush was beaten into yeast dough and baked in small rings, to be split apart when baked and toasted. Back in 1747, Hannah Glasse had lectured readers on the correct way to eat a muffin: "Do not touch them with a knife, either to spread or cut them open, if you do they will be as heavy as lead."

2 teaspoons sugar
½ teaspoon dried yeast
1 cup warm milk
2 cups cooked mush (2 cups cornmeal mixed
    with 2 cups water, boiled for 15 minutes)
1 tablespoon butter
2 teaspoons salt
5 cups all-purpose flour

Cream the yeast with the sugar in the warm milk. Leave to bubble up for 5 minutes. Add the butter to the mush and pour this into the yeast. Mix. Add the salt and 4 cups of flour and combine to make a slightly soft dough. Add as much of the remaining flour as is needed to make a dough that will clear the sides of the bowl. Knead well for 5 minutes and put to rest in a clean oiled bowl. Leave until the dough is doubled in size. Punch down and form into 18 round balls.

Roll each ball into a muffin shape and set 2" apart on a greased cookie sheet. Cover with foil. Leave to rise until they are not quite doubled in size, about 20 minutes. Bake in a slow 325°F oven. To serve, split in two with a fork and pull apart to toast. Lots of butter is needed. *Makes 12 "slipperdowns."*

# A Miraculous Loaf

Adapted from: Sarah J. Hale, *The Good Housekeeper*, 1841, pg. 19

## For the Salt Rising Starter

1½ *cups hot water*
1 *medium potato, peeled and sliced thin*
2 *tablespoons cornmeal*
1 *teaspoon sugar*
½ *teaspoon salt*

## For the Bread

¼ *teaspoon baking soda*
½ *cup warm milk*
1 *tablespoon melted butter*
1 *teaspoon salt*
5–5½ *cups flour*

Mrs. Hale considered the art of making good bread to be the most important one in cookery. This salt rising bread is a miracle indeed. It relies upon a starter made from potato, which is of a more unpredictable character than dried yeast, but bakers of old knew the temperamental character of each of their yeasts and were prepared to discard a batch of dough that did not rise as expected.

 To *Make the Starter*: Mix the ingredients and pour into a warmed jar or bowl that has room for the starter to bubble up. Cover with a lid or plate. Stand it in a warm place until the starter bubbles up—12 hours or more. If it bubbles at all, make the bread. If not, discard this batch of starter and try again.

To *Make the Bread*: Strain the liquid from the starter and discard the potatoes. Add the liquid to the soda, milk, melted butter, and salt. Mix. Stir in about 2 cups of the flour and beat until satiny. Stir in the remaining flour—1 cup at a time—until a soft dough is formed. Turn the dough onto a floured surface and knead vigorously for 10 minutes. Shape the dough into a large plump roll and set it in a well-buttered stoneware bread pan. Cover and let rise again until doubled in size. This may take as long as 4 hours. Bake in a preheated 425°F oven for 45 minutes, until golden brown. Cool. *Makes 1 loaf.*

# SYLVESTER GRAHAM BREAD

Adapted from: Sarah J. Hale, *The Good Housekeeper*, 1841, pg. 27

The Reverend Sylvester Graham was a self-styled physician who, during the 1830s, toured America to lecture on the benefits of eating brown bread baked from coarse wheat flour. This was a progressive and not entirely successful crusade. Historically, whole wheat bread was seen as inferior and unscrupulous bakers were known to try to create a whiter bread, and to "improve" their product by the addition of whiting (bones and plaster of Paris). Sarah J. Hale was a sympathetic supporter of Mr. Graham, and probably did more by her efforts to encourage the eating of brown bread than did the fanatical Mr. Graham.

1 package dry yeast
¾ cup warm milk
1 teaspoon sugar
2¼ cups boiling water
2 cups old fashioned oats
3½ cups whole wheat flour
½ cup molasses
2 tablespoons butter
1 tablespoon salt
3 cups all-purpose flour

Whisk the yeast in the warm milk and sugar. Let it bubble for 5 minutes. In a large mixing bowl, pour the boiling water over the oats and let it stand for 5 minutes. Warm the molasses, butter, and salt in a saucepan until the butter is melted, then add to the yeast. Add this to the flour mixture. Stir and gradually add the whole-wheat flour and 2 cups of the all-purpose flour.

Turn the dough onto a floured counter and add as much of the remaining flour as is needed to make a stiff dough. Knead for 10 minutes. Divide into two loaves and place in buttered bread pans. Cover and let dough rise in a warm place until the dough has risen to the tops of the pans. Bake in a 375°F oven for 45 minutes, until the bread sounds hollow when tapped. Cool on racks. *Makes 2 loaves.*

# SWEET AND STICKY CINNAMON BUNS

Adapted from: Catharine Beecher, *Miss Beecher's Domestic Receipt Book*, 1846, pg. 94

1½ cups sugar

3 tablespoons cinnamon

2 packages active dry yeast

1 cup warm water

⅔ cup sugar

½ cup milk

⅔ cup melted butter

2 teaspoons salt

2 eggs beaten

8 cups flour

½ cup melted butter

1½ cups chopped pecans

½ cup melted butter

## ICING

6 tablespoons hot water

2 teaspoons vanilla extract

2 cups powdered sugar

Buns as an art form are most closely associated with "the City of Brotherly Love," Philadelphia. It was on the banks of the Delaware River, near the present Reading Terminal Market, where the farmers, fishermen, and hunters first gathered to trade and sell their wares. Eventually the market began to retail the Pennsylvania Dutch baked goods, and the sticky bun was born.

Mix the 1½ cups sugar and cinnamon and set aside. Whisk the yeast and ⅔ cup sugar in the cup of warm water and let proof. In a large bowl, mix together the milk, the yeast-sugar, ⅔ cup melted butter, salt and eggs. Add 7 cups of flour and mix to form a soft dough. Turn the dough out onto a floured surface and knead for 6 minutes, then place the dough in a cleaned and oiled bowl, cover and let rise until doubled in bulk.

Punch down the dough and let rest for 5 minutes while you coat a large shallow baking pan with another ½ cup melted butter. Roll out the dough into a rectangle measuring 15" x 20". Brush the final ½ cup butter over the dough, sprinkle with the cinnamon sugar mixture and the pecans. Roll up the dough tightly and cut the roll into 15 fat slices, using a sharp long-handled knife. Set the rolls side by side in the pan; the edges should touch. Set aside to rise for ½ hour. Bake in a 375°F oven for 25 minutes, until golden brown.

To make the icing, combine the hot water, vanilla extract, and powdered sugar and beat until smooth. When the rolls are cooled, drizzle the icing over the top. Serve at room temperature. *Makes 15 cinnamon buns.*

# LEMON CAKE

Adapted from: Catharine Beecher, *Miss Beecher's Domestic Receipt Book*, 1846, pg. 142

Lemons came to the New World in 1493, brought by Columbus's second voyage and planted thereafter throughout Haiti, and eventually Florida in the 1560s and California in the 1730s. Catharine Beecher's recipe for lemon cake is preferred here for its intense, lemony, sweet tart taste that is heightened by the glaze.

1 stick unsalted butter
1 cup plus 2 tablespoons granulated sugar
4 large eggs, separated
juice of 1 lemon and zest of 2 lemons
1 teaspoon almond extract
¼ cup milk
1 teaspoon baking powder
2 cups all-purpose flour, sifted
⅛ teaspoon salt

## GLAZE

1 cup powdered sugar
2 tablespoons lemon juice
grated zest of 1 lemon

 Preheat oven to 375°F. Line a 9" cake pan with parchment paper and spray with nonstick spray. In your food processor, blend the butter and 1 cup sugar until light and creamy. Add the egg yolks, one at a time, then the lemon juice, zest, the almond extract, and the milk.

Mix the salt, baking powder, and flour and add this mixture slowly to the creamed mixture.

In a separate bowl, beat the egg whites until they stand in stiff peaks. Sprinkle over the extra 2 tablespoons granulated sugar and combine the egg white mixture to the batter. Pour the lemon batter into the cake pan and bake for 30 minutes until light golden brown.

Let the cake cool in the pan for 5 minutes, then invert the pan and allow the cake to cool completely.

To make the glaze, whisk the sugar, lemon juice, and zest together and pour the glaze slowly over the cake, letting it drip over the sides. *Makes 1 cake.*

# A Ginger Cake for Lafayette

Adapted from: Sarah J. Hale, *The Good Housekeeper*, 1841, pg. 99

2 cups flour

1 teaspoon baking powder

¼ teaspoon salt

1 tablespoon ginger

½ teaspoon ground ginger

½ teaspoon cinnamon

½ teaspoon allspice

1 stick unsalted butter

½ cup dark brown sugar

3 large eggs

½ teaspoon vanilla

¾ cup molasses

¼ cup milk

½ cup coarsely chopped walnuts

2 tablespoons brandy

In the 19th century many cakes were named for the famous, and the French Revolutionary hero, Lafayette, came in for a goodly share. Mrs. Hale was still using pearl ash in her instructions, but the rising agent had its share of problems. It was hard to dissolve and mix evenly; any baker who has added too much soda to a recipe knows how the result can taste acid and is often discolored. Many cookbook authors were suspicious of putting chemical agents in food, and Mrs. Hale was one of them. We have substituted baking powder in this recipe, and added nuts and brandy to produce a moist and subtle flavor to this spicy cake.

 Preheat the oven to 350°F. Butter and flour a loaf pan. Mix together the flour, salt, baking powder, ginger, spices, and salt. Beat together the butter and the sugar until creamy, and add the eggs one at a time. Add the milk, molasses, and vanilla. Add the dry ingredients. Fold in the nuts and the brandy until just combined. Spoon the batter into the pan and bake in the middle of the oven for 40 minutes until golden brown. Cool in the pan for 10 minutes before turning out. Keeps well. *Serves 8.*

# "1-2-3-4" CUP CAKES

Adapted from: Lydia Maria Child, *The Frugal Housewife*, 1841, pg. 71

"**A**s easy as counting to four!" A cup of this, two cups of that, and so on. The name probably came from the ingredients used, rather than because the cakes were baked in cup-sized pans. Cup cakes weren't necessarily small, although they were easy to cook when they were and found favor with a housekeeper using her oven to full advantage. Small cakes could be finished off in an oven that was cooling down from the week's bread baking with little risk of burning the delicate crust.

1 cup butter
2 cups sugar
4 eggs
1 teaspoon vanilla essence
3 cups flour
½ cup ground almonds
½ cup currants
1 tablespoon lemon zest

Cream the sugar and butter together until creamy. Add the eggs and vanilla gradually. Sift the flour and gently fold it into the creamed mixture alternately with the ground almonds. Lastly, fold in the zest and currants, and stir gently. Put the batter in small cupcake pans and bake for 20 minutes until golden. When cool, the cupcakes may be iced and decorated with small crystallized fruits, violets, and so on. *Makes 12 cupcakes.*

# COMPOSITION CAKE

Adapted from: Sarah J. Hale, *The Good Housekeeper*, 1841, pg. 99

3 sticks butter

¾ cup brown sugar

1 cup sugar

6 eggs

3 cups flour

½ teaspoon salt

¾ cup brandy flavored with 1 tablespoon
    orange and 1 tablespoon lemon zest

Making butter was one of the house-
wifely chores completed by the 19th
century housewife and instructions were
included in cookbooks like Mrs. Hale's and
Mrs. Child's. Descriptions include details
of packing the butter in a clean, scalded
firkin, covered with brine. If you were
lucky enough to procure supplies from a
trusted farmer in the spring, you were
fortunate. Otherwise, the task of making
your own butter from cream fell to the
woman of the house. Cakes composed of
butter were therefore something special.
They were often much improved by the
addition of homemade brandy. Mrs. Child
suggests keeping a bottle of brandy flavored with lemon and orange peel to use
in puddings and pies.

Cream the butter and sugars together until fluffy. Add the eggs one by
one, beating well. Add the flour, sifted with the salt, and mix lightly.
Finally add the brandy. Pour the batter into a greased and floured loaf
pan or Bundt pan. Bake at 350°F for 45 minutes, or until a toothpick inserted in the
middle comes out clean. *Makes 1 large loaf.*

# QUAKING CUSTARD

Adapted from: Sarah J. Hale, *The Good Housekeeper*, 1841, pg. 94

A "Quaking Custard" shivering delicately on a bone china plate today is something of a rarity, but in the early 19th century, they were popular as desserts. The dish was more difficult to achieve then, because of the vicissitudes of the old brick ovens, which sometimes did not hold the temperature long enough for the custard to solidify. The addition of breadcrumbs, as in this recipe, made the pudding more solid. When fine cream was available from the dairy, the custard must have been a delicate and delicious end to one of the heavier meals of the period.

3 egg yolks

1 cup light cream

2 tablespoons sugar

2 tablespoons rosewater (alt: 1 tablespoon almond or vanilla essence)

½ teaspoon nutmeg

1 cup breadcrumbs, using homemade white bread

2 tablespoons melted butter

2 tablespoons currants, soaked in ½ tablespoon brandy

6 chopped dates

½ cup walnuts, chopped

## SAUCE

3 tablespoons redcurrant jelly

2 tablespoons butter

2 tablespoons brown sugar

Beat the eggs and cream together until light. Add the sugar, rosewater, nutmeg, and breadcrumbs, and mix until all are incorporated. Stir in the butter and the fruits and nuts. Cover and set aside for 2 hours, then pour into a buttered ovenproof baking dish. Bake at 350°F for 45 minutes, until the top is golden.

*To Make the Sauce:* Melt the butter with the sugar and jelly and simmer for 5 minutes. Pour warm over the pudding. *Serves 6.*

# New England Style Rhubarb Cake

Adapted from: Catharine Beecher, *Miss Beecher's Domestic Receipt Book*, 1841, pg. 00

2 cups fresh rhubarb, washed and trimmed
    and cut into ½" pieces
1 cup sugar plus 3 tablespoons
1 cup all-purpose flour
freshly grated zest from 1 orange
1 teaspoon nutmeg
1 teaspoon cinnamon
1 teaspoon baking soda
¼ teaspoon salt
4 tablespoons unsalted butter, cut into
    small pieces
1 egg and 1 tablespoon milk, combined
freshly squeezed orange juice from 1 orange

Rhubarb was a popular fruit in the early 19th century. Lydia Maria Child liked the early appearance of rhubarb in the spring, when there was little else to put in a pie, but she complained that rhubarb pies were dear "for they take an enormous quantity of sugar." Still, pioneer women made their families eat rhubarb (also called "Persian Apple" or simply "Spring Fruit") because it was "a broom for the system." Mrs. Hale and Miss Beecher concurred with Mrs. Child—rhubarb would continue to make appearances in medicinal books, but eaten in this succulent cake, adapted from a recipe from Catharine Beecher, it became a treat and not medicine at all.

Butter a 13"x9" baking dish. Preheat the oven to 350°F. Arrange the rhubarb pieces in the dish and sprinkle them with ¾ cup of the sugar, the nutmeg, cinnamon, orange zest, and 2 tablespoons of flour.

Combine the remaining flour, 2 tablespoons of the remaining sugar, the baking soda and salt. Then add the unsalted butter, rubbing it into the flour until it resembles breadcrumbs. Pour in the egg/milk mixture and form into a soft dough. Spoon this over the rhubarb and spread it smooth with a spatula. Bake for 25 minutes.

Mix the orange juice and the remaining sugar together and brush over the cake. Bake for 15 minutes more. Cool the cake for 5 minutes before loosening it from the dish and turning it upside down on a plate. Serve at once. *Serves 6.*

# CAPE COD BEACH PLUM PIE

Adapted from: Catharine Beecher, *Miss Beecher's Domestic Receipt Book*, 1841, pg. 00

From New England to Virginia this hardy perennial lives in the beach littoral and once a year offers a small tart fruit from its scrubby plants. The making of the tarts was part of the spring renewal for many in the Rhode Island colony, and the lore persisted down to the day of the reformer Catharine Beecher.

4 cups wild beach plums, washed and stoned

2 tablespoons orange marmalade

1 tablespoon lemon juice

⅔ cup sugar or to taste

⅓ cup arrowroot

½ cup flour

½ cup brown sugar

½ teaspoon ginger

½ teaspoon nutmeg

½ teaspoon cinnamon

4 tablespoon unsalted butter cut into pieces

1 frozen pie shell

 Mix the plums with the marmalade, lemon juice, sugar, and arrowroot and set aside to marinate for 30 minutes, stirring once.

Make the topping by mixing the flour, sugar, and spices together. Rub in the butter bits.

Pour the plum mixture into a buttered pie plate, and sprinkle with the topping. Bake for 45 minutes at 375°F until the filling bubbles. Cool and serve with cream. *Serves 8.*

# RICE SNOWBALLS

Adapted from: Sarah J. Hale, *The Good Housekeeper*, 1841, pg. 79

*4 large Granny Smith apples*
*4 tablespoons grated lemon peel*
*1 teaspoon cinnamon*
*2 tablespoons brown sugar*
*2 cups short-grain or pudding rice,*
  *cooked in milk*

## SAUCE

*2 tablespoons melted butter*
*2 tablespoons brown sugar*
*2 tablespoons sweet dessert wine*

Boiled puddings cooked in a cloth made frequent appearances in cookbooks that preached economy and good housekeeping. With a bit of careful planning, a kettle of water that simmered on the hearth could cook an entire family's meal, not only easing the cook's task but economizing on fuel. A joint of mutton boiled with a few vegetables could be ready for dinner, followed by a pudding of suet or a cornmeal mush for supper. These rice snowballs were more fanciful, but still required no special attention except an occasional prod to make sure the puddings did not stick to the pan.

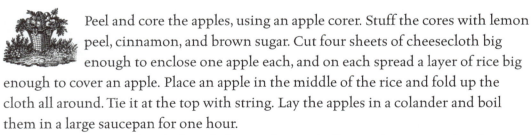 Peel and core the apples, using an apple corer. Stuff the cores with lemon peel, cinnamon, and brown sugar. Cut four sheets of cheesecloth big enough to enclose one apple each, and on each spread a layer of rice big enough to cover an apple. Place an apple in the middle of the rice and fold up the cloth all around. Tie it at the top with string. Lay the apples in a colander and boil them in a large saucepan for one hour.

To serve, remove the cloth and place each snowball on a plate, covered with a sauce made of melted butter, brown sugar, and sweet wine. *Serves 4.*

## Chapter Four

# Cooking on Two Fronts: From Frontier to Fireplace

Mrs. T. J. Crowen, *American Lady's Cookery Book*, 1847
Anna Collins, *The Great Western Cook Book*, 1857
Sarah J. Hale, Ed., Recipes from *Godey's Lady's Book*, 1860-1865
Dr. A. W. Chase, *Dr. Chase's Recipes, or, Information for Everybody*, 1864
Marion Harland, *Common Sense in the Household*, 1873
*Confederate Receipt Book*, 1863

The lure of the new frontier persuaded settlers in the thousands to head West in the years before the Civil War. For these hardy pioneers, eating was a matter of survival rather than good cooking, but as houses were built and primitive settlements became established townships, dining became more of a ritual and the market for new cookbooks correspondingly expanded.

Many pioneer families carried *Dr. Chase's Recipes, or, Information for Everybody* with them in the wagon west, giving it pride of place along with the Bible in their cramped quarters. The book became a sort of official owner's manual for survival on the frontier. Dr. Chase himself was a publicist par excellence, at the peak of his popularity suggesting that over 4 million souls owned a copy of his book. Hyperbole apart, the book was an encyclopedic tome that gave information and advice to a young, homesteading population who daily faced the challenges of finding and preparing food for their families. On the trail, the housewife spit roasted wild game over a campfire and was grateful for whatever her man shot, and carefully nurtured a sourdough so that she could knock up a batch of biscuits. One tale, probably not apocryphal, had a hardy housewife save her crock of sourdough as the wagon went down on a river crossing—this before any other possession! Once arrived at her destination, it might be months before she had a roof over her head and years before she took delivery of one of the new-fangled iron stoves for the kitchen.

It is hard to over estimate the revolution that the iron stove produced in the lives of busy housewives, and almost harder to understand the suspicion with which it was initially greeted. When President Fillmore had a stove installed in the White House in 1854, his chef walked out in protest, exclaiming that he could not cook on such a contraption. He clung stubbornly to the morass of hooks, cranes, hanging pots, and spits that were required to prepare a dinner over the fire, rather than embrace the new technology. The fact was, these early stoves were veritable monsters, with a myriad dampers and flues and a temperament enough to try the patience of any housewife. Despite all this, they were still a huge improvement in convenience and efficiency over the open hearth and eventually, of course, they became standard issue. To celebrate the new predictability possible when cooking in an oven with a regulated temperature, cookbooks like Marion Harland's *Common Sense in the Household* (1873) and Mrs. Crowen's *American Lady's Cookery Book* (1847), included a vast number of recipes for baked goods, especially cakes.

Although many of the recipes were still for the loaf cakes that were of English origin (we'd call these enriched yeast breads and not cakes), housewives accepted the use of baking soda and cream of tartar as leaven for their cake batters. Pearl ash, as introduced to bakers by Amelia Simmons fifty years previous, was now outmoded. The rules of cake baking were more or less codified by this time, and it was now a matter of imagination to decide what ingredients to include. The cake recipes in this chapter suggest just a handful of the possibilities.

America's love affair with baking has continued to this day and it had its roots in cookbooks of this period. Marion Harland's approach was the "Stand facing the oven" one that was used a hundred years later by another famous cookbook author, Irma Rombauer. Equally astute were Mrs. Harland's savvy advice columns in magazines such as *Home-Maker* and *Housekeeper's Weekly* that won her a loyal readership for her full-length cookbooks.

The reader's recipes in the best selling magazine *Godey's Lady's Book* also leaned heavily on the breads, cakes, and pies that America loved to bake and eat. The recipes were largely from rural homes and were, for the most part, traditional. The women who sent in their contributions for publication by Mrs. Hale took great pride in the skills of their mothers and grandmothers.

This was "not for profit" recipe writing at its best and the trend soon reached mammoth proportions. Communities all over the war-torn country put together collections of recipes that were often sold in aid of a charity—the improvement of hospitals or to help the families of wounded veterans. The subject of charitable or community cookbooks is dealt with in our next chapter.

The deprivations of the War generated a rash of nostalgic, fond recollections for food that could not be enjoyed by the South and their boys away on the battlefield. Mrs. Harland made mouths water with recipes in *Common Sense in the Household* for fried chicken, light and fluffy biscuits, and mashed Neshannock potatoes. It all made welcome reading for Southern cooks who were forced to make an art form of substitution: water melon syrup for molasses; ground crackers instead of apples in the pie; roasted and skinned peanuts for hot chocolate; and sassafras bark and huckleberry instead of black tea. Out of this deprivation was born a flowering of Southern and soul cooking that burst forth after the war in many fine regional cookbooks.

The celebrities of this period were the unsung heroines of frontier and fireplace, who struggled against the odds in difficult circumstances to produce meals for their families, whether over a campfire in the West, in an iron stove in a Northern kitchen, or over a hearth down South. What they cooked is recorded in this unique collection of cookbooks, written on two fronts.

# UNCLE JIMMY'S AUTHENTIC BRUNSWICK STEW

Adapted from: Marion Harland, *Common Sense in the Household*, 1873

In 1828, Dr. Creed Haskins, running for the legislature, needed a show-stopper for his political rally. He called on that infamous raconteur, bootlegger, and man-about-the-woods, Uncle Jimmy Matthews, to do the honors with a colossal production of Jimmy's trademark squirrel stew. Uncle Jimmy did the trick—Haskins got re-elected, and the voters of Brunswick County, Virginia, claimed they had never eaten so good!

2 squirrels, dressed and cut into serving pieces
   (alt: chicken can also be used)
1½ teaspoons salt
1 cup red potatoes, peeled and chopped
6 large tomatoes, skinned, peeled, and chopped
1 pound fresh, shelled lima beans
1 cup chopped onion
1¾ cups corn from the cob
1 teaspoon sugar
½ teaspoon salt
¼ teaspoon pepper
½ teaspoon red pepper
½ teaspoon oregano

Place the squirrels (or chicken) in a large Dutch oven, cover with water, add salt and bring to a boil. Reduce the heat to a simmer and cook for 1 hour. Drain, reserving broth and the cooked meat separately. Skim the fat from the broth, return to the Dutch oven, and reduce to 2 cups. Add the potatoes and cook 10 minutes. Add the tomatoes, lima beans, onion, and simmer for 20 minutes. Stir in the corn and remaining ingredients. Return the cooked meat to the pot and continue to simmer for 15 minutes more. Adjust the seasonings and serve in individual bowls. *Serves 8.*

# FRIED CHICKEN THE COMMON SENSE WAY

Adapted from: Marion Harland, *Common Sense in the Household*, 1873

*1 plump young chicken, cut up*
*1 clove garlic, split*
*1½ to 2 pounds lard*
*1 cup flour*
*salt and pepper*
*1 cup cream*

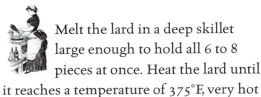

Melt the lard in a deep skillet large enough to hold all 6 to 8 pieces at once. Heat the lard until it reaches a temperature of 375°F, very hot but not smoking.

Pat the chicken pieces dry and rub each one with a split garlic clove. Season them with salt and pepper. Dip them into the flour, turning to coat each piece evenly, and shake off the excess.

Fry them all in the pan together, starting with the drumsticks first, then count to 5, then the thighs, then the breasts, skin-side down. Turn with tongs until they color richly and evenly. Total frying pan time should be 12 minutes, maximum, from the first drumstick to the removal of all. Remove the chicken pieces from the fat and lay on paper towels to drain. Put them in a warm oven to keep warm while you make the cream gravy.

Take 2 tablespoons of the hot fat and make a roux by adding 2 tablespoons flour. Pour the cream in a thin stream into the pan and bring the gravy to a boil, stirring all the time. Season and serve poured over the chicken. *Serves 4-6.*

Fried chicken is featured in all the cookbooks of the period and each cook had his or her own favorite recipe. Like all dishes, it was seasonal and most often served in the spring and early summer when the flock was culled. Lard was the frying medium of choice and gave unbeatable results. It remained the leader of the pack until late century when its position was challenged by synthetic substitutes, one of which was Cottolene. Lard by this time was being blamed for the preponderance of dyspeptic stomachs that abounded in America. In the cookbooks of this period, many recipes are condemned or recommended because they inflame sensitive stomachs. Nowadays there are other reasons for not frying in lard; your most recent cholesterol readings will guide you as to how often to enjoy this delight.

# POTTED PIGEON

Adapted from: The pages of *Godey's Lady's Book*, 1865

In the days following the Civil War, percussion cap shotguns were generally available for shooting birds in an afternoon's sport. Following a bash or two at the feathers, one might eventually expect a light repast with a morsel of bread, a glass of cider from the cellar, and in well-provisioned estates a jar of potted pigeon. As early as 1860, Underwood & Co. was shipping canned and deviled ham to markets across the country, but it was an old fashioned custom to make one's own fresh game terrines.

2 cups pigeon breasts and legs, cooked
⅔ cup butter
¼ teaspoon allspice
a pinch of cayenne
1 tablespoon brandy
salt and pepper to taste
aspic to cover

Remove the skin and bones from the cold, cooked game birds and chop the meat finely. Working in batches, pound the meat in a mortar with the butter until the paste is quite smooth. Season to taste with the allspice, cayenne, brandy, the salt and the pepper.

Pack the mixture into several small ceramic jars, seal with aspic, cover and tie down with string.

Serve one jar to each diner with a broad knife, a manchet of bread, and a quaff of cider. *Serves 4.*

# YANKEE BEANS

Adapted from: Mrs. T. J. Crowen, *American Lady's Cookery Book*, 1847, p. 115

2 quarts dried navy beans
1 pound corned pork
1 teaspoon red pepper flakes
2 teaspoons cayenne pepper
salt and pepper
2 teaspoons butter bits
2 teaspoons flour

Beans in one form or another, almost always with pork, were a dietary staple during the middle of the century. Rations in the Union army included two ounces of beans daily, along with 12 ounces of salt pork. Pilgrim women often used the slow-baking technique for the pork and beans on a Saturday so as to be available for Sunday meals without a Sabbath conflict. And the U.S. Navy was so consistently a provider of the light-colored beans to its seamen that in common parlance the "navy" bean was born.

 Soak the beans overnight. In a Dutch oven place the drained beans and cover with fresh water. Score the pork rind all over with a sharp knife and turn it with tongs in a hot pan until is colored richly and evenly. Add to the Dutch oven with the spices, cover, and bring to a boil. Reduce the heat and simmer for 2 hours, until the beans are tender.

In a lightly buttered loaf pan, put in the drained beans with a little of the liquor. Lay the pork on top and press it down to cover. Dot the top with the butter bits and sprinkle over the flour. Set in a moderate oven and bake for one hour. *Serves 12.*

# FRENCH PILAU

Adapted from: The pages of *Godey's Lady's Book*, 1862, p. 140

Noted food historian, the late Karen Hess, did invaluable work on the origins of rice growing in the Carolinas. She concluded that it was slaves whose knowledge of rice cultivation established the industry, which died out after emancipation. "Pilaf" came to this country via two sources. One was from the slaves who called the dish "Hoppin' John," and the other was via the French Huguenots who fled from religious persecution to America and brought the dish with them. French rice growing had a long tradition behind it, although it was never as widespread as it became in the Carolinas.

*1 chicken, jointed*
*1 medium onion, chopped*
*2 cloves garlic, peeled and minced*
*4 tablespoons butter*
*1 cup basmati rice*
*2 thick slices smoked ham*
*8 oz. smoked sausage, sliced*
*2 cups chicken stock*
*fresh herbs: parsley, rosemary, thyme, chopped*
*salt and pepper*
*4 oz. mushrooms, cleaned and chopped*

Stew the chicken for 1 hour until tender. Remove and reserve the cooking liquor. When cool enough to handle, remove the meat from the bones.

In a skillet, fry the onion and garlic in the butter, add the rice and stir to coat the grains. Add the sliced ham and sausage. Gradually add the stock to the pan and bring to a boil. Lower the heat, cover and simmer for 10 minutes. Off the heat, allow the rice to stand for an additional 10 minutes to absorb the liquid. Fry the mushrooms in a little extra butter and add to the skillet, along with the chicken meat and herbs. Season well and stir to combine. Let stand at the side of the fire for at least 5 minutes until ready to serve. The pilau should be dry. *Serves 4.*

# SCALLOPED OYSTERS

Adapted from: The pages of *Godey's Lady's Book*, 1862, p. 132

1½ pints oysters with their liquor
1 cup stale white breadcrumbs
4 tablespoons melted butter
½ teaspoon salt
½ teaspoon pepper
½ cup cream
Worcestershire sauce

As shad had been commonplace in American cuisine and in her cookbooks, by the War years, oysters had become ubiquitous. They were consumed in vast quantities at oyster bars across the nation. By 1840, annual shipments of oysters from the Chesapeake Bay to Philadelphia had reached four thousand tons and by 1859, residents in New York City spent more on oysters than butcher's meat. This dish of scalloped oysters cooked well "in front of a nice clear fire," as the *Godey's* reader suggests.

 Drain the oysters, but save the liquor. Toss the breadcrumbs lightly with the butter. Butter the bottom of a small gratin dish and spread ⅓ of the crumbs into it, then cover with half the oysters. Salt and pepper. Repeat. Mix the reserved liquor with enough of the cream to make 1 cup, season with salt and pepper and Worcestershire sauce, and pour this over the oysters. Top with the last breadcrumbs and bake in a 350°F oven for 45 minutes. Serve at once. *Makes 4 servings.*

# Salmon Trout and Adirondack Poetry

Adapted from: Marion Harland, *Common Sense in the Household*, 1873, p. 64

"Salmon Trout," no matter where you catch them, are not salmon at all, but rather anadromous brook or brown trout that have probably spent some time in the ocean and then returned up river to be caught by grateful sportsmen and women. Their large size is what provoked the curious common name, and often their flesh has a slightly pink hue, but a trout they remain. In the right circumstances, perhaps with Winslow Homer behind his easel on the far bank, the normally sensible Marion Harland may be forgiven for the poetic rush she felt upon dining on fresh poached trout.

*"Those who have eaten this prince of game fish in the Adirondacks within an hour after he has left the lake will agree with me that he never has such justice done him at any other time as when baked in cream. He will take kindly to the creamy bath—let no sharp spiced sauces come near him. They would but mar his native richness. Salt him lightly should he need it, eat and be happy."*

## To Do Justice to A Large Trout

1 large lake trout, 2 lbs. or better, gilled and
    oven-ready
3 cups cream
2 tablespoons butter
parsley and lemon for garnish

 In a large oven roasting pan, arrange the fish on its side, add the cream to reach halfway up the side of the fish, and send to a preheated 325°F oven on the center rack.

Taking care that the cream does not boil, baste the fish occasionally until it is done, and the flesh behind the gills flakes easily to the teasing of a knifepoint, about 40 minutes, or 10 minutes per inch of thickness of the fish at the thickest point.

Remove the fish from the oven and quickly separate the serving fillets with a fish knife. Add a bit of butter, salt and pepper if necessary, and lemon and parsley for garnish. *Serves 4.*

# Oyster Vol-au-Vents

Adapted from: Marion Harland, *Common Sense in the Household*, 1873, p. 80

*1 quart fresh oysters*
*1 cup clam juice or fish stock*
*2 tablespoons butter*
*2 tablespoons flour*
*2 tablespoons cream*
*salt and pepper*

## Puff Pastry

*3 cups unbleached all-purpose flour*
*1½ teaspoons salt*
*3 sticks cold butter cut in cubes*
*9 tablespoons ice water mixed with 2 teaspoons*
    *lemon juice*

The journey of the oyster on American tables was an odyssey. It began in the wigwams of the Wampanoag Indians and traveled to the oyster saloon bars of New York, and thence to the dining rooms of big cities and small towns all across the country. By 1859, residents in New York spent more on oysters than on meat. There are more recipes for oysters in the cookbooks than any other seafood.

Set the oysters in a saucepan covered with fish broth or clam juice. Bring the pot to a boil, skim the froth, and stir in the butter rubbed with the flour. Keep stirring and when the liquor thickens, add the cream and seasonings. Simmer gently for 2 minutes. Remove from the heat and cool.

To make the puff pastry, combine the dry ingredients, add the butter cubes and rub together with fingertips to form meal-like texture. Pour in the liquid and stir to form a rough dough. Wrap and chill for 1 hour. Remove from the icebox and roll out lightly to a rectangle, fold in 3 like a letter, and repeat once more. Chill until needed.

Roll out half the chilled pastry to ½" thickness. Cut the vol-au-vent shells as follows. Using a cookie cutter of 3½" diameter, cut out circles and place half on a cookie sheet. Using a smaller cutter of 2" diameter, cut out the centers of the remaining pastry circles to make rings. Place each ring on one of the larger circles and press lightly. Paint the vol au vents with egg wash and bake in a 400°F oven for 15 minutes, until the pastry is puffed. Fill each vol au vent with warm sauced oysters.

*Makes 12 vol-au-vents.*

# THE HISTORICAL PEPPER POT SOUP

Adapted from: The pages of *Godey's Lady's Book*, 1860 and 1861, p. 68

This soup was fed to Washington's famished troops in 1777 as they over-wintered and prepared to repulse the British. A hearty mix of tripe, hot peppers, and scraps of meat, this soup is attributed miraculous powers. It is a dish with West Indian origins and it is thought that Africans serving alongside the Continental Army played a part in the soup's concoction. "Pepper Pot" was so popular that the recipe appeared for two years in a row in *Godey's Lady's Book*. This, from the second version, has been made genteel by substituting ham and chicken for the tripe.

1 pound lean ham
1 chicken, jointed and skin removed
2 onions, chopped
2 large potatoes, peeled and chopped
1 cup celery, chopped
1 cup green pepper, chopped
4 tablespoons butter
5 cups stock
salt and pepper
cayenne to taste
½ cup cream blended with 3 tablespoons flour

 Simmer the chicken in the stock for 1 hour. Cook the vegetables in the butter until soft and add to the pan along with the ham. Cook for a half hour, then remove the chicken meat from the bones and return the meat to the pan. Thicken the soup with the cream, season to taste with salt, pepper, and cayenne. Serve piping hot in bowls. *Serves 6.*

# Rabbit Soup

Adapted from: The pages of *Godey's Lady's Book*, 1861, p. 173

2 rabbits
2 tablespoons flour
2 onions, chopped
2 carrots, chopped
1 teaspoon grated nutmeg
3 tablespoons butter
4 cups chicken or veal stock
salt and pepper
1 teaspoon marjoram
1 tablespoon redcurrant jelly

Godey's magazine was targeted to women in the expanding middle class of the mid-19th century. They were readers who sent in their recipes, an idea that was new in the publishing industry and another "first" for Mrs. Sarah J. Hale, the magazine's remarkable editor. The readership was largely rural and this was reflected in the recipes. "Rabbit Soup" was familiar to readers both North and South. This particular recipe, sent in during 1861, is substantial enough to be eaten as a stew.

Joint the rabbits and dredge lightly in flour. Fry in butter until golden, remove, and put in a large pot. Fry the onions in the same fat and add to the pan along with the carrots, nutmeg, stock, and marjoram. Season with salt and pepper. Cover the pan and cook in a moderate oven for 2 hours, until the meat is almost falling off the bone. Strain the soup to remove the bones and shred the rabbit meat. Return the soup to the pot, bring back to the boil and thicken, if needed, with a roux. Add the jelly and season well. Serve with croutons of fried bread. *Serves 8.*

# ℋEIRLOOM ℒUCCOTASH

Adapted from: Marion Harland, *Common Sense in the Household*, 1873, p. 173

It is often said that, in honor of their Indian guests at the first Thanksgiving dinner, the Pilgrims served a thick porridge of corn, beans, and bear grease called succotash. (Which proves that if you stand close enough to the fires of history, the smoke gets in your eyes.) Lima beans, although very popular today, if not to say mandatory, in succotash definitely were not at that first party. Limas (*phaseolus lunatus*) need a rather long 80-day growing period, which Plymouth couldn't offer. Nevertheless, Marion Harland knew what her readers expected in 1873, and here is succotash the way it should have been when your grandmother was a girl, and always has been ever since, no matter the facts.

2 cups fresh lima beans
1 cup water
2 cups fresh corn kernels
½ cup cream
4 tablespoons butter
salt and pepper

 Boil the beans in water until tender; the water will almost evaporate. Add corn, cover, and cook over high heat for 5 minutes shaking frequently. Add the cream and butter and stir to coat. Season to taste and serve. *Serves 4.*

# HOMINY CROQUETTES

Adapted from: Marion Harland, *Common Sense in the Household*, 1873, p. 236

1 cup canned hominy (yellow or white)
1 tablespoon butter, melted and cooled
1 cup whole milk
1 teaspoon sugar
1 egg, beaten
2 tablespoons flour
½ cup breadcrumbs, made from stale
     white bread

Hominy is the whole kernel of the corn, shucked off at its juicy ripeness, and preserved by soaking it in homemade lye. In the 19th century, this was part of the household chores, and relied on a regular supply of lye that the lady of the house made from wood ash and water. Mrs. Marion Harland was the pen name of a successful Southern novelist, who turned her hand to writing cookbooks after the Civil War. This one sold over one million copies between 1871 and 1892.

Put the hominy in a small bowl and add the melted butter. Combine, then add the milk, beating to form a soft paste. Add the sugar and egg. Chill this mixture for 30 minutes, then form into oval balls with floured hands. Dip each ball in egg and then in crumbs. Fry in hot oil. *Serves 4.*

# OLD 49er's Sourdough

Adapted from: Dr. A.W. Chase, *Dr. Chase's Recipes*, 1864, p. 486

Before yeast was available in foil wrappers and packages, a few bread cooks realized they could preserve a supply of starter dough, use a few handfuls to start a loaf each day, and then replenish the starter with fresh flour and water. That starter was a precious commodity, and many a crock traveled West to Oregon on a rattling, rickety wagon, held tight in the lap of the family daughter, and protected from all the hazards of the trail. During the California gold rush of 1849, the miners had nothing else but "sourdough" as this bread was called, so they made a virtue of it. Today the sourdough of San Francisco is highly prized.

## STARTER

1½ cups lukewarm milk, whole preferred
¼ teaspoon dried yeast
1 teaspoon clover honey
2 cups unbleached white flour
¼ cup spring water

## THE BREAD

1 cup Starter
2 cups unbleached flour
2 teaspoons salt
1 cup warm water
1 tablespoon olive oil

 *To Make the Starter:* Put the yeast in a bowl with the milk, honey, and 1 cup of flour and whisk to combine. Cover closely with plastic wrap and set in a warm place to ferment for 72 hours. After 24 hours, and again after 48 hours, stir down the starter and let it recover volume. Whisk in the rest of the flour, cover again, and let the dough rise for another 2 hours. Transfer the starter to a glass jar. Keep tightly covered in the refrigerator for up to 1 month, replenishing after each use with ½ cup each of water and flour.

*To Make the Loaf:* Remove 1 cup of the starter and bring to room temperature. Beat the starter into the warm water, add salt and oil, and stir in the flour. Make a shaggy dough, turn out onto a counter and knead vigorously for 10 minutes until the dough is smooth and pliant. Add more spoonfuls of flour as needed. Place in an oiled bowl, cover, and allow to rise. The dough may take 4 hours to double in bulk. Punch down, form into a large round loaf and rise again until puffy. Slash the loaf 4 times with a sharp knife and bake 40 minutes in a preheated 450°F oven until golden brown. Cool before tearing into hunks to eat. *Serves 8.*

# MULE TRAIN CORN BREAD

Adapted from: Anna Collins, *The Great Western Cook Book*, 1857, p. 132

¾ cup finely diced bacon

2 cups cornmeal

1½ teaspoon baking powder

½ teaspoon baking soda

1 teaspoon salt

2 eggs

1 cup buttermilk

2 tablespoons bacon drippings

The 1400 hundred mile wagon train trek from the Missouri River to California was not a trip to be undertaken lightly. Special knowledge of the trail, the Indians, and the weather qualified certain men to lead these undertakings, for a fee. One of the most remarkable was Captain Randolph B. Marcy, veteran of many trips, who wrote *The Prairie Traveler: A Handbook for Overland Expeditions*. In it he bemoaned the extravagance of some of his charges, one party in particular from New York who had loaded their wagon with champagne, olives, and sweetmeats from the delicatessen, only to throw it all out en route. The Captain liked bacon for the trip, and extolled its use as fat, meat, and cooking medium. This is the cornbread for the wagon trail.

Fry the bacon for 10 minutes until crisp. Drain and reserve fat. Mix the cornmeal, baking powder, baking soda, and salt in a bowl. Beat in the eggs and buttermilk, then the bacon drippings. Add the finely diced bacon to the batter. Pour into a buttered pan and bake for 25 minutes in a 400°F oven. *Serves 4-6.*

# BUCKWHEAT SHORT CAKES

Adapted from: Dr. A.W. Chase, *Dr. Chase's Recipes*, 1864, p. 289

The frontier encyclopedia was a vocation and a career to Dr. Alvin Wood Chase. By this great book, *Dr. Chase's Recipes, or, Information for Everybody*, he meant to educate, illuminate, and motivate an entire nation. Not since Gervase Markham, writing in 1615, has one author in one volume established "departments" of learning for merchants, tanners, harness makers, gunsmiths, barbers, and cooks. It was all there if you would only turn the page and become enlightened. Neither was he bashful about recipes for the kitchen, and with the panache of a master salesman he has transformed a common griddle cake into the magnificent creation you see before you.

1 cup milk
1 package dried yeast
2 eggs, separated
½ cup sour cream
1 cup each of buckwheat and all-purpose
    flours, combined
½ teaspoon salt

Warm the milk and put it in a small bowl with the yeast; whisk to combine. Separate the eggs and stir the yolks together with the sour cream into the yeast. Add the flour and salt and stir to make a thick batter. Cover the bowl and leave for 1 hour until bubbly.

Whisk the egg whites until stiff and fold them into the batter. Brush a baking sheet with butter and drop spoonfuls of batter onto the sheet 2" apart. Bake in a preheated 350°F oven for about 15 minutes until golden brown, then flip and cook the other side for another 15 minutes total. Eat warm with syrup or honey and more butter. *Serves 8 for breakfast.*

# The First Baguette

Adapted from: Mrs. T. J. Crowen, *American Lady's Cookery Book*, 1847, p. 162

### Sponge Starter

⅛ teaspoon dried yeast
¾ cup warm water
1 cup lower protein unbleached flour

### Dough

½ teaspoon dried yeast
½ cup water
2 cups flour mixed with 1 teaspoon salt
1 egg white, beaten with 1 tablespoon water

 Combine the ingredients for the starter and stir to make a thick batter. Cover the bowl and leave for 4 hours until the batter is double in size.

To make the dough, add the yeast and the water to the sponge and stir. Add the flour to form a shaggy dough. Knead the dough vigorously for about 10 minutes until the dough is smooth and satiny. To determine if the dough is sufficiently kneaded, stretch a piece thin with your fingers. If it tears, continue to knead for another 5 minutes. This is called the windowpane test. Let the dough rise, covered, for 1½ hours.

Turn the dough out onto the work surface and form 2 baguettes, each about 15" long. Place the formed loaves on a parchment-covered baking sheet, cover loosely with a plastic bag sealed at the top, and leave to rise overnight in a refrigerator. When you are ready to bake, preheat the oven to 500°F along with the baking stone. Place a baking pan on the bottom shelf. Allow the loaves to remain at room temperature for 45 minutes, then slash the tops 5 times with a very sharp knife, and brush the surface with egg white glaze. Pour boiling water into the baking pan. Carefully slide the baguettes onto the hot stone and bake for 15 minutes total, turning the loaves after 10 minutes. Cool before eating. *Makes 2 loaves.*

The incomparable French baguette, that long, crusty golden loaf so familiar in modern Parisian street scenes, is the product of what was originally an imported Viennese bread oven. And it only achieved that remarkable crust, color, and texture because of engineering wizardry that included internal steam injectors and sloping oven floors. Mrs. T. J. Crowen wrote about the technique in her mid-19th century bible of baking. She described the manner in which the water vapor falls back from the roof of the oven and gives the crust its beautiful tint. For years now, modern American home bakers have been trying to replicate the same procedure, with the inimitable Julia Child shouting instructions about pans of boiling water and heavy stones from the background.

# Monsieur Giron's Snow Drift Cake

Adapted from: Marion Harland, *Common Sense in the Household*, 1873, p. 332

For an American hero fifty years after the battles, the parades went on and on. The General Marquis de Lafayette and his wife were lionized across America in that soldier's tour of 1825. Every door was opened and every patriot lined the streets. For the Kentucky banquet honoring the great man, Monsieur Giron, a celebrated baker, developed a white cake that was such a success that the cake itself became a celebrity. Silver or "snow drift" cakes such as this, derive their lightness from well-beaten egg whites.

*1 cup unsalted butter*

*2 cups white sugar*

*1 cup milk*

*3 cups flour, sifted*

*3 teaspoons baking powder*

*1 cup blanched almonds, ground in a food processor to resemble coarse flour*

*6 egg whites*

*1 teaspoon vanilla extract*

Preheat the oven to 350°F. Grease and flour a Bundt cake pan. Cream the butter and sugar until smooth and creamy, add the milk, the sifted flour, and baking powder alternately to make a smooth batter. Stir in the almond flour and vanilla extract. Beat the egg whites until stiff and carefully fold these into the batter using a metal spoon.

Pour the batter into the prepared pan and bake for 1 hour. A toothpick inserted in the cake will come out clean. Cool before sprinkling with powdered sugar. *Serves 8.*

# TALL LAYERED CARAMEL CAKE

Adapted from: Marion Harland, *Common Sense in the Household*, 1873, p. 323

3 cups sugar

1½ cups butter

1 cup milk

4½ cups flour

5 eggs

1 teaspoon soda

2 teaspoons cream of tartar

## CARAMEL FILLING

1½ cups brown sugar

½ cup milk

1 cups molasses

4 tablespoons butter

1 tablespoon flour

2 tablespoons cold water

2 oz. good semisweet chocolate

1 teaspoon vanilla extract

This tall, southern-style layer cake was a typical example of celebration food. In this era before modern rising agents, much of the cake's success depended upon the quality of the eggs used—and their freshness. Marion Harland gave the conventional wisdom of the day and advised her readers to use the following test:

"A fresh egg placed in water will sink to the bottom. In breaking eggs, do not break them over the vessel in which they are to be beaten. Break them, one by one, over a saucer, so that if you come across a defective one, you will not spoil the rest by mixing it with them."

*To Make the Cake:* Beat the sugar and butter together until they are light and fluffy. Beat the eggs and add them one at a time to the batter. Sift the flour with the soda and cream of tartar, and fold the mixture into the batter alternately with the milk. Pour the batter into 2 greased and floured cake tins. Bake in a 350°F oven for 30 minutes until the cakes are golden brown. Let them cool for 5 minutes in the pans before turning them out to cool.

*To Prepare the Filling:* Put all the ingredients except the chocolate and vanilla in a small pan and bring to a boil. Cook for 5 minutes until a thick custard is formed. Beat in the vanilla and chocolate and let melt. Cool before using to fill the cake and frost the top. Best eaten the same day. *Makes one layer cake.*

# RICE FLOUR ORANGE COOKIES

Adapted from: Marion Harland, *Common Sense in the Household*, 1873, p. 336

Cakes, cookies, and *teacakes* were terms used interchangeably in early 19th century recipes. One classic receipt incorporated rice flour, and the orange-flavored cookie is specially short and crumbly as a result. Those who like Scottish shortbread will recognize the texture. Rice flour may be either brown or white. The white gives a more tender and moist cookie. Orange and rose flower waters were still popular as flavorings for baked goods at this time.

*2 eggs*
*1 cup powdered sugar*
*juice and rind of 1 orange*
*1 tablespoon orange flower water*
*1 stick unsalted butter*
*1 cup rice flour*
*1 cup all-purpose flour*

Whisk the eggs and sugar to a foam, add the orange juice and water, and beat well. In a separate bowl, beat the butter until it is soft, then beat into the sugar mixture. Sift the flours together and add to the batter along with the orange rind. When the batter is smooth, drop spoonfuls onto a greased cookie sheet. Bake in a 350°F oven for 10 minutes, until the cookies are lightly colored. *Makes 16 cookies.*

# Pioneer Bride's Cake

Adapted from: Anna Collins, *The Great Western Cook Book*, 1857, p. 120

¼ cup sherry

2 cups chopped candied peel

2 cups golden raisins

2 cups currants

½ cup candied cherries

1 cup stewed blueberries

3 cups flour

½ teaspoon baking powder

2 teaspoons mixed sweet spice

2 cups dark brown sugar

1 cup butter

5 eggs, beaten

1 cup ground almonds

1 recipe marzipan (see p. 46)

## Royal Icing

6 cups confectioner's sugar

4 egg whites

1 tablespoon lemon juice

For Anna Collins, writing as she was from the Utopian community of New Harmony, Indiana, an American wedding cake meant a rich, spiced cake, similar to an English fruitcake and iced with marzipan and frosting. Sometimes, these festive cakes were called black cakes, on account of the molasses used to sweeten the batter. Another variation was to add blueberries to the mix; the resulting batter was dark and fruit enriched.

 Combine the dried fruits with the sherry, then add the blueberries and mix. Set aside. Sift the flour with the spices and baking powder and set aside. Line a 9" round cake tin with wax paper and flour it lightly. Cream the sugar and butter together until fluffy. Gradually add the beaten eggs. Add the fruit alternately with the flour mixture until combined. Finally fold in the ground almonds. Spoon the batter into the pan and bake in a 325°F oven for 2 hours until a toothpick inserted in the center comes out clean. Cool completely, then ice with marzipan and royal icing as desired.

Roll half the marzipan into a circle big enough to fit the top of the cake. Brush the cake with melted redcurrant jelly and lay on the marzipan. Repeat with a strip of marzipan long enough to roll around the cake completely. Seal the edges and let the marzipan harden for 24 hours.

Make the icing by sifting the powdered sugar into a large bowl and adding the egg whites slowly, whisking and then stirring to form a white icing that will hold its shape. Add the lemon juice and beat. While the icing is still spreadable, coat the top and sides of the cake. Let the cake rest for 24 hours before eating. *Makes 1 cake.*

# THE NIGHTINGALE'S PUDDING

Adapted from: The pages of *Godey's Lady's Book*, 1865, p. 226

It was P. T. Barnum, showman extraordinaire, who launched the unprecedented media campaign that promoted Jenny Lind's American tour in 1850. In the crush to see her, newspapers reported, coats were torn, headdresses crushed, and ladies carried off in a swoon. And in her honor was created a lubricating singer's soup that was a liaison of sago, eggs, and cream, an entrée of oysters and ham, and this pudding.

*1 loaf brioche bread, one day old (see p. 40)*
*10 apples*
*½ cup lemon juice*
*1 cup sugar*
*1 teaspoon cinnamon*
*½ stick unsalted butter*

Cut the crust off the bread and make breadcrumbs. Peel and slice the apples and sprinkle them with lemon juice. Butter a round casserole dish generously and lay in about ¼ of the crumbs. Top with ¼ of the apples, sprinkle with sugar and cinnamon, and repeat until all the layers are used. Cut the butter into small pieces and sprinkle over the top of the pudding. Bake in a 350°F oven for 1 hour. Serve with lots of cream. *Serves 6.*

# MOCK APPLE PIE

Adapted from: *Confederate Receipt Book*, 1863, p. 19

2 recipes Short Crust Pie Dough (*see p. 50*)

2 cups sugar

1½ cups water

2 teaspoons cream of tartar

1 lemon, both zest and juice

24 buttery crackers

2 tablespoons butter

1 egg

1 teaspoon nutmeg

1 teaspoon cinnamon

There was a time in the South following the Civil War when fruit of any kind, and sometimes even food itself, was hard to come by. It is well-known that sometimes starving soldiers would sprinkle gunpowder on their steaks to approximate the taste of salt and pepper. And for dessert, using the abundant crackers on hand to build a mock apple pie was right in keeping with the tradition. One hundred years later the Ritz cracker company followed tradition and announced a variation of this recipe on the back of their box, using their buttery crackers to make "a modern mock apple pie."

 Place the sugar, cream of tartar, and water in a saucepan and bring to a boil. Lower the heat and simmer for 10 minutes. Add the lemon juice and zest, then cool.

Roll out half the pastry and line a pie plate. Crush the crackers roughly and place in the pastry shell, then pour over the syrup. Dot with the butter. Beat the egg and pour over the filling. Roll out the remaining pastry and place over the pie. Do not seal the edges. Slit the top of the pie. Bake at 425°F for 30 minutes until the crust is golden. Cool the pie, then gently remove the lid, sprinkle the nutmeg and cinnamon over the filling and replace the lid. Serve cold with ice cream. *Serves 6.*

# Boston Cream Pie

Adapted from: The pages of *Godey's Lady's Book*, 1865, p. 186

In Boston during the Civil War, the Parker House Hotel was such a model of prestige and success that they not only hired a French chef, named Sanzian, but he created the "Boston Cream Pie" for the fascination of an adoring clientele. To facilitate analysis one should be aware that this "pie" is actually a cake, which features a pastry, split and filled with a sweetened creamy custard, and covered in a chocolate glaze.

## Filling

2 cups cream

1 vanilla bean, crushed

3" cinnamon stick

¼ cup sugar

4 egg yolks

## Sponge Cake

2 large eggs

⅔ cup sugar

1 teaspoon vanilla extract

1 cup cake flour

1 teaspoon baking powder

¼ teaspoon salt

½ cup milk

½ stick unsalted butter, cut in pieces

## Glaze

¼ cup heavy cream

3 oz. semisweet chocolate

 *To Make the Filling:* Bring the cream, cinnamon stick, and vanilla bean to a boil in a small saucepan. Remove from the heat, add the sugar and stir. Set aside for 1 hour. Strain the cold cream into the saucepan and heat gently until almost boiling. One by one add the yolks. Whisk, then strain into the pie plate. Nestle the pie plate in a roasting pan and fill the pan with boiling water about halfway up the sides of the pie plate. Cook in a 325°F oven for 20 minutes until the custard is set.

*To Make the Cake:* Butter a 9" cake pan and line the bottom with waxed paper. Beat the eggs, then beat in the sugar. Add the vanilla and the dry ingredients, beating gently to incorporate. Meanwhile bring the milk and butter to a simmer and when boiling, add slowly to the cake batter. As soon as the batter is smooth, turn it into the cake pan and bake for 25 minutes until golden brown. Cool. To assemble the cake, split it in half. Spoon the cooled custard over the bottom half and then top with the other half.

*To Make the Glaze:* Bring the cream to a simmer over medium heat; stir in the chocolate and melt. Remove from the heat and continue to stir until the glaze is smooth. Pour over the cake, spreading evenly. Chill the cake for an hour to set the glaze. Eat the same day. *Serves 10.*

# Sweet Potato Pie

Adapted from: The pages of *Godey's Lady's Book*, 1865, p. 193

1 deep-dish pie crust, uncooked (see p. 50)
1½ cups sweet potatoes, cooked and mashed
1 stick unsalted butter, melted
1 cup sugar
½ cup maple syrup
3 tablespoons flour
3 eggs, beaten
⅔ cup cream
2 teaspoons lemon juice
1 teaspoon vanilla extract

"Sweet Potato Pie" today is a signature dish of the soul food movement, but in its technique, it follows on the tradition of the batter puddings and flans that often appeared in historic English cookbooks. It is an excellent example of how the old methods and the new foods came together in America and were celebrated by writers like Marguerite Hunter (*The Melrose Plantation Cookbook*), Lettice Bryan (*The Kentucky Housewife*) and other writers drawing strength and sustenance from African American cuisine.

 Combine the filling ingredients and pour into the pie crust. Bake at 350°F for 40 minutes, until a knife inserted in the middle comes out clean. Serve warm or room temperature. *Serves 6.*

# Wartime Ice Cream

ADAPTED FROM: The pages of *Godey's Lady's Book*, 1862, p. 232

The Civil War did not stop developments in America's diet. There were plenty of "firsts"; for instance, flavored soda waters as well as the counters where they were served became popular, and Gail Borden perfected his system of condensing milk. So important was this development that the Union Army commandeered the entire output of his factory and issued the canned milk to its soldiers for whom it became a staple. Recipes for wartime ice cream used Borden's milk when cream was not available; in fact, even the stern Mrs. Hale, the editor of *Godey's Lady's Book*, admitted that ice cream had become such a necessity of life that the newly invented home ice cream freezer was assured a market amongst her readers.

1 whole pineapple
2 cups white sugar
1 cup whole milk
4 eggs
2 cans condensed milk

 Pare the pineapple, chop it fine and pulverize to extract the juice. Sprinkle the juice with half the sugar and let stand for ½ hour to melt the sugar. Bring the whole milk to a boil and add the eggs, not letting the mixture boil after this point. Stir the remaining sugar into the milk and whisk until thickened. Add the condensed milk and pineapple juice mixture and beat well. Freeze in the ice cream freezer until set and firm. Small pieces of pineapple flesh may be added. *Makes 1 pint ice cream.*

# Cheese Puff Straws, Mid~Century Style

Adapted from: Anna Collins, *The Great Western Cook Book*, 1857, p. 135

3 cups flour
1½ tablespoons sugar
1½ teaspoons salt
3 sticks butter
9 tablespoons ice water
2 teaspoons lemon juice
1 cup fresh grated Parmesan

Cheese straws were the epitome of the genteel ladies luncheon, stacked pyramid-style and served with tea or coffee. They made a surprise entry in Mrs. Collins' otherwise down-to-earth cookbook. The first appearance of cheese straws in print was in 1894, in a church cookbook titled *Recipes Tried and True* published by the First Presbyterian Church in Ohio, but Anna Collins' recipe was identical in all but name. She explained the technique of dusting the pastry with grated cheese and folding the dough, envelope style, into the layers, which explode upon baking. Mrs. Collins did not specify the cheese, but nowadays, Parmesan is preferred.

 Combine the dry ingredients. Cut in the cold butter and toss to combine. Sprinkle the ice water and lemon juice over and gather into a rough ball. Chill covered for 1 hour.

Unwrap the dough, roll out on a floured counter, and fold into 3, like a business letter. Repeat the process twice, chilling the dough for 15 minutes between turns. Chill again for 15 minutes at the end.

To make the straws, roll out the pastry to ½" thick. Sprinkle with the grated cheese and cut into ¾" strips. Twist each strip corkscrew style and lay on a baking sheet 1" apart. Bake 20 minutes in a 425°F oven. Cool on wire racks. *Makes 24 straws.*

CHAPTER FIVE

# MY COMMUNITY COOKS

Mrs. M. E. Porter, *Mrs. Porter's New Southern Cookery Book*, 1871

*Presbyterian Cook Book*, 1873

*Favorite Dishes*, Comp. by Carrie V. Shuman, 1893

*The Blue Grass Cook Book*, Comp. by Minnie C. Fox, 1904

Mrs. Estelle Woods Wilcox, Ed., *Buckeye Cookery, And Practical Housekeeping*, 1877

Mrs. Simon Kander, Ed., *The Settlement Cook Book*, 1901

The original community cookbooks grew out of fundraising efforts during the War. Church groups and women's organizations all across America collected recipes and sold them to each other to raise money for various good causes. The idea was modest and the resulting cookbook very often a quirky collection of favorite dishes with vague instructions, even vaguer measurements, and no attempt at standardization. The charm of these cookbooks was as much in the telling as the details, for there were anecdotes and recollections galore dotted amongst the recipes. Community cookbooks often offer a fascinating historical glimpse into both dishes and days gone by.

From this modest start, however, two cookbooks stand head and shoulders above the rest. It should come as no surprise that the women behind both of these hugely successful cookbooks were extraordinary personalities. Lizzie Black Kander's *The Settlement Cook Book* (1901) and Estelle Wilcox's *Buckeye Cookery* (1877) both became run-away bestsellers. *The Settlement Cook Book* is now, one hundred years later, in its 35th edition and has even spawned a knock off, *The New Settlement Cook Book*. *Buckeye Cookery* was first published in Marysville, Ohio, but was so successful that, to find a larger market, it was translated into German and was even published in a Southern version, *The Dixie Cook Book*. It sold out in all three editions.

Mrs. Kander might be surprised, even startled, at the reincarnation of her classic cookbook in its latest edition. The book began life as an exercise in assimilation, teaching recent immigrants to Milwaukee how to cook typical American dishes. Two million copies and a hundred years later, *The New Settlement Cook Book* celebrates culinary diversity and offers a plethora of international dishes. Such was the name recognition of the title, however, that the new project succeeded.

Mrs. Kander was the conscientious daughter of German Jewish immigrants and she ran a Settlement house in Milwaukee. There were similar enterprises in many Western towns that offered aid to the vast influx of immigrants in late 19th century America. In the fifty years between 1866 and 1915, there were a total of 25 million immigrants, at first from Ireland and Germany, later from Italy, Russia, and Poland.

Mrs. Kander's earliest attempts to secure funding for her recipe book from the conservative gentlemen of the Settlement Board fell on deaf, not to say unhelpful, ears. They—the gentlemen in question—would be glad to share in any profits but declined the princely sum of $18 to fund Mrs. Kander's booklet.

The rebuff was just what the determined and civic-minded Mrs. Kander needed; she funded the publication of *The Settlement Cook Book* herself. It was a beginner's manual, with simple instructions and unpretentious recipes. Some of the most mouthwatering are the kuchen, tortes, and stollens with which Mrs. Kander must have been most familiar. Ultimately, the compilation and production of *The Settlement Cook Book* became a full time career for Mrs. Kander.

The women of the First Congregational Church of Marysville, Ohio, wanted to raise some money to repair their church, so Estelle Wilcox took on the job of gathering recipes and compiling a cookbook. In the spirit of the true community cookbook, the names of individual cooks were given with each recipe, giving the first edition, titled *The Centennial Buckeye Cook Book* (1876) a truly personal touch.

The recipes echoed many of the classics from an earlier age and that were beloved to contributors: Mrs. Child, Mrs. Hale, and Miss Leslie all made appearances. There was even a recipe taken from Amelia Simmons for "Old Hartford Election Cake" with an acknowledgment of its antiquity. "Self-Freezing Ice Cream" came from Marion Harland. Not all the recipes were achievable; Governor Safford of Arizona contributed enchiladas, interestingly described at this early date as "one of the national dishes," but sadly unworkable.

Esther Wilcox was a shrewd businesswoman. She quickly realized the potential of the book, bought the copyright and turned her back on the modest charitable background. (The church, however, did get its repairs.) At the same time she bought into the catapulting market for women's magazines. The total number of monthlies produced in the U.S. grew fivefold between 1860 and 1900, to over 1,800 titles. All included a mandatory section on cooking with appropriate recipes. Mrs. Wilcox's contribution was "The Housekeeper." Between the magazine and the many subsequent editions of *Buckeye Cookery*, she became a force of reckoning in the cookbook publishing industry.

Of equal charm were the many smaller community-based publications that were spawned in these years. Between the end of the Civil War and the end of the First World War, over 3,000 titles appeared under the banner "charity cookbooks." The causes they represented were various. Some were political: women's suffrage, for instance. Others were written to coincide with the fairs and expositions that were held in America in the late 19th century and which were popular public entertainments.

*Favorite Dishes*, for instance, was written for the World's Colombian Exposition held in Chicago in 1893, which attracted

28 million visitors. This handsome volume contained 300 auto-graphed recipes.

Still other cookbooks celebrated the specialties of the region. It is possible here to mention but two. *The Blue Grass Cook Book* was suffused with the essence of Kentucky cooking; not just "Blue Grass Ham," but "Deviled Lobster," "Tutti Frutti Ice Cream," and "Bourbon Whisky Punch." *The Presbyterian Cook Book* from Dayton, Ohio, contained a myriad of fascinating pudding recipes with tantalizing names such as "Piccolomini," "Wapsie Pudding," and "Young America Pudding."

One retrospective view of community cookbooks is to see them as a final stand against what was to become the brand name cooking of the 20th century. We've already seen how magazines and newspapers exploded, providing pages to be filled with advertisements for brand name products. Added to this was a constantly expanding, constantly improving railway service that made it possible to ship foods cross-country. Cooking began to slide into a conformity and homogeneity in which more and more people across the country cooked the same food.

Community cookbooks were a last gasp of individuality before the great ladies of the domestic science movement, like Fannie Farmer, took over at the turn of the century.

# CHICKEN MARENGO ~ A GENERAL'S LAST WISH

Adapted from: Mrs. Kander, *The Settlement Cook Book*, 1901, p. 398

Lots of stories surround the creation of this famous dish. Reportedly, Napoleon ordered a meal right before the Battle of Marengo, 1800—a battle he regarded as his finest victory. His cook, however, was terrified; supplies in camp were low. He sent out soldiers to forage supplies and what they came back with was the ingredients for his famous dish: chicken, tomatoes, olives, and crayfish. The jigger of brandy that finishes the dish was taken from Napoleon's own flask. Tall tale or not, the recipe duly was recorded by French chef Louis Andot in 1841 (sans tomatoes) and then by Fouret and Viart in *Le Cuisinier Royal*, 1842 (avec tomatoes). It's a good story and the recipe is well worth cooking for its own sake.

1 chicken, cut up
½ cup olive oil
1 onion, thinly sliced
1 cup dry white wine
1 cup chicken stock
2 garlic cloves, crushed
1 cup tomatoes, skinned and chopped
salt and pepper
1 teaspoon thyme
1 bay leaf
1 cup pitted black olives
2 tablespoons cognac
2 tablespoons lemon juice
1 dozen boiled crayfish (or to taste)
toast and chopped parsley to garnish

Sauté the chicken pieces in hot oil until golden brown. In the same skillet, sauté the onion. Add the wine and scrape the pan to get up all the juices. Replace the chicken in the pot, add the garlic, the stock, the tomatoes and herbs, cover and simmer until the chicken is tender, about 45 minutes. Remove the chicken to finish the sauce.

Boil down the stock until it is reduced to 1 cup. Add olives, sprinkle with cognac and lemon juice, return the chicken and heat through. To serve, place the chicken on plates and pour over the sauce. Garnish with the crayfish and toast, and scatter thickly with parsley. *Serves 4.*

# CHICKEN PIE WITH SHORT BEAN CRUST

Adapted from: Mrs. Esther Wilcox, *Buckeye Cookery*, 1877, p. 181

## CRUST

2 cups white beans, mashed

½ stick cold butter

3 cups flour

1 teaspoon salt

3 tablespoons ice water

## FILLING

1 cooked chicken, jointed and boned

2 green peppers

1 onion

1 garlic clove, crushed

2 tablespoons butter

2 tablespoons flour

1 cup chicken broth, hot

salt and pepper

egg wash

Early in the 19th century, cookbook authors like Sarah J. Hale were concerned about the digestive effects of eating rich pie dough. A number of cooks who contributed recipes to *Buckeye Cookery* suggested making pie dough with mashed potatoes, or beans in place of butter and lard. The trick was, in Esther Wilcox's words, to "preserve tenacity in the dough." It was a good plan, she suggested, "to make a puff paste for the top crust and for the under crust use less shortening." You can use whatever variety of bean you like, and it makes sense to use canned beans, which can be quickly drained and mashed without the trouble of long cooking first.

 Mash the beans until they are quite smooth. Cut the butter into the flour and salt, and then add the white beans. Sprinkle over the water, a tablespoon at a time, and combine to form a soft dough. Wrap and chill until stiff.

Sauté the sliced green peppers, onion, and garlic until soft. Add the chicken pieces and simmer until lightly colored for 10 minutes. Make a roux with the flour and butter and stir in the hot stock to make a smooth sauce. Add salt and pepper, and then stir into the chicken.

Divide the dough into 2 pieces, one larger than the other. Roll out the larger to fit the bottom of the pie dish. Tip in the filling, and then roll out the remaining piece of dough and place it on top. Seal the edges and brush with egg wash. Bake in 425°F oven for 20 minutes, then lower the heat to 350°F and continue to cook for 25 minutes. *Makes 1 pie.*

# SALMIS OF PHEASANTS

Adapted from: Mrs. M. E. Porter, *Mrs. Porter's New Southern Cookery Book*, 1871, p. 128

"Salmis of Pheasants," or for that matter any other game bird, is a cooking technique that brings the heightened essence of the bird's flavor to the table. This method was so much a part of good living in the 19th century that writing soon after the Civil War, Mrs. Porter could describe the technique as "simple and inexpensive." As a party dish it can largely be prepared ahead of time, and then crowned with the glorious sauce, just the way Commodore Vanderbilt insisted.

*2 pheasants*
*1 stick celery, diced*
*1 carrot, diced*
*1 onion, diced*
*chicken or veal stock*
*1 bay leaf*
*1 cup white wine*
*salt and pepper*
*1 tablespoon redcurrant jelly*
*1 teaspoon thyme*
*1 teaspoon crushed juniper berries*
*2 tablespoons heavy cream*
*parsley and croutons to garnish*

Roast the pheasants surrounded by the diced vegetables for 30 minutes until the juices of the birds still run clear. Remove from the oven and when cool enough to handle, joint the birds.

Put the carcass into a clean pot, along with the vegetables and juices from the roasting pan. Add enough chicken or veal stock to cover and simmer for 1 hour. Strain the stock, pressing the carcass and vegetables to get as much of the flavor as possible. Reduce the stock over high heat until you have 1 cup. Add the wine, redcurrant jelly, and seasonings, including thyme and juniper berries. Simmer and then stir in the cream.

Return the pheasant pieces to the pan, cover tightly and cook gently for 20 minutes more, until the pheasant is cooked. Do not allow to boil. Serve the salmis in hot bowls, garnished with croutons and parsley. *Serves 6.*

# AN EPICURE'S GAME ENTRÉE, BUCKEYE STYLE

Adapted from: Mrs. Esther Wilcox, *Buckeye Cookery*, 1877, p. 143

4 birds in season (*pheasants, guinea fowl or
  prairie chicken*), oven-ready
large pieces of onion
2 tablespoons butter
2 tablespoons olive oil
½ teaspoon nutmeg
½ teaspoon red pepper flakes
½ cup flour mixed with ½ teaspoon allspice
salt and pepper
1 cup game stock (*or chicken stock*)
1 cup red wine
½ cup cream

At the one end of the scale was the extravagant consumption that went on at Delmonico's Restaurant in New York, where Diamond Jim Brady dined on such delicacies as "Guinea Fowl Georgian Style." At the other end was Mrs. Godard who contributed her method of baking prairie chickens to *Buckeye Cookery* in 1877. Game was still an important article of diet in the late 19th century. Its availability in the markets of New York was colorfully described by Thomas De Voe in 1867 when he listed the many species of wild fowl offered for sale, and condemned the wanton destruction of birds killed merely for the sport or for a few pence profit. Steaming the birds, then roasting in Buckeye fashion is a guaranteed method of a savory result, no matter the bag, and whether you are dining in New York or in a Buckeye forest.

 Wash and dry the picked birds. Stuff each bird with a piece of onion and season with salt and pepper. Tie the legs and wings in place. Place in a steamer or colander set over a pan of boiling water and steam for 1 hour or until the juices run clear. Remove the birds to a roasting pan, smear with butter and olive oil, and sprinkle with the nutmeg, red pepper, and more salt and pepper. Sprinkle a little flour over the tops and pour the stock and red wine around. Roast for another half hour until the birds are golden brown and fork tender. Use the pan juices to make a rich sauce thickened with the ½ cup cream. Serve with applesauce or currant jelly. *Serve 4.*

# Kentucky Baked Ham

Adapted from: Minnie Fox, *The Blue Grass Cook Book*, 1904, p. 99

This old treasure of Southern cooking attests to the rich contribution black women made to a storied cuisine. Minnie Fox was born in Bourbon County, Kentucky, and the original book was full of photographs of African American women at work. The recipes range from the traditional, such as this local ham, to the decadently rich, like "Tutti Frutti Ice Cream" and "Caramel Layer Cake." Many of them are named after the cooks who produced them in the kitchens of Kentucky. Bake this ham and you are baking a legacy.

10 lb. Magnolia Kentucky ham
2 cups flour, mixed to a paste with 2 cups water
1 cup brown sugar
1 egg yolk
2 cups breadcrumbs
24 whole cloves

 Soak the ham for 36 hours, changing the water each day. Make a stiff dough of the flour and water and envelop the ham with it, using your fingers to seal. Put the ham in a baking pan and pour a cup or so of water in the bottom so that the ham does not stick. Cook in a 350°F oven for 5 hours or until an internal temperature of 111° is achieved.

Remove the ham and break away the crust. Skin the ham and remove all but a ¼" layer of fat. Mix the brown sugar and egg yolk together and paste over the surface of the ham. Sprinkle the breadcrumbs over and press to adhere. Stick the cloves into the ham at even intervals all over. Brown in a 375°F oven for 30 minutes. Serve hot or cold. *Makes 24 servings, sliced.*

# OLD CAPE COD CLAM PIE

Adapted from: Mrs. A. Wilson in *Buckeye Cookery*, 1877, p. 259

2 recipes Shortcrust Pastry (see p. 50)
2 cups clam meat from 3 pints clams
¼ cup clam juice
2 medium potatoes, cooked and diced
1 egg, beaten
1 cup light cream
½ cup cracker crumbs
1 tablespoon butter
salt and pepper

Clams were early on an important industry for New England coastal residents, and before the colonists arrived, Native Americans used the *quahog*, or hard shell clam, not just as food but as a medium of exchange and for sealing friendships. Sometimes the shells were made into belts known as *wampum*. By the time Mrs. Wilson offered her recipe for publication, canned clams were available nationwide. They would be ideal in this recipe if the fresh are not to be had.

Line a pie dish with pastry. Put in a layer of clams, a few potatoes, salt and pepper, and repeat until the clams are used. Beat together the egg, clam juice, cream, and the cracker crumbs, and pour over the clams. Top with bits of butter and lay on the top layer of pastry. Cut slits in the top to allow the steam to escape and bake at 350°F for 1 hour. *Serves 4.*

# CRISPY CODFISH BALLS

Adapted from: Mrs. Shearer in *Buckeye Cookery*, 1877, p. 131

Cod has been called the beef of centuries past. It was such a popular item of commerce in New England that it appeared symbolically on coins, letterheads, and legal documents. There is a huge pine carving of the "sacred cod" that hangs in the Massachusetts Hall of Representatives. This recipe, contributed by Mrs. Shearer to the *Buckeye Cookery*, had changed little since the days when Mary Randolph in Virginia described mixing the fish with boiled parsnips, onions, and brandy and frying the patties in butter. It was a sublime treatment for a modest fish. We've added the Southern treatment to the Northern dish, with all due respect to Mrs. Shearer.

*1 pound codfish, boiled until the flesh flakes from the bones*
*1 large potato, peeled, cubed, and boiled tender*
*2 parsnips, peeled and boiled tender*
*1 clove garlic, minced*
*½ onion chopped*
*1 tablespoon butter*
*1 tablespoon brandy*
*salt and pepper*
*chopped fresh parsley*
*1 egg beaten*

Mix the warm fish with the warm potatoes and parsnip, and mash. Sauté the garlic and onion in the butter and add to the fish with the brandy, salt and pepper, and parsley. Use as much of the egg as necessary to make patties or balls. Fry in hot lard until golden brown. Serve with a cold pickle or tartar sauce, and lemon wedges. *Serves 4.*

# Deviled Lobster

Adapted from: Mrs. J. C. Staughan in *The Blue Grass Cook Book*, 1904, p. 46

4 cooked lobster tails, meat removed
2 tablespoons butter
2 tablespoons flour
2 cups cream
½ teaspoon mustard
½ teaspoon cayenne
salt and pepper
½ cup fine white breadcrumbs

In Europe, lobster was the food of kings, but it was not until 1880 that the public fancy was caught by the American lobster. What had been merely the bait food for New England fishermen was now offered on chic menus in New York, and also featured heavily in "most popular recipes" in all the charitable cookbooks in this chapter. Whole lobsters were most generally featured, but nowadays either fresh or fresh frozen tails are a convenient substitute to dealing with the whole creature.

Cut the meat into dice. Wash and dry the shells, which will be the containers for the meat. Melt the butter and add the flour, stirring to make a roux. Stir in the cream and make a smooth cream sauce. Season with mustard, salt and pepper, and cayenne, then add the lobster meat. Fill the shells; set each in a gratin dish and sprinkle with breadcrumbs. Brown for 5 minutes under a broiler, and be careful not to burn. *Serves 4.*

# TURTLE BEAN SOUP ~ HENRY WARD BEECHER'S FAVORITE

Adapted from: Mrs. H. C. Clark in *Buckeye Cookery*, 1877, p. 269

The charm of charity or community cookbooks lies in their personal touch. In this recipe, for instance, the famous wife of Henry Ward Beecher, mother of Catharine and Harriet (both famous cookbook authors featured in this book) adds her own comment, which makes the recipe special. "After straining [the soup] I sometimes return the soup to the digester, bring to a boil and break in four or five eggs and as soon as the whites have set a very little, dish the soup and bring to the table with the slightly cooked eggs floating on top."

3 cups turtle beans

2 quarts beef stock

8 tomatoes

1 onion, chopped

1 stick celery, chopped

1 carrot, chopped

½ cup tomato ketchup

4 eggs

salt and pepper

Put the beans to soak overnight. Next morning, rinse in clean water and put to boil in the beef stock. Cook for 2 hours, then add the tomatoes roughly chopped, the vegetables, and the ketchup. Simmer another 2 hours. Strain the soup, rubbing through enough of the beans to thicken and season well. Return to the stock pot. Break as many eggs as there are diners in the soup. Cook for 5 minutes until the egg whites have firmed. To serve, ladle 1 egg into each bowl and pour soup gently on top. A little minced parsley can garnish the top. *Serves 4.*

# RUSSIAN BORSCHT

Adapted from: Mrs. Kander, *The Settlement Cook Book*, 1901, p. 509

1 chicken
3 quarts boiling water
½ cup lima beans
2 beets, peeled and cut into strips
2 tablespoons butter
1 pound tomatoes
2 onions, peeled
2 apples, peeled and sliced
2 potatoes, peeled and cubed
2 sticks celery, diced
1 teaspoon salt
1 teaspoon pepper
3 tablespoons butter
3 tablespoons flour

Borscht soup was one of those favorites that Russian immigrants didn't want to leave behind when they came to America; so, despite the fact that Mrs. Kander taught American dishes in her class, she included four variations on the beetroot soup in her cookbook. There was a reason: Mrs. Kander thought the recipe might be lost, as grandparents and parents were no longer there to provide their experience of how to cook the soup. The same went for other heirloom dishes that were preserved for posterity and aspiring cooks in subsequent editions of *The Settlement*.

Poach the chicken for 2 hours in the water with the lima beans. Fry the beet in butter, add the tomatoes, and simmer them in some of the poaching stock from the chicken for an hour. Fry the remaining vegetables and apples until they are golden, then add them to the beets. Simmer for 15 minutes, then add the salt and pepper. Remove the chicken meat from the bones and return to the pan. Mix the chicken stock and the beetroot mixture, bring the soup to a boil and simmer for 20 minutes. Add the chicken meat. Thicken the soup with the *beurre manie*, made from beating the 3 tablespoons of butter into the 3 tablespoons of flour. Serve the soup very hot with sour cream on top. *Serves 8.*

# Made~at~home Golden Chicken Soup with Barley

Adapted from: Mrs. Kander, *The Settlement Cook Book*, 1901, p. 66

Barley was revered by the Chinese as one of five sacred plants, but its reputation as a food in America has never been high. Here, it was valued only as essential to the beer brewing industry. In England back in medieval times, the grain was used to make bread but was only eaten by the poor, who could not afford the white bread of the rich. From there, it was a downhill struggle for the grain, despite the fact that barley is low in fat and high in vitamins and fiber. In soup, it holds up to a long simmer without becoming mush, as Campbell's soup company discovered. The first canned soups took to the stores in 1896, and soon it was much more convenient to use the can opener than to bring out the soup kettle and start a simmer on the back of the stove.

*1 chicken (Mrs. Kander specifies an old hen)*
*1 onion, chopped*
*1 carrot, chopped*
*1 stalk celery, chopped*
*6 cups good chicken stock*
*1 cup pearl barley*
*2 tablespoons fresh herbs: rosemary, parsley and sage, chopped*
*salt and pepper*
*garlic bread slices*

 Simmer the chicken in the stock with the chopped vegetables for 1½ hours until the meat is falling off the bones. Strip the meat and return to the strained stock. Meanwhile, cook the barley separately in water, drain, and put in the stock for another ½ hour of cooking. Just before serving, stir in the fresh herbs, and season well with salt and pepper. Serve the soup ladled over slices of garlic bread. *Serves 6.*

# Salsify or Oyster Plant

Adapted from: Esther Wilcox, *Buckeye Cookery*, 1877, p. 295

1 salsify root, peeled
water to cover
piece of salt codfish
juice of 1 lemon
salt and pepper
1 tablespoon butter mixed with
    1 tablespoon flour
pinch of fresh grated nutmeg
4 slices of buttered toast

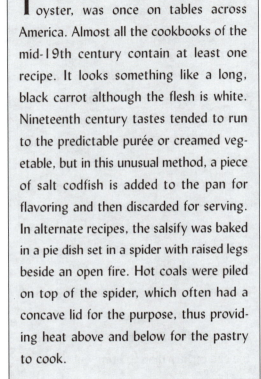

This vegetable, which has the flavor of oyster, was once on tables across America. Almost all the cookbooks of the mid-19th century contain at least one recipe. It looks something like a long, black carrot although the flesh is white. Nineteenth century tastes tended to run to the predictable purée or creamed vegetable, but in this unusual method, a piece of salt codfish is added to the pan for flavoring and then discarded for serving. In alternate recipes, the salsify was baked in a pie dish set in a spider with raised legs beside an open fire. Hot coals were piled on top of the spider, which often had a concave lid for the purpose, thus providing heat above and below for the pastry to cook.

 Boil the salsify root in water to cover with the salt codfish, lemon juice, salt and pepper. When tender, remove and discard the fish, reserving the liquid. Drain the salsify, slice thickly, and put in a shallow buttered baking pan. Keep warm. Make a roux with the butter and flour, and use to make a sauce with ½ cup of the reserved liquid. Season with nutmeg. Pour the sauce over the salsify and serve with buttered toast.

*Advice on making the toast:* "Few know how to prepare it nicely. Take bread not too fresh, cut thin and evenly, trim off the crust edges; first warm each side of the bread, then present the first side again to the fire until it takes on a rich, even brown color; treat the other side the same way; butter and serve immediately. Or... dip each slice of toast in boiling hot water (slightly salted), spread with butter, cover and keep hot."
*Serves 4.*

# GUINEA SQUASH OR FRIED EGGPLANT

Adapted from: Esther Wilcox, *Buckeye Cookery*, 1877, p. 287

First introduced to America by Thomas Jefferson, the eggplant was initially grown as an ornamental flowering plant. Like its South American cousin, the tomato, it was at first viewed with suspicion and suspected of producing insanity in those who dared eat it. Mary Randolph cooked eggplant back in Virginia in the 1820s, presumably encouraged to do so by her cousin Jefferson. Her treatment was to boil the guinea squash (an alternate name for the fruit), purée it and fry it in little patties. By 1877, it was widely known that to rid the eggplant of its bitter taste, the slices must first be salted then fried crisp. In this treatment, we have added the Italian tomato sauce and Parmesan cheese to produce a classic Parmigiano, a little ahead of its time but in the spirit of the recipe.

2 large purple eggplant, peeled and
    sliced ½" thick

salt

1 pound ripe tomatoes, peeled and chopped

1 clove garlic

1 bunch basil

salt and pepper

1 cup flour

8 oz. grated Parmesan cheese

olive oil

 Sprinkle the eggplant slices with salt and let drain on a paper towel-lined rack for 45 minutes. Squeeze the slices to remove excess moisture, then pat dry. Make a thick tomato sauce by boiling the tomatoes and garlic, with minimal salt and plenty of pepper, and add the roughly chopped basil leaves. Dip each eggplant slice in flour, shake off the excess and fry both sides in hot olive oil for about 2 minutes a side until the slices are golden. Try not to add too much extra oil. The pan will need cleaning with a towel from time to time. Layer the eggplant and tomato sauce alternately in a shallow casserole, sprinkling each layer with the Parmesan cheese. Finish with more basil and more cheese and bake for 45 minutes in a 375°F oven. The top should be crusty. Serves 4.

# Best Boston Brown Steamed Bread

Adapted from: Mrs. H. S. Stevens in *Buckeye Cookery*, 1877, p. 16

1 cup cornmeal
1 cup rye flour
½ cup graham flour
½ cup white flour
1 cup sweet milk
1 cup sour milk
1 teaspoon salt
1 teaspoon baking soda
¾ cup molasses
1 cup raisins (optional)

Mrs. Stevens struck a warm and personal note in the recipe she contributed for "Boston Brown Bread." "This recipe has never been known to fail," she writes, and goes on to tell us how she serves the bread. In her preface to *Buckeye Cookery*, Esther Wilcox wrote that the book was made up of "the choicest bits of the best experience of hundreds who have long traveled the round of household duties… lovingly, with heart and hand fully enlisted in the work." It was a chief selling point for this wildly popular cookbook. This recipe probably came into Mrs. Steven's hands from her mother, who would have baked the bread from memory and not from a cookbook at all. A sense of pride informs the writing.

Grease the inside of a 16 oz. coffee can. Sift the flours together and beat in the molasses and milks, salt, and soda. If you are using the raisins, add them now. Put the batter into the coffee can; it should not quite fill the can. Secure the top with a lid or wrap very tight with buttered foil. Set the can upright in a pan full of boiling water and cook for 2 hours, checking every 30 minutes to make sure the water level is not too low. A skewer inserted in the loaf should come out clean. Carefully remove the bread from the can and cool for 10 minutes before slicing. Eat with baked beans or else as a pudding with whipped cream. *Makes 1 loaf.*

# An Aristocratic Sally Lunn

Adapted from: Mrs. H. B. Sherman in *Buckeye Cookery*, 1877, p. 25

Stories cluster around this aristocrat of breads. The most popular has it as migrating from England to the colonies, named after the proprietress who baked it in Bath, England, for patrons who had come to take the famous waters. The original Sally Lunn was a Huguenot refugee from France, and it's therefore no surprise that the bread she baked was very similar to a French brioche. Southern recipes use a yeast-risen dough, but Mrs. Sherman, who hailed from Milwaukee, recommended a quick-rising batter and no doubt appreciated the ease of mixing that the modern rising agents afforded.

*2 tablespoons sugar*
*4 tablespoons butter*
*2 eggs*
*1 teaspoon soda*
*2 cups milk*
*½ teaspoon salt*
*2 teaspoons cream of tartar*
*1 cup all-purpose flour*

 Beat the sugar and butter together, then add the eggs. Mix the soda and milk together, and add to the batter. Stir the cream of tartar and salt with the flour, and sift into the mixture. Mix lightly and turn into a buttered loaf pan. Bake for 1 hour at 350°F. *Makes 1 loaf.*

# KAFFEE KUCHEN

Adapted from: Mrs. Kander, *The Settlement Cook Book*, 1901, p. 27

## THE SCHNECKEN

2 packets dried yeast

½ cup sugar

2 cups warm milk

1 stick unsalted butter, melted and divided in 2

1 teaspoon nutmeg

1 teaspoon salt

2 eggs, beaten

5 cups flour

2 cups dried prunes, chopped

2 teaspoons cinnamon

1 cup brown sugar

The term coffee cake is from the Germans, an Americanization of "*kaffee kuchen*." In *The Settlement Cook Book*, Mrs. Kander's aim was to make the young girls in her settlement house feel comfortable living in their new and adopted country, but it was unthinkable that they should do without their *kuchen*. She wisely devoted a full chapter to making the special butter-enriched dough. Traditionally, the dough was yeast risen but once baking powder became available in the 1850s, shortcuts followed. There isn't one right or wrong way to make this cake, but Mrs. Kander's recipe was the one published in America and so earns pride of place in this chapter.

 Whisk 1 cup milk, half the sugar, and the yeast together and leave to proof for 5 minutes. Into the remaining milk, mix half the melted butter, the remaining sugar, salt, and nutmeg. Beat. Add the yeast, then add the eggs. Add 4 cups flour and mix to make a sticky dough. Add enough of the remaining flour to make a smooth dough. Cover and let rise until doubled in bulk.

Divide the dough into 2 pieces. Roll each out to ½" thick and brush with the remaining melted butter. Top with the chopped prunes and sprinkle with cinnamon and brown sugar. Roll up tightly and cut into 1" thick slices with a sharp knife. Put the slices side by side in a 9"x13" buttered baking pan; they should just touch. Cover and let rise until the slices are puffy, about 30 minutes. Bake the kuchen slices for 20 minutes at 350°F. To serve, pull apart the slices. *Makes 12 slices kuchen.*

# A Rhyming Cake

Adapted from: *Presbyterian Cook Book, Ohio, 1875, p. 312*

Substantial numbers of rhyming recipes were found in the local fund raising cookbooks and they generally singled out those foods with patriotic and traditional significance. Thus poetic pork and beans were described in the *Presbyterian Cook Book*. *Buckeye Cookery* quoted the Rev. Sidney Smith's elaborate poetic recital that was a recipe for salad dressing disguised. These were the days before technological entertainment had taken over our lives, when conversation and letter writing, charade games and reading aloud were seen as important daily matters. It didn't seem in the least pretentious to glorify a recipe or indeed, a product, in verse. In that spirit, here is a "Corn Pound Cake" with a few words of poesy by which to cook it. The full text can be found in *The Way We Cook in East Hampton, Long Island* (1916).

2 cups yellow cornmeal
1 cup cake flour
½ teaspoon salt
1 teaspoon nutmeg
1 teaspoon cinnamon
2 sticks butter
2 cups white sugar
1 egg
1 tablespoon rosewater
1 tablespoon whisky

"When you've nothing in for tea
This the very thing will be
All the men that I have seen
Say it is of all cakes queen
Good enough for any king
That a husband home may bring;
Warming up the human stove,
Cheering up the hearts you love;
Get a husband what he likes
And save a hundred household strikes."

 Combine the sifted cornmeal, flour, salt, and spices in a bowl. Beat the butter and sugar until creamy and gradually add the egg. An electric mixer makes short work of the batter. Slowly add the dry ingredients, then the rosewater and whisky. Scrape the batter into a well-buttered 9" round cake pan, smooth the top and cover with parchment paper. Bake in a preheated 350°F oven for 1 hour until a toothpick inserted in the center comes out clean. *Makes 1 cake.*

# Black Walnut and Coconut Bars

Adapted from: Mrs. Kander, *The Settlement Cook Book*, 1901, p. 209

½ cup butter
½ cup brown sugar
1 cup flour

## WALNUT AND COCONUT TOPPING

3 tablespoons flour
½ teaspoon baking powder
½ cup shredded coconut
1 cup black walnuts (or regular), chopped
2 eggs
1 cup brown sugar
1 teaspoon vanilla

"A full cookie jar is a sign of a hospitable household," reads an early edition of *The Settlement Cook Book*. The cookie chapter was divided in sections for rolled cookies, molded cookies, drop cookies, kisses and macaroons, and bar cookies. Some of the recipes had changed little (except for spelling) since Amelia Simmons' Recipe for "Jumbles" in 1796 and Mary Randolph's "Macaroone" in 1824. Both jumbals and macaroons make an appearance in *The Settlement Cook Book*. Jumbals were a tender, buttery cookie and macaroons were traditionally made from almonds and flavored with rose water, but bar cookies were a more recent addition to the jar and far more elaborate than either of the earlier cookbook authors could have contemplated.

 Beat the sugar and butter together and blend in the flour. Spread this paste into a greased 9" square pan. Bake at 375°F for 20 minutes. While the cake is baking, prepare the topping. Sift the flour and baking powder together and add the walnuts and coconut. In a separate bowl, combine the eggs, sugar, and vanilla and add to the dry mixture. Beat well and pour batter over baked crust. Bake at 375°F for 20 minutes. Allow to cool in the pan for 5 minutes, then cut into squares. *Makes 12 bars.*

# A Chocolate Marble Cake

Adapted from: Mrs. J. A. Riddle in *Buckeye Cookery*, 1877, p. 66

American recipes of the last decades of the century were full of fanciful cake creations called marbled cakes. The technique was straightforward: spoonfuls of batter were dropped into a pan and remained somewhat separate as the cake cooked. When cut, a mélange of different colors and flavors were revealed. The earliest recipes used molasses to darken part of the batter, but *Buckeye Cookery* had a more modern interpretation that used chocolate. The candy was still considered a luxury to be eaten in small squares after a meal, rather than melted in quantity in a cake. Chocolate marble cake in 1877 would have been a cake reserved for a birthday party and our modern frosting an unthinkable extravagance.

## White Cake

½ cup butter

1 cup sugar

1½ cups cake flour

3 egg whites, beaten stiff

2 teaspoons baking powder

½ cup milk

1 teaspoon vanilla

## Chocolate Cake

½ cup butter

1 cup sugar

1½ cup cake flour

3 whole eggs, beaten

⅓ cup cocoa

2 teaspoons baking powder

½ cup milk

1 teaspoon vanilla

## Frosting

½ stick unsalted butter

4 ounces unsweetened chocolate, melted

2 cups confectioner's sugar, sifted

2 teaspoons vanilla

¼ cup cream

 For each cake, which should be mixed separately, cream the sugar and butter until smooth and add the eggs. Gradually stir in the sifted flour and spices and fold in the milk. For the dark cake, add the cocoa powder with the flour. Using a deep 7" cake pan, buttered and lined with wax paper, spoon layers of white and chocolate batter into the pan. There should be 4 layers. Bake for 1 hour at 350°F. Cool and frost with the chocolate frosting.

*To Make the Frosting:* Mix the melted chocolate with the butter and beat until satiny. Add the sugar and vanilla and beat again until the frosting thickens. Cover and chill for 30 minutes. Spread thickly over the top and sides of the cake. *Makes 1 cake.*

# NOT YOUR CORNER STORE CHARLOTTE RUSSE

Adapted from: Mrs. H. B. Sherman in *Buckeye Cookery*, 1877, p. 86

*40 ladyfingers*
*1-ounce packet gelatin*
*2 cups milk, ½ cup reserved*
*1 large egg and 1 egg yolk*
*1 cup sugar*
*1 teaspoon vanilla*
*2 cups heavy cream*
*1 tablespoon rosewater*
*½ cup redcurrant jelly*
*candied violets and blanched almonds*

Mrs. H. B. Sherman contributed a number of recipes to *Buckeye Cookery*. She worked hard to do so. In a casual phrase dropped in at the start of her preparations to make the popular cream dessert "Charlotte Russe," she says "one quart milk, six ounces sugar, two ounces isinglass; put all into a saucepan and on the stove." She neglects to mention that she had to prepare the isinglass herself from scratch. This transparent gelatin-like substance was used 100 years ago to set jellies and was indispensable in a kitchen that loved to eat desserts like the "russe." Mrs. H. B. Sherman used the sturgeon fish, which gave up isinglass from the air bladder when boiled. Perhaps this explains why the confection was eagerly snapped up from the corner candy store, where it was displayed in glass containers for those sweet-deprived customers who lacked the dedication of Mrs. H. B. Sherman.

Line a charlotte russe mold with ladyfingers and set aside. Make a custard by dissolving the gelatin in the ½ cup milk. Bring the 1½ cups milk almost to a boil, then remove from the heat and whisk in the gelatin, the sugar, the whole egg, and egg yolk. Beat until a smooth custard is formed. Beat in the vanilla. Cover the custard until needed. Whisk the heavy cream over ice and when it is frothy, fold gently into the cooled custard. Spread a layer of redcurrant jelly into the bottom of the lined mold. Top with the custard and chill until needed. Decorate with more whipped cream, candied violets, and almonds. *Serves 8.*

# Apfel Strudel

Adapted from: Mrs. Kander, *The Settlement Cook Book*, 1901, p. 456

In the days of home baking, it was considered a high compliment to be told that you had a light hand with the pastry. Some cooks just had a knack with strudel dough, which had to be rolled out and then tossed and pulled and stretched to make a paper thin dough that enclosed a sweet filling, usually apples. There was an art to it; recipes could only hint at the magic involved. Nowadays, few of us have the time to prepare a strudel from scratch, so frozen filo pastry leaves are a godsend. If you feel up to tackling the original, consult Mrs. Kander and remember the golden rule for strudel, which is (unlike other pastries) keep the room warm and not cold.

*1 packet frozen filo dough*
*1 cup fresh breadcrumbs*
*1 cup unsalted butter, melted and divided*
*4 cups Granny Smith apples, peeled and*
  *sliced thin*
*1 cup raisins*
*¾ cup blanched almonds, toasted*
*1 cup sugar mixed with 1 teaspoon cinnamon*

 Defrost the filo dough according to package directions. Lay a large clean cloth over the counter and sprinkle it with flour. Lay the filo sheets end-on-end on top of the cloth to make a sheet measuring about 20" x 24"; brush water over the edges of the pastry to join the edges.

To make the filling, fry the breadcrumbs in ¼ cup of the butter, mix with the blanched and toasted almonds, the raisins, the apples, sugar and cinnamon. Brush the pastry with the other ½ cup melted butter. Spread the filling evenly over the pastry to within 1" of the edges all around, and 2" from the nearest edge. Beginning with this edge, flip the pastry over the filling, then fold over the sides. Continue to roll carefully, using the cloth to turn the dough. When you come to the end, brush the edge with water so that it will stick to the dough. Slide the strudel onto a cookie sheet. Brush with the remaining butter. Bake at 350°F for 35 minutes until golden brown. Strudel is best eaten at once, with cream. *Makes 1 large strudel.*

# TUTTI FRUTTI ICE CREAM

Adapted from: Mrs. M. Bashford in *The Blue Grass Cook Book*, 1904, p. 232

6 egg yolks

4 cups whole milk

2 cups sugar

1 cup raisins

½ cup brandy

1 pound blanched almonds, ground

1 cup strawberry preserves

1 teaspoon vanilla

3 pints heavy cream

whole strawberries to garnish

Despite some cranky 19th century medical advice that suggested eating ice after a meal would cause everything from digestive failure to colic, Americans gobbled up ice cream by the gallon and increasingly as the century progressed, they were gobbling it up on the streets. Mass produced ice cream consumption rose from an estimated 4,000 gallons in 1859 to 24,000 gallons in 1869.

Making ice cream at home had always been labor intensive. But ice cream was truly democratized when the home freezer arrived in 1846, invented by a woman, Nancy Johnson. Ice cream was turned out in every imaginable flavor and one of the classic favorites was this "Tutti Frutti," eaten in Kentucky when the summer crop of fresh, homegrown strawberries was at its peak.

 Plump the raisins overnight in the brandy. The following day, make the custard. Bring the milk to a boiling point over low heat. Beat the egg and sugar together in a bowl and slowly pour the warmed milk into the bowl, beating well. Pour the custard back into the cleaned pan and stir over a low heat until a thickened custard is made. Pour the hot custard over the raisins, almonds, and preserves. Add the vanilla. Cool, then freeze. When half frozen, whip the heavy cream and add it to the ice cream. Stir well and freeze, stirring often until frozen. Serve in sundae glasses, decorated with fresh strawberries. *Serves 6.*

# CHOW CHOW PICKLES

Adapted from: Mrs. Ada Estelle Bever in *Buckeye Cookery*, 1877, p. 226

Esther Wilcox had begun her project in Ohio, having graduated from the Female College of Ohio Wesleyan University, but she married and moved to Minneapolis where she finished and published the book. Her success moved her to start a domestic advice magazine called simply *The Housekeeper*. Within a decade, the publication had reached a circulation of 120,000 and from its pages, Mrs. Wilcox drew recipes from readers with which to update *Buckeye Cookery*. Thus the culinary effect of ethnic and national backgrounds was clearly evident in the recipes, which were from all over America.

*4 pounds green tomatoes, thickly sliced*
*1 cup salt dissolved in 4 cups water*
*1 pound green beans, chopped*
*2 pound small white onions*
*1 large head cabbage, chopped*
*2 large green peppers, sliced*
*4 tablespoons white mustard seed*
*2 tablespoons whole cloves*
*4 tablespoons powdered mustard*
*1 tablespoon allspice*
*16 oz. brown sugar*
*1 oz. turmeric*
*white vinegar to cover*

Slice the tomatoes thickly and leave them in brine of salt and water overnight. The next day, drain the tomatoes, discarding the brine. Chop the tomatoes and put in a kettle with the rest of the vegetables. Mix all the spices and put them into the kettle along with the vinegar. Boil gently for 1 hour, then place in sterilized jars. Seal. Serve the "Chow Chow" with cold meats or on hot dogs. *Makes 8 16-oz. jars.*

# Italian Bread Boat Sandwiches

Adapted from: Mrs. Kander, *The Settlement Cook Book*, 1901, p. 497

1 loaf of Italian bread
½ cup milk
1 egg
1½ cups cooked, smoked turkey
1 cup diced celery
⅓ cup olives, sliced
½ cup mayonnaise
salt and pepper
2 hard boiled eggs, sliced

American sandwiches outgrew their dainty English cousins. Instead of being served as a teatime morsel, they became robust vehicles for hot fillings of all kinds. Rather than eaten sitting down, with a lace napkin, they were taken on the run. Sandwiches were the epitome of American society. By the time Mrs. Kander put out *The Settlement Cook Book* to an astonished audience of gentlemen officials who had refused to back the project, she had a full selection of toasted sandwiches. It was truly a case of "eat your words."

Cut the top crust off the loaf and scoop out the crumbs. Mark the boat into the desired number of servings, using a sharp knife and cutting almost through to the bottom crust. Soften the breadcrumbs in the milk, blend in the eggs and seasonings, and add the turkey meat and other ingredients. Fill the cavity of the loaf, top with egg slices and replace the crust. Brush the outside of the loaf with melted butter. Wrap in foil and bake in a 425°F oven for 20 minutes until golden brown. Serve hot. *Makes 1 loaf.*

## Chapter Six

# America's Kitchen

Women's Centennial Committee, *The National Cookery Book*, 1876
Mrs. Esther Allen Howland, *The American Economical Housekeeper*, 1845
Gustav Peters, *Die Geschickte Hausfrau*, 1848
Mrs. Isabella Beeton, *Book of Household Management*, 1861
Mrs. Esther Levy, *Jewish Cookery Book*, 1871
Henriette Davidis, *Henriette Davidis' Practical Cook Book*, 1897

As the occasion of America's 100th birthday approached, plans were made for the Centennial Exposition in Philadelphia. The organizers called upon the Ladies of the Women's Executive Committee to produce a cookbook worthy of the occasion, to be sold at the Exposition and to celebrate America's kitchen.

Mrs. Elizabeth Duane Gillespie was appointed President of the project. As the great-granddaughter of Benjamin Franklin, she was well connected in Philadelphia society and an obvious choice. Mrs. Gillespie was determined to play an active role in the promotion of "Women's Events" in the Centennial celebrations.

The fund-raising efforts of the Committee were especially successful and within short order, a Women's Pavilion was designed to exhibit women's work (many

visitors said it was the most interesting exhibit at the Exposition).
A newspaper, *New Century for Women*, was compiled and pub-
lished, and Mrs. Gillespie announced the pending creation of a
Museum of Art in Philadelphia. The museum opened in 1878.

*The National Cookery Book* was just one of Mrs. Gillespie's proj-
ects. It was to be a grand affair with recipes from every state in the
Union. A community cookbook with national appeal, in fact, that
would answer the question asked by foreigners about America's
national dishes. Thousands of recipes poured in from women all
over the United States, as varied as the immigrants who flocked to
America during the late 19th century. Over 25 million souls
arrived on our shores between 1865 and 1915, at first from Ireland
and Germany, later from Italy, Poland, and Russia.

Mrs. Gillespie wrote in her appeal to the housewives of America, "No recipe will be considered too homely if characteristic of
the country. Our aim is to give the true flavor of American life in
all its varieties." The cooks of America did not disappoint. The
recipes were eventually winnowed down to about 950 and the
dishes represented every aspect of cookery. An entire chapter was
devoted to corn, another to wild game; the soup chapter offered
gumbos and chowders, and there was the expected abundance of
breakfast breads, puddings, and cakes. *The National Cookery Book*
truly celebrated the roots of the American kitchen.

The German influence on American cooking was especially
strong. It is estimated that during the 19th century, ten percent of
all Americans were German-speaking. Given this figure, it was
surprising that German-American cookbooks were so slow to be
published in America. The most widely read was *Henriette Davidis'
Practical Cook Book*, which was already a best seller in its own country when it came to America. German classics such as meat loaf,
sticky buns, pretzels, and pickles had already become American
favorites and were featured in the first English translation of the
book in 1897.

During the 1840s, when Gustav Peters was gathering material
for his cookbook, *Die Geschickte Hausfrau*, as many as 40 percent of
Pennsylvania spoke a dialect of German that was distinctive to the
Pennsylvania Dutch. The local housewives were suspicious of

new-fangled iron cooking stoves, so the recipes in *Die Geschickte Hausfrau* were all based on open-hearth and bake oven cookery. The recipes were distinctive and delightful, scrapple and shoofly pie being classics still beloved today.

Jewish immigrants coming to America also brought traditional dishes that were European in origin, such as herring in sour cream, bagels, and borscht. Esther Levy's *Jewish Cookery Book* (1871) gave recipes for these and other favorites.

Rounding out our survey of America's kitchen is a book familiar to all by name: Isabella Beeton's classic *Book of Household Management*. Known affectionately as just "Mrs. Beeton," the book was English in concept and considered the seminal Victorian cookbook. Influenced no doubt by the standard image of Queen Victoria, the general impression of Isabella Beeton was of an ample matronly figure of stern appearance. She was in fact a beautiful young woman who lived a tragically short life. Of all the books reviewed in this chapter, hers was imbued with personality, and it turned her into a celebrity with universal name recognition.

Mrs. Beeton's advice on domestic issues was all part of a package that was not really so different from that of Gervase Markham 250 years earlier. Mrs. Beeton's housewife was the manager of a complex household, just as her Elizabethan counterpart had been. Mrs. Beeton expected readers of her book to be prosperous, middle class ladies who employed servants to do the work for her, and Gervase Markham had written for just such a woman back in 1615.

What had changed was the concentration on gentility and refinement that was such a preoccupation with the Victorians. Mrs. Beeton's model wife and housekeeper had to know about far more than cookery, and she might well have recourse to one of the many etiquette manuals that flooded the market at the end of the 19th century. "Let the mistress of every house rise to the responsibility of its management; so that, in doing her duty to all around her, she may receive the genuine reward of respect, love and affection!" was how Mrs. Beeton summed up the task confronting the housewife of our period.

One hundred years into the history of American cooking seemed a symbolic moment to celebrate the national cuisine in a single book, *The National Cookery Book,* but the truth was that American cooking was extraordinarily diverse and there was no one single cuisine. This chapter and the next celebrate the regional differences that gave American cooking its rich heritage.

# Stars and Stripes Meat Loaf

Adapted from: *The National Cookery Book*, 1876, p. 74

The National Cookery Book was published in the centennial year, 1876. The recipes celebrated almost a century of American cookbook writing. There is a strong English presence—about half of the recipes are the puddings, pies, and soups that came over with the English colonists. But since the year in which Amelia Simmons wrote her pioneering and distinctly American volume *American Cookery*, which we reviewed in chapter one, new ingredients and adaptations from the cookery of diverse cultural groups had transformed American cookery. One such American invention made its first print appearance in *The National Cookery Book*. As you might expect, it was the centennial meatloaf, served with a dollop of that other American standby, a homemade tomato sauce, or ketchup.

## Meatloaf

2 pound fillet of veal

½ pound ground pork fat

1 onion, minced

2 eggs, beaten

1 cup soft white breadcrumbs

¼ cup fresh thyme, oregano, and
    parsley, chopped

salt and pepper

1 cup homemade tomato sauce

## Homemade Tomato Sauce

4 pounds fresh ripe tomatoes

½ cup brown sugar

½ cup malt vinegar

salt and pepper

*To Make the Meat Loaf:* Grind the veal and mix it with the pork fat, onion, eggs, breadcrumbs, and herbs. Season to taste with salt and pepper. Use your hands to mold it into a loaf. Put it in a baking pan and spread with tomato sauce. Bake for 1 hour at 350°F. Serve with additional brown gravy. *Serves 6.*

*To Make the Tomato Sauce:* Chop the washed tomatoes and put them in a large pan. Add the sugar and vinegar and bring them to a boil. Simmer, stirring often to prevent sticking. When the sauce is thickened, remove from the heat, season to taste with salt and pepper, and strain through a sieve to remove the skins and seeds. Put in sterilized glass jars to store. Best kept in the icebox. *Makes 1 meat loaf.*

# Venison Pasty

Adapted from: *The National Cookery Book, 1876, p. 101*

## Rich Paste Pastry

3 cups flour

1 teaspoon salt

2 sticks butter

½ cup ice water

1 teaspoon lemon juice

## Venison Pasty

4 cups venison meat, trimmed, cubed

3 cups venison stock (alt: game stock or
  beef stock)

1 cup onion, chopped

salt and pepper to taste

½ teaspoon mace

4 tablespoons butter

2 tablespoons flour

½ cup red wine

The provident Centennial kitchen always had recipes for leftovers, and this entry, which originally called for venison neck and breast meat trimmings, is improved by the choice of the more select cuts of meat, the round or even the shoulder. Carrying the issue further, this meat pie, or pasty, acts as a worthy vehicle for squirrel, rabbit, and a host of mixed bag ingredients, including fish fillets. The pastry here is generic, and can be substituted for recipes of any age or era that call for a thick, heavy crust.

 To Make the Pastry: Mix the dry ingredients and cut in the butter until the mixture resembles cornmeal. Add the ice water and the lemon juice a little at a time to form a dough. Wrap the dough in plastic and chill for 2 hours.

To Make the Pasty: In a saucepan, combine the meat, onion, seasonings, and the stock, and simmer for 20 minutes. Make a roux with the butter and flour and whip into the liquid.

Continue the simmer until the liquid is reduced to a heavy gravy. Line a pie pan with the Rich Paste Pastry. Add the red wine to the venison sauce, then pour venison meat and sauce into the pie pan. Cover the top with a pastry lid and bake in a 325°F oven until the crust is a golden brown. *Serves 4.*

# Epsom Downs Pigeon Pie

Adapted from: Isabella Beeton, *Book of Household Management*, 1861, p. 482

Isabella Beeton was the oldest of 21 children whose stepfather was a functionary for the Epsom Downs racetrack, where the original Derby horse race was run each year. She and her siblings ran wild over the track and up and down the Epsom Downs Grandstand that overlooked the home stretch. Like every racecourse in America, the infield was home to a great gaggle of pigeons, a very useful convenience on days when the ponies didn't cooperate at the betting window. As a consequence, Mrs. Beeton grew up with a pigeon in the pot. This recipe is always a winner; sufficient for 5 or 6 persons, its seasonable at any time.

1½ lb. rump steak
½ cup flour seasoned with ½ teaspoon salt
2 cups pigeon meat (from 3 pigeons)
3 slices ham
4 egg yolks
1 cup good stock (approximately)
1 small onion, chopped
2 tablespoons butter

## Quick Puff Paste

3 cups all-purpose flour   1½ cups cold butter, cubed
1½ tablespoons sugar   9 tablespoons ice water
1½ teaspoons salt   2 teaspoons lemon juice

 First, make the pastry. Combine the flour, sugar, and salt. Rub the butter into the flour, sprinkle over the ice water and the lemon juice, and press until the mixture clumps together. Wrap and chill. Turn the chilled dough onto the counter and roll it into a large rectangle. Fold into thirds, turn and repeat, chilling again if necessary.

*To Make the Pie*: Cut the steak into bite-sized pieces, roll in seasoned flour, and brown in hot butter. Turn the pieces into a deep pie dish. Repeat the process with the pigeon meat and lay it on top of the steak. Lay the slices of ham over. Soften the chopped onion in the butter and spread over the meat. Beat the egg yolks together and pour over the meat. Pour the stock around and season the dish with salt and pepper. On a chilled counter, lightly roll out the paste to make a lid and a strip of pastry to place around the rim of the dish. Position the rim first, then cover with the lid, forming a decorative border with your fingers. Brush the pastry with egg.

*Optional Extra From Mrs. Beeton*: "Use 3 pigeon feet and place them in a hole in the top of the crust for decoration, this will show what kind of pie it is."

Bake the pie at 400°F for ½ hour. Then cover (when the crust is golden brown) and lower the oven to 375°F. Continue baking for an additional 1 hour. *Serves 6.*

# Idaho Smothered Quail

Adapted from: *The National Cookery Book*, 1876, p. 135

8 quail
salt and pepper
½ cup stock
½ cup Madeira
4 tablespoons butter
¼ cup cream

For as long as quail have been shot and eaten, cooks have sought a way to prepare the tiny bird so that the flesh does not dry out before the meat is cooked. Quail have been wrapped in bacon, in vine leaves, and in pork caul, amongst others. An old timer's recipe from Idaho, given in *The National Cookery Book*, suggested putting the quail into the hot ashes and embers, cooking them to a literal crisp and then defeathering and skinning. Luckily this was to be carried out in the open air, as the smell of scorched feather is enough to drive diners miles away from camp! A better approach is to use the Dutch oven, which offers the best hope of baking the quail to a succulent doneness. Eaten straight from the pot—with the fingers and sucking the meat from the bones—is outdoor eating at its Idaho best.

 Set the Dutch oven in the hot coals and allow ample time for heating. Put the butter in the oven and when it is hot, turn the quail over in it and allow them to turn golden brown, about 5 minutes. Pour in the stock and the Madeira, and salt and pepper. Replace the lid and cook the quail for 15 minutes. Take the quail out and set on hot plates while you prepare the sauce. There should be 1 cup of liquid. If there is more, reduce. If there is less, add white wine. Off heat, stir in the cream to thicken the sauce. Check the seasoning and smother the bird with sauce. *Serves 4.*

# GREEK DELMAS

Adapted from: *The National Cookery Book*, 1876, p. 65

These lamb birds, chopped and cuddled in sauce and savory spices and shrouded in a cabbage leaf, are essentially Greek, where they are called *dolmas*, but neither the editors nor the Women's Executive Committee who greeted President Ulysses S. Grant to the opening of this exposition in 1876 would ever admit it. Nor would they concede that the intent behind the recipe was to remove the filling from the cabbage and eat it. The classic delma included both the cabbage and filling as part of the dish. We have added a tomato and feta cheese sauce that brings the dish a new urgency that even Greek chef Nicholas Tselementes would have admired.

2 lbs. roast lamb, chopped and well-seasoned

1 cup basmati rice, cooked in 2 cups chicken stock

1 small onion, chopped

2 cloves garlic, minced

2 tablespoons olive oil

½ cup Greek black olives, minced

1 teaspoon each: salt, pepper, marjoram, cayenne

1 egg, beaten

1 large firm savoy cabbage

2 cups tomato sauce (see p. 75)

2 cups crumbled feta cheese

Sauté the onion and garlic in the oil until soft. Mix the cold rice with the meat and onion mixture. Add the olives, herbs, salt, pepper, and enough of the beaten egg to make a stuffing for the cabbage leaves.

To prepare the cabbage, bring a large pot of water to boil. Lower the cabbage into the water in a colander and boil for 5 minutes. Lift out the colander and peel off the outer leaves, rinsing each under cold water before laying on paper towels to dry. Return the whole cabbage to the pot and repeat the process until you have 16 leaves.

Cut a notch at the base of each leaf to remove the fleshy stalk. Place a sausage of lamb mixture in the bottom half of the leaf and roll up tightly. Place the rolls side by side in a buttered casserole dish. Pour over the tomato sauce, cover, and bake in a 350°F oven for 1 hour. Remove the cover, sprinkle the feta cheese over, and return to the oven for another 15 minutes. *Serves 4.*

# Hunter's Bigos

Adapted from: *The National Cookery Book*, 1876, p. 159

2 lbs. sauerkraut (canned or homemade)

1½ cups beef stock

4 Granny Smith apples, peeled and sliced

2 large onions, halved

½ cup dry white wine

½ chicken

½ duck

1 lb. loin venison

½ lb. piece of ham

salt and pepper

½ cup olive oil

2 tablespoons flour

2 tablespoons butter

Following the culinary trail investigated by food historian William Woys Weaver, we learn how much the dish known as "sauerkraut" became a part of the Pennsylvania Dutch culture before the Civil War. *Sauerkraut Yankees* is the name of his book, and the term was also adopted in a pejorative way by Confederate soldiers during the war. Sauerkraut has many uses, of course, and its addition to this dish of hunter's stew—a polish bigos—is traditional.

 Put the sauerkraut on to stew gently with the stock, apples, and half onions. In a skillet, brown the meats and then the remaining onions in the olive oil. Pour in the wine and stir it well, then cover the pan and cook for 30 minutes. Remove the meat and take it off the bone. Transfer half the sauerkraut into a large pan, put the meat on top and cover with the remaining sauerkraut. Pour over the liquid in which the sauerkraut cooked. Season with salt and pepper. Cover the pan and simmer for 1 hour. Check the liquid from time to time and add more wine if needed.

Make a roux with the butter and flour and use it to thicken the stock. Allow to simmer for another ½ hour until the bigos is thick and smooth. Serve piping hot in bowls with crusty bread. *Serves 8.*

# RED SNAPPER IN TOMATO SAUCE

Adapted from: Mrs. Esther Levy, *Jewish Cookery Book*, 1871, p. 40

In 1871, when the Jewish community in Philadelphia numbered about 12,000, this landmark book was published. The Jewish cooking revealed here was Ashkenazic with a colorful array of vividly seasoned dishes, especially those using cayenne pepper. Another remarkable feature for this narrowly focused book was the surprising deference to quintessential American dishes, such as succotash and corn bread. This delicious treatment of a great Gulf fish is well prepared in a typical manner.

*1 red snapper, 5-6 lbs., scaled and cleaned*
*3 cups fish stock*
*1 cup dry white wine*
*2 onions, chopped*
*1 stick celery, chopped*
*1 carrot, chopped*
*4 tomatoes, peeled and chopped*
*½ cup cream*
*2 teaspoons flour*
*½ teaspoon cayenne*
*salt and pepper*
*lemon and parsley for garnish*

 Put the stock, wine, onions, celery, and carrot in a fish kettle and bring to a boil. Lower the heat and place the fish in the kettle. Simmer for 8 minutes per pound, about 30 minutes for a 5-lb. fish. Carefully take the fish out and lay on a warm serving platter.

Put the tomatoes in the liquid in the kettle and boil for 10 minutes. Strain the liquid, pressing the vegetables down to extract all the juices. Boil down the liquid until there is 1 cup, then thicken with a flour and cream roux. Season with the cayenne, salt and pepper, and pour the hot sauce over the fish to serve. Garnish with lemon quarters and parsley over rice. *Serves 4.*

# Baltimore Oyster Pie

Adapted from: *The National Cookery Book*, 1876, p. 50

1 recipe rough puff paste (*see p. 177*)
2 pints oysters, shucked
6 tablespoons butter, cut into little bits
½ cup fine white breadcrumbs
1 cup cream
salt and pepper
pinch mace and nutmeg

The merry blast of the "fishorn" signaled the approach of the huckster's wagon, rattling down the small town streets all over land-locked Pennsylvania and Ohio, where the recipe for this pie originates. Fresh shad, cod, mackerel, clams, and oysters were hawked along the road from town to farm in special wagons fitted out with ice and seaweed to keep the fish fresh. To attract even more attention, the hucksters often chimed in a jingle about whatever they were selling that day. By mid-century, canals and railroads had re-carved the geography of the upstate communities, but hucksters continued to flourish along the by-roads, even into the early 20th century, in living memory of today's grandmothers.

Mix the oysters with the breadcrumbs, the cream, and the seasonings. Put them in a deep pie plate. Dot the pie with the butter bits. Roll out the chilled pastry and make a lid to cover the plate. Make slits in the top, brush the pastry with beaten egg, and bake for 1 hour in a 375°F oven until golden. *Serves 6.*

# CARP WITH POLISH SAUCE

Adapted from: Henriette Davidis, *Henriette Davidis' Practical Cook Book*, 1897, p. 207

Big freshwater carp are the pride and passion of fishermen all over Europe, from Isaak Walton to the Lord High Mayor of Krakow. There, carp are holiday food and eaten ceremoniously on Christmas Eve with all the trimmings and lots of company. Henriette Davidis could hardly have foreseen that in the decade following the American publication of her book, carp hatcheries established by the American government would stock the fish in every suitable river and lake, nor the enormous success of that environmental niche.

4 cups fresh carp fish, scaled and cut into large chunks

3 cups beer

3 cups water

3 carrots, chopped

1 parsnip, chopped

3 onions, chopped

1 single stalk of celery, sliced

1 teaspoon ginger

1 teaspoon cloves, ground

2 bay leaves

4 black peppercorns

3 tablespoons butter

1 lemon, cut in cubes, seeded, and tied in cheesecloth

⅓ cup vinegar (plus up to 1 cup carp blood from the butchering)

1 cup red wine

1 cup gingerbread or crumbled *Pfefferkuchen* (alt: wheat bread)

salt and pepper to taste

In a Dutch oven on top of the stove, make a broth with the beer, water, carrots, parsnip, onions, and celery seasoned with the ginger, cloves, bay leaves, and peppercorns. Bring the stock to a boil, reduce, and simmer for 30 minutes.

Add the cut-up fish, butter, lemon, and vinegar. Cover the pot tightly and cook for 15 minutes or longer until the fish is tender. Remove the fish to serving platters and keep warm.

Reserve the cooking liquid, and to it add the red wine and the gingerbread. Reduce the sauce until it is quite thick. Serve the fish with sauce over. *Serves 4.*

# PERCH STEWED WITH WINE

Adapted from: Isabella Beeton, *Book of Household Management*, 1861, p. 191

2 whole perch, fresh
4 cups fish stock (alt: clam juice)
1 cup dry sherry
1 bay leaf
1 garlic clove
1 cup parsley, chopped
2 cloves
salt and pepper
2 tablespoons butter and 2 tablespoons flour
pepper, nutmeg, and anchovy paste to flavor

Mrs. Beeton was vitally interested in the details of each fish and bird for which she recommended a recipe. She commented that the perch was extremely voracious and had the peculiarity of being gregarious. That characteristic was seized upon by The Schuylkill Fishing Company, a sportsmen's fishing club formed near Philadelphia in 1732, whose banner flag was emblazoned with a crown and three perch in white against a red background. It was true when General Washington and General Lafayette dined there, and it is true today, the club members were all voracious and gregarious.

Scale the fish and dress by removing the gills, cheeks, dorsal and gill fins. Lay the fish side by side in a large roasting pan with sufficient stock and sherry to just cover them. Add the bay leaf, garlic, parsley, cloves, salt and pepper, and simmer on the top of the oven until tender. The flesh should just flake at the thickest point to the tip of a knife. Remove the fish carefully and reserve on warm serving plates.

To make a sauce, take the reserved poaching liquid, add 2 tablespoons each of butter and flour for thickening. For flavoring, add a dash of fresh pepper, a few grindings of nutmeg, and ¼ teaspoon of anchovy paste and stir while reducing the liquid over a brisk heat to the desired quantity. Pour over each fish and serve. *Serves 2.*

# Hot Potato Soup

Adapted from: Henriette Davidis, *Henriette Davidis' Practical Cook Book*, 1897, p. 33

Presbyterian Scotch Irish settlers brought the spud with them to Londonderry, New Hampshire, in 1719. From that modest beginning the cultivation of this vegetable tuber spread to other colonies throughout the Northeast, initially, and then nationwide. In the early days, the potato was grown as a crop rotation relief for fields drained down by the constant demands of corn production, but a wave of German immigrants brought their reliable potato recipes with them, both soup and salad, and the spud was back in demand.

*8 large potatoes, washed and skinned*
*water for parboiling potatoes*
*10 cups water for soup*
*2 cups game or beef trimmings, fresh or roasted*
*4 lbs. fresh or roasted beef or game bones*
*1 onion, chopped roughly*
*1 celery stalk, chopped roughly*
*1 large leek, chopped with leaves*
*2 tablespoons flour*
*2 tablespoons butter*
*salt and pepper*
*1 cup parsley, finely chopped*

Start a stock by combining the 10 cups of water with the bones and meat trimmings, onion, celery, and leek in a stock pot; bring to a boil, then reduce the heat and simmer slowly for 1 hour.

Half an hour before the stock is ready, peel the potatoes, and chop roughly. In a separate saucepan, bring sufficient fresh water to cover the potatoes to a boil, add the chopped potatoes, reduce the heat to medium, and cook the potatoes until almost soft. Remove and strain, reserving the potatoes.

Strain the stockpot, reserving the liquid and discarding the meat and bones. Combine 8 cups of the reserved stock and the partially cooked potatoes in the stockpot and continue to simmer until the potatoes are quite soft, then mash.

In the meantime, in a small skillet make a roux from the butter and flour and cook over low heat until brown. Combine the roux with a small amount of stock outside the pot, then return to the stockpot and allow it to thicken. Adjust the seasonings with salt and pepper, stir in the parsley, then serve with bits of toasted bread. *Serves 6.*

# THE PRINCE OF WALES SOUP

Adapted from: Isabella Beeton, *Book of Household Management*, 1861, p. 77

1 shin of beef (alt: 4 lbs. veal shank cut in
    2" cross sections, or 4 oxtails)

8 quarts beer

1 small cabbage, quartered

6 carrots, roughly chopped

4 turnips, roughly chopped

3 potatoes, roughly chopped

2 onions, quartered

salt and pepper

2 tablespoons fresh chopped herbs: parsley,
    thyme, and rosemary

The idea of public charity is never far from the hearts of well-meaning cooks, and so it was that on the eve of the birthday celebration for England's Prince of Wales, Mrs. Beeton and her pals concocted this enormous soup as a gift to feed to the poor of the city. The many hundreds who supped that day were soon forgotten, but the Princes' legacy of indulgence and hedonism endured for generations, lending a certain irony, if not savor, to Mrs. Beeton's efforts. Nevertheless, in the spirit of Victorian charity, Mrs. Beeton wanted us to have the recipe, and likewise, we want to pass it on, albeit in this reduced version for a savory oxtail soup at your neighborhood block party.

 Boil a shin of beef (or the alternative) for 3 hours in the beer until the meat falls off the bone. Set in the refrigerator overnight and the next day, take off the fat. Chop the vegetables and boil them in the reserved stock until tender. Press the cooked vegetables through a sieve, or process in a food processor for 30 seconds. Return the purée to the pot, add the shredded meat, and season well with salt, pepper, and chopped fresh herbs. Serve piping hot. *Serves 8.*

# A SPECIFIC FOR FRESH HERB SOUP

Adapted from: Henriette Davidis, *Henriette Davidis' Practical Cook Book*, 1897, p. 40

Dutch and German cooking in the American Midwest got a tremendous impetus first from George Girardey, and then from Henriette Davidis, both writing in German and later translated into English. In each case, the lists of culinary herbs used was long and colorful and the dishes they made more colorful still, reflecting a cultural affinity for fresh herbs. A chilled version of the Davidis original is given here, with the addition of fresh thyme and chives and the substitution of vegetable for the beef stock. Fresh herbs ensure that the delicate flavor is preserved.

1 large onion, chopped
1 tablespoon vegetable oil
1 tablespoon flour
4 cups vegetable stock
1 cup dry white wine
2 cups fresh parsley leaves
1 cup fresh chervil leaves
1 cup fresh spinach leaves
2 tablespoons fresh thyme leaves
2 tablespoons fresh sorrel leaves
1 egg yolk
⅔ cup low fat sour cream
salt and pepper
1 tablespoon lemon juice

Cook the chopped onion in the oil until soft but not colored. Stir in the flour and cook for 3 minutes. Stir in the stock and the wine, and simmer until slightly thickened. Remove from the heat and stir in the fresh herbs, all washed and chopped. Allow to stand until cool, then purée the soup briefly until smooth. Return to the pan and heat slowly; whisk in the egg yolk, sour cream, and salt and pepper. Return the soup to a tureen and chill for about 2 hours, but not more than 24 hours. Serve sprinkled with lemon juice. *Serves 4.*

# OXTAIL SOUP

Adapted from: Isabella Beeton, *Book of Household Management*, 1861, p. 92

2 oxtails, skinned

3 quarts water

2 slices ham

2 tablespoons butter

2 carrots

2 turnips

2 onions

1 leek

1 head of celery

1 bunch of savory herbs: parsley, thyme, oregano

1 bay leaf

12 whole peppercorns

4 cloves

1 tablespoon salt

2 tablespoons ketchup

1 glass port wine

Following the enthusiastic lead of Chef Alexis Soyer (soup for the troops in the Crimean War), and Florence Nightingale (the gas ovens of the Reform Club in London), and Mrs. Beeton's announcement of the newly created bouillon cube, soup had become respectable and was featured on most American restaurant menus. Mrs. Beeton recognized that this popular British soup, even thickened with ketchup and port wine, would become a standard worldwide.

 Cut up the oxtails, separating them at the joints, wash and reserve. Cut the vegetables into slices. In a stewpan, melt the butter and over a sharp fire color the oxtails for 2 to 3 minutes. Add the ham slices. Add the sliced vegetables, the peppercorns, cloves, and herbs and brown the vegetables for 2 minutes, stirring. Add 1 cup of the water and continue shaking for 3 additional minutes until the vegetable juices are drawn.

Fill the pan with the remaining water and bring to a boil. Add the salt. Reduce the heat and continue to simmer for 4 hours, skimming regularly, until the oxtails are tender. Remove and reserve the oxtails. Strain the broth.

If the broth is to be used for stock, then freeze in 1-pint containers. For oxtail soup, thicken the broth with flour and flavor with ketchup and port wine. Return the oxtails to the soup, simmer for 5 minutes, and serve. *Serves 10.*

# PARSNIP PANCAKES

Adapted from: Gustav Peters, *Die Geschickte Hausfrau*, 1848, p. 78

Nineteenth century cooks boiled their vegetables longer than we do. And there was a reason, apart from ignorance. Vegetable varieties were selected and grown for shelf or storage life, so they tended to be tougher and needed more cooking. Parsnips, for instance, are boiled "one to two hours" in *Die Geschickte Hausfrau* (*The Handy Housewife*) after which they were not good for much except mashing. Parsnips were once more popular and easier to store than potatoes, and had fewer problems with disease, blight, and insects. In this simple example, young parsnips are grated raw and made into little pancakes to be eaten with sour cream and fresh nutmeg, and served with roast pork.

1 pound tender parsnips
2 eggs, beaten
½ onion, grated
1 cup flour
salt and pepper
½ cup vegetable oil

 Shred the parsnips on a grater into a bowl. Mix in the onion, eggs, flour, salt and pepper, and stir until smooth. Heat the vegetable oil in a heavy nonstick frying pan. Pour in heaped tablespoons of the batter and cook until the whiskery edges of the pancakes turn golden brown. Turn the pancakes and cook the other side. Serve with sour cream. *Serves 4.*

# BREAKFAST LAPLAND ROLLS

Adapted from: *The National Cookery Book*, 1876, p. 171

3 eggs, separated
¼ teaspoon salt
1 cup flour
1 cup milk
1 tablespoon melted butter

> Thus through the long ages
> Advancement was slow
> While kings and their pages
> Ate charcoal or dough
> And both were contented
> With second class loaves
> Until man invented
> … Peninsular stoves …

So read a little booklet of the period, advertising the cast iron cook stove. But not all cooks embraced the iron monster. We find plenty of recipes in the *The National Cookery Book* for griddle or flatbreads cooked over the fire, like the traditional johnnycake and these laplands, which were a Southern specialty. The johnnycake was baked on a flat board before the fire, whereas these popover-like rolls had to be dropped in spoonfuls on a hot griddle, and then rushed to table before they fell.

Beat together the egg yolks with the flour, salt, and milk, then stir in the melted butter. Fold in the stiffly beaten egg whites and drop spoonfuls of batter onto a piping hot and greased griddle pan. Cook for about 10 minutes, until puffed and golden, being careful not to burn. Serve hot with butter and honey. *Makes 12 small laplands.*

# Carolina Loaf Rice Bread

Adapted from: Mrs. Howland, *The American Economical Housekeeper*, 1845, p. 15

By the middle of the 19th century, rice was available in stores and markets across this nation. Conscientious cooks such as Mrs. Howland realized the unique qualities of bread made with this starchy grain, and recommended it for the specific application of making sandwiches intended to be eaten during long trips. This quaint notion may have originated with one Lady Llanover, corresponding from Wales, but Mrs. Howland was won over by the pleasing nutty texture. We use a modern hybrid basmati rice here, which produces a pleasant colored loaf.

½ cup basmati rice
2¾ cups water
6 cups bread flour
1 teaspoon active dried yeast
2 teaspoons salt

Cook the rice in half the water until the rice is tender. Remove from the heat and set aside, covered, to cool.

In a large mixing bowl, stir the yeast into the rice and 2 cups of the flour, and make a thick batter. Cover and let rise for 1 hour until doubled in size. Stir down, add the salt, the remaining water, and the remaining flour and knead for 8 minutes until a smooth, satiny dough is formed. Grease 2 loaf pans. Divide the dough in half and form into 2 loaves; put in the prepared pans. Cover and let rise for 1 hour. Bake in a 375°F oven for 45 to 50 minutes until the loaves are lightly golden and sound hollow when tapped on the bottom. Cool before eating. *Makes 2 loaves.*

# SAVARIN

Adapted from: *The National Cookery Book*, 1876, p. 271

1 tablespoon dried yeast
¼ cup sugar
½ cup water
3 cups all-purpose flour
½ teaspoon salt
4 large eggs, beaten
grated zest of 1 orange and 1 lemon
2 sticks unsalted butter
1 tablespoon cream

## SYRUP

½ cup dark rum
2 tablespoons maraschino liqueur
¼ cup sugar

There is a lugubrious and slightly salacious character to the stories recounting the origins of "savarin," a rum-soaked sweet bread from Poland. Legend has it that the savarin, or the "baba," its near cousin, were invented by an exiled Polish king who enlivened his stale bread by dipping it in rum. The King named it after his favorite hero, Ali Baba, who dipped nearly everything in rum, or the Babylonian version thereof. Savarins are baked in a special ring mold and then soaked in rum syrup.

Cream the yeast with the sugar and water and allow to stand until frothy. Add the salt and flour to the yeast and beat well. Now add the beaten eggs, the zest, and the softened butter, one piece at a time. Add the cream at the end to make a soft batter. Place the batter into a large buttered ring mold and cover. Let it rise until the batter reaches the top of the pan, and bake in a 375°F oven for about 35 minutes, until the savarin is golden brown. Remove and cool.

To make the syrup, stir together the rum, the maraschino, and the sugar. Pour this syrup over the cake, but do not wet too much. If you want, fill the center of the cake with sweetened cream and fresh fruits. *Makes 1 savarin.*

# Sportsman's Outdoor Cake

Adapted from: *The National Cookery Book*, 1876, p. 136

Open air cooking always offers a revealing glimpse into the recreational habits of the American sportsman. One and a half centuries ago, roughing it for dinner was described in the following words.

"Indian meal is easily carried, and makes a very palatable addition to a dinner in the woods. Pour boiling water over the meal to scald it. Make the mixture stiff enough to shape. Add a little salt. When you have finished frying your meat or fish, make up little cakes of this dough and drop them into the hot pan and brown them." Also: "Get your Indian guide to find a smooth sapling, peel off the bark, scrape it smooth and then you have your rolling pin. Take one of the boards from the bottom of your boat, cover it with a napkin and then you have a good pasteboard. You can cut the paste into cakes and fry them as you would in civilised life."

I've heard about hunting camps like that, but this pound cake is too good and too delicate to make the trip. Cornmeal is a brilliant ingredient, and used sparingly, the product can bake up a cake that is every bit as toothsome as a loaf made with flour.

*2 sticks unsalted butter*
*2 cups sugar*
*2 cups white cornmeal*
*1 cup cake flour*
*1 teaspoon fresh nutmeg, grated*
*1 teaspoon cinnamon*
*6 eggs, beaten*
*1 tablespoon whisky*

Cream the sugar and butter together until smooth and fluffy. Add the sifted dry ingredients alternately with the beaten eggs. Beat well. Lastly, stir in the whisky. Spoon the batter into a buttered loaf pan and smooth the top with a wet spoon. Bake in a 350°F oven until the cake is browned and a skewer inserted in the middle comes out clean. Cool before turning the cake out on a wire rack. Stand overnight before serving. *Makes 1 large cake.*

# Lebkuchen or Honey Cookies

Adapted from: Henriette Davidis, *Henriette Davidis' Practical Cook Book*, 1897, p. 407

2 cups honey
1 cup almonds, blanched and ground fine
2 teaspoons cinnamon
2 teaspoons nutmeg
grated zest of 1 orange and 1 lemon
2 cups flour
2 teaspoons baking powder
½ cup cherry cordial

Honey may be man's oldest source of sugar, and food history from the origins of mead to the Pharaohs' last drop attest to the ubiquity of the sweetener. Certainly the German lebkuchen and other imported cookies were developed with honey as their main ingredient, and have been reproduced by the immigrant populations in largely undiluted form. The maple, cane, and ultimately beet-based sugars, the last developed by a German chemist in 1747, came too late to intrude on this inherited glimmer of the good old days.

Be careful with these traditional German lebkuchen because the honey in the recipe causes them to brown more quickly.

Put the honey on the stove over low heat. When melted, stir in the almonds, the spices, and the zests. Remove from the heat, and add the flour and baking powder sifted together. Lastly, stir in the cherry cordial. While the dough is still warm, roll it out about ¼" thick and cut into round cookies. Lay them on a buttered baking tray, with the edges just touching. Let the cookies get quite cold, then bake them in a 350°F oven for 18 to 20 minutes, watching carefully. Break them apart while they are warm, dust with powdered sugar, and let cool.
*Makes 18 cookies.*

# Rhode Island Cherry Slump

Adapted from: Gustav Peters, *Die Geschickte Hausfrau*, 1848, pp. 118 and 122

*Die Geschickte Hausfrau*, translated as *The Handy Housewife*, was one of the first truly ethnic cookbooks published in America. Written in German, the book was hugely popular with early settlers of Teutonic lineage, and catered to their favorite dishes, including sweet cherry pies flavored with maple syrup and baked in a crust of yeast-risen pastry such as this. The name "slump" comes from the uneven way in which the dough will rise and fall across the surface during baking.

## The Slump Crust

1 tablespoon yeast
1 tablespoon sugar
¾ cup milk
2 cups flour
3 tablespoons butter

## The Slump

4 cups cherries, stoned
1 cup brown sugar
1 teaspoon nutmeg
1 teaspoon cinnamon
1 egg, beaten
additional sugar

Make the crust by whisking the yeast and sugar into the warmed milk. When it is bubbly, add the flour and the butter cut up into little pieces. Mix well, turn out onto a floured surface, and knead lightly until smooth. Place in an oiled bowl, cover, and let rise for 1 hour.

Meanwhile, prepare the cherries. Boil the washed fruit in as little water as possible, add the sugar and spices, and stir to avoid sticking. Cook until the cherries are tender, about ½ hour. Cool.

Turn the risen dough onto the counter and roll out half into a large round. Line a pie plate. Tip in the cherries with their cooking liquid. Cover with the second round of dough. Brush with beaten egg, sprinkle with additional sugar, and bake in a 375°F oven for 1 hour, until golden brown. *Makes 1 pie.*

# Apple Brown Betty

Adapted from: Isabella Beeton, *Book of Household Management*, 1861, p. 623

12 large Granny Smith apples
4 tablespoons melted butter and 1 tablespoon
    butter cut into bits
1 teaspoon nutmeg
1 teaspoon cinnamon
1½ cups brown sugar
grated rind of 1 lemon
2 cups breadcrumbs

"What's its name?" they asked, squirming a small finger toward the still hot crust. "Crisps, buckles, grunts, slumps, sonkers, bettys," came the distracted answer from the kitchen, all these being regional variations on puddings using seasonal fruits and berries. "Consonance has as much to do with the naming of dishes as provenance" someone once observed, and so it will always be with the "Brown Betty"; your special anecdote excepted.

Pare, core, and slice the apples and stew with just enough water to cover until soft. Add the melted butter, the spices, sugar, and lemon rind. Beat to a smooth pulp.

In a buttered pie dish, put a layer of breadcrumbs, then the apples, and another layer of breadcrumbs. Dot the top with the remaining bits of butter. Bake for ½ hour at 350°F. Serve warm with cream. *Serves 4.*

# All Aboard! for Shoofly Pie

Adapted from: Gustav Peters, *Die Geschickte Hausfrau*, 1848, p. 230

The selfsame genius that inspired the creation and patent of the Pullman railroad dining car on American railroads extended to every aspect of the traveling experience, including the menu! In the decades following 1868, the golden era of train travel flourished and one might expect lovely china and distinctive menus featuring local dishes from the country-side seen out the window. One such was the "Shoofly Pie" found on the menu of the Pennsylvania Railroad's "Broadway Ltd." The dish had been a standard for 40 years in the Pennsylvania Dutch community, made from "barrel" molasses, to which the flies are partial—hence the name.

1 pie crust, unbaked

## Crumb Mixture
2 cups flour
¾ cup brown sugar
⅓ cup shortening
1 teaspoon nutmeg
1 teaspoon cinnamon

## Filling
1 cup molasses
½ cup brown sugar
2 eggs
1 teaspoon baking soda dissolved in 1 cup hot water

Mix the crumb ingredients together in a bowl and reserve. Mix the filling ingredients until well blended, and pour into the pie crust-lined plate. Sprinkle the crumb mixture over the top. Bake in a 400°F oven for 10 minutes, then lower the heat to 350°F and bake for an additional 45 minutes. Serve cool with whipped cream or vanilla ice cream. *Makes 1 pie.*

# PAN DOWDY

Adapted from: *The National Cookery Book*, 1876, p. 203

2 recipes pastry (see p. 50)
4 cups apples, pared, cored, and quarterd
1 teaspoon cinnamon
2 cups sugar
1 cup apple cider

Without even the presumption of an elaborate name, the "pan dowdy" conjures scenes of cast iron stoves, kitchen window sills with pies cooling, and the ineffable rightness of apples and cinnamon crushed in rich crust. There was no "holding back" in those days, and a frumpy, dowdy crushed pie lid was all the more proof of the treasure in store for the lucky diner.

Line a 9" round pie plate with pastry and fill it with the apples. Sprinkle over the cinnamon, sugar, and cider. Cover the filling with a pastry lid. Bake at 350°F for 1 hour. Remove from the oven and, with a fork, break through the crust vigorously mixing it with the apples. "To be eaten with cream," the instructions read! *Makes 1 pan dowdy.*

# BÉCHAMEL SAUCE

Adapted from: Henriette Davidis, *Henriette Davidis' Practical Cook Book*, 1897, p. 353

In the 17th century, béchamel sauce was a complicated mixture of vegetables, wines, and meats, often made from ham and partridge. François Pierre de La Varenne, chef to Louis XIV, gets credit for the idea, including the extended reduction of the sauce to produce the desired consistency. The use of cream and vegetables here reveals that Mrs. Davidis was of the old French school in her view of this now quite modern sauce.

3 cups water
3 onions, sliced thinly
1 cup carrots, diced
1 cup kohlrabi, diced (alt: celery)
1 cup lean ham, cubed
1 tablespoon flour
1 tablespoon butter
2 cups milk
2 cups cream
¼ cup mushrooms, finely chopped
salt and pepper

In a large saucepan over medium-high heat, stew the onions, carrots, kohlrabi, and ham in the 3 cups of water until the latter is tender. Rub the flour and butter together to form a beurre manie, then add to the stew together with the milk and cream. Let the mixture reach a near-boil and watch for 4 minutes without allowing the cream to scorch.

Strain the mixture through a sieve, and then add the mushroom bits. Adjust the seasonings with salt and freshly cracked black pepper, and warm before serving. *Makes 2 cups of sauce.*

# GINGER BEER

Adapted from: Isabella Beeton, *Book of Household Management*, 1861, p. 889

2 lemons
2 fresh ginger roots
1 tablespoon cream of tartar
2 lbs. sugar
3 gallons boiling water
2 tablespoons brewers' yeast

"Ginger Beer" is a euphemism for mildly alcoholic or small beer, and in fact this popular drink is often made with no residual alcohol whatsoever. In olden days, ginger beer was highly prized for medicinal purposes on account of the sprightly and exotic taste of the imported ginger root (*Zingiber officinale*). With the advance of mass marketing in the 1890s, and the availability of sturdy glass bottles, ginger beer was transmogrified into ginger ale, which became the dominant flavor until the 1920s when colas were introduced.

Peel and juice the lemons, reserving the peel. Chop the peel and lemon pulp and combine with the juice in a large earthen crock, 5 gallons capacity or more. Peel and crush the ginger and add to the crock, together with the cream of tartar and the sugar. Pour 3 gallons of boiling water over this. Let it stand for 30 minutes, or until warm. Add the yeast and stir the mixture well. Cover the crock and keep it at 65° to 85°F all night.

The next day, skim off the surface yeast and decant the liquor into one or more separate pans, leaving the sediment behind. Pour the liquor into 8 to 10 quart bottles and cap securely. Store the bottles away from light or heat and allow them to ferment for 3 days; then they are fit for use. Storage life is reduced if less sugar is used. *Makes 8-10 quarts.*

## Chapter Seven

# Roots Are Everywhere

Mrs. Abby Fisher, *What Mrs. Fisher Knows About Old Southern Cooking*, 1881
Rufus Estes, *Good Things to Eat*, 1911
François Mignon and Clementine Hunter, *Melrose Plantation Cookbook*, 1956
Encarnación Pinedo, *El Cocinero Español (The Spanish Cook)*, 1898
Lafcadio Hearn, *La Cuisine Creole*, 1885
Mrs. Lettice Bryan, *The Kentucky Housewife*, 1839

The ferment of cookbook publishing in America reached unprecedented levels in the South, as the voices of African American and Hispanic cooks and the genius of the Creole and Cajun kitchens were heard for the first time.

The skills of the great black cooks had long gone unacknowledged, even though their influence was reflected in the dishes served up daily to their white masters. Literacy levels lagged so far behind that of whites that, as late as 1890, two thirds of blacks in America were illiterate. Small wonder, then, that cookbooks written by blacks did not appear until 1881, when Mrs. Abby Fisher, a former slave, published *What Mrs. Fisher Knows About Old Southern Cooking*. The book began with an apology reminiscent of Amelia Simmon's disclaimer at the front of *American Cookery* nearly a century earlier, in 1796. Mrs. Fisher wrote, "Not being able to read or write myself and my husband also having been without the advantages of education, caused me to doubt whether I would be able to present a work that would give perfect satisfaction."

Mrs. Fisher had been encouraged to write her book by the ladies of San Francisco, who flocked to buy her wonderful preserves and pickles. Before the advent of iceboxes and freezers, and before the speedy shipment of produce by train, families ate fresh produce in the summer and put up food the rest of the year. There was a concentration of recipes for preserved goods and Mrs. Fisher was a master of the art. To her goes the honor of authoring the oldest known African American cookbook published in America.

As colorful and unique were the recollections of Clementine Hunter, the semi-literate granddaughter of slaves, whose skills were inherited from a line of great Creole African American chefs. Although the *Melrose Plantation Cookbook* was not published until 1956, the recipes came from a time sixty years earlier. They described the high Creole style of cooking in the Joyous Coast region in Northern Louisiana.

In the closing decades of the century, when Clementine was growing up, game was abundant across America and especially in Louisiana where a man might kill a couple of hundred pigeon or duck in an evening's sport. The very names of the recipes reflect the richness of the living: "Eggplant Bourre Brochette," "Cote Joyeuse de Pain," and "Parsnip Beignet."

Rufus Estes was born a slave in Murray County, Tennessee, in 1857, and was given the name of his master, D. J. Estes. At the age of eleven, Rufus was doing odd jobs to take care of his mother, since his six brothers had all been killed in the War. The story of his gradual rise to respected chef and maître d' on the Pullman cars makes poignant reading. His book *Good Things to Eat* (1911) was testimony to the sophistication of his cuisine, which, though it had roots in the best Anglo cuisine, also showed his knowledge of French cooking.

There had been no record of Creole cooking until an eccentric journalist named Lafcadio Hearn set down the recipes he had collected from his year of eating in New Orleans. Creole cooking had its origins in France, for the earliest settlers in Louisiana were the French who came in 1699, and who brought with them a sophisticated cuisine that would lend its subtle flavors and delicate sauces to the abundant produce of their new home. Crabs, oysters, shrimp, red snapper, and pompano were the Southern equivalents of the eels and codfish eaten in the North and, like the colonists who settled New England, the early French learned from Native Americans how to use the bounty of Louisiana's fields and streams.

The official birth of Creole Cooking is often cited as 1722. Just four years after the founding of New Orleans, fifty women staged what became known as "The Petticoat Rebellion" at the Governor's Palace. The women were complaining about the lack of traditional foods, in particular they pined for the taste of fine, white bread. The Governor's response was brisk. He sent his housekeeper, Madame Langlois, to teach the ladies how to bake with corn meal and how to use file to thicken and flavor their stews.

Lafcadio Hearn came to New Orleans at a time when there was an awakening of Creole consciousness. *La Cuisine Creole* was planned in time for the World Industrial Exposition in 1884, which was to be hosted in New Orleans, but a series of printing delays cheated Hearn of his anticipated market and the book was not a success. The eccentric journalist soon left America, settling eventually in the East and writing about the food of Japan and China. Today, the achievements of Hearn are recognized as the first attempt to make a systematic presentation of the renowned Creole cuisine.

Encarnación Pinedo was nothing short of a heroine. There were only a handful of Latinas who published their works in the period following the conquest of Alto, California, and she was the only cookbook writer. But El *Cocinero Español* suffered the fate of other books written in a recently conquered language. It languished in private libraries.

Recent efforts on the part of food historians have rescued Encarnación Pinedo, however, and restored her work to the place it deserves as California's first and most extensive Spanish language cookbook. Pinedo loved the fruits and vegetables of her home state, and they appeared in abundance in her recipes. She also gave us the first major collection of Mexican recipes, complete with the aggressive spicing that was so very different from what her Northern neighbors were eating at the time!

Mrs. Lettice Bryan makes a belated appearance in this chapter, for her book *The Kentucky Housewife*. This book was first published back in 1839, when housewife books were all the rage. In some ways, Mrs. Bryan's work was typical of the trend, for there were standard recipes for many of the dishes already encountered in this book, such as chowders, roasted meats, pies, and cakes galore. What set her book apart and earned it a place on kitchen shelves throughout the 19th century was her inclusion of Native American and African recipes.

Alongside all these cookery books that gave recipes for ethnic and regional dishes, women's magazines boomed in the last quarter of the 19th century. Between 1860 and 1900, the number of titles produced in the United States increased fivefold to number 1,800. Titles such as *The Woman's Home Companion* (founded 1873), *Ladies Home Journal* (1883) and *Good Housekeeping* (1885) all carried articles on cooking and housekeeping.

President Rutherford B. Hayes characterized America at this time as being in a period "when old questions are settled and the new ones are not yet brought forward." Cookbook writing fell into this category. The recipes in this chapter were written in the old idiosyncratic style, using paragraphs and with little attempt at precise measurement or detailed instruction. The great change would occur in the new century, when larger than life personalities such as Fannie Farmer and Sarah Rorer emerged to take cookbook writing onto a whole new level. The era of the "level measurement" was about to explode in America's kitchens and on the pages of her cookbooks.

# CALIFORNIA CHILI PIE

Adapted from: Encarnación Pinedo, *El Cocinero Español*, 1898, p. 66

Writing in San Francisco in 1898, Encarnación Pinedo announced the first Hispanic statement on the food of California. Naturally, the subject extended to imports of every flavor, including this large meat pastry dish, or "cake," which eventually became known as a casserole. The original title of the book, used here, was supplanted with a recently translated reprint, by Dan Strehl, entitled *Encarnación's Kitchen*, which trims the thousand plus recipes of the original Spanish version and leaves behind much of the repressed hostility relating to the Yankee invasion of Pinedo's homeland.

*2 recipes shortcrust pastry (see p. 50)*

## THE PICADILLO

*4 garlic cloves*
*3 tablespoons peanut oil*
*2 cups beef, chopped*
*2 cups onions, chopped*
*1 cup tomatoes, chopped*
*4 green chilies Anaheim, chopped*
*½ teaspoon cumin, ground*
*½ teaspoon oregano, ground*
*salt and pepper to taste*

## THE CHICKEN SAUCE

*1 chicken, boiled*
*2 onions, sliced thinly*
*3 tomatoes, finely chopped*
*4 poblano peppers, skinned*
*⅓ cup seedless raisins*
*⅓ cup black olives, chopped*
*½ teaspoon cayenne pepper*
*¼ teaspoon oregano, ground*
*¼ teaspoon cumin, ground*

*To Make the Picadillo*: Fry the garlic in the oil until it begins to color. Add the beef bits to the skillet, then in turn the onions, tomatoes, and green chilies. Cook over moderate heat stirring frequently and, as the meat colors, add in the spices. Mix thoroughly and reserve.

*To Make the Chicken Sauce*: Cut up the boiled chicken and reserve. Fry the onions in oil and add the tomatoes, poblanos, olives, raisins, and spices. Add the chicken pieces and cook an additional 15 minutes.

Make the pasteles by lining a 9"x13" baking dish with a pastry dough, then a layer of picadillo, then a layer of the chicken sauce, then another layer of picadillo. Cover with a pastry lid, brush with beaten egg, and bake in a 325°F oven until the crust is brown, about 1 hour. *Serves 6.*

# ROLLED RIB ROAST

Adapted from: Rufus Estes, *Good Things to Eat*, 1911, p. 20

2 lbs. beef rib-eye steak, 1½" thick, trimmed
    of outside fat and bone
4 tablespoons butter
4 tablespoons olive oil
⅓ cup onions, minced
⅓ cup celery, minced
¼ cup carrots, minced
1 cup brandy
salt and freshly cracked black pepper
1 cup parsley, chopped, for garnish

Rufus Estes came into his full stature as man, chef, and maître d'hotel for the Pullman railroad service in 1883 at the age of 26. From that point forward his early life—born as a slave, toiling for his aged mother, and lack of education—were mere background incidents. Estes was the man of poise and experience who assured the comfort and pleasure of his special Pullman passengers from President Grover Cleveland to the pianist Paderewski, as they hurried across the American stage. Estes knew and demanded from his staff a well-finished meal for his patrons, and this jolly "rib" roast, which has no ribs at all, was prepared ahead of time and broiled to perfection on the train, to meet the highest restaurant standards of the day.

 Thoroughly tenderize the trimmed steak with a "bata carne" (or meat hammer) until the meat is ½" thick. Salt and pepper both sides of the meat, using the freshly cracked pepper. Trim the meat again to make a regular rectangle, then roll tightly and secure with kitchen string.

In an ample oven roasting pan, melt the butter on a top burner of the stove, add the olive oil, and brown the roast on all sides and at both ends. Remove the pan from the heat and introduce the mirepoix of onions, celery, and carrots and splash the brandy in the bottom of the pan. Baste the roast with the melted butter.

In a 350°F oven, introduce the roast and cook for 35 minutes or until the roast reaches an internal temperature of 145°F, basting regularly with the pan juices. Remove and allow the roast to stand 10 minutes before carving. Reduce the juices for sauce. *Serves 4.*

# Roast Woodcock with Spiced Peach Butter

Adapted from: Mrs. Lettice Bryan, *The Kentucky Housewife*, 1839, pp. 130 and 175

Peaches were an early commercial crop in America, with orchardists such as William Prince of Flushing, Long Island, offering saplings that produced uniformly juicy fleshed fruit. Thomas Jefferson was one of his most knowledgeable customers. But the growing market economy required a more resilient fruit, a peach that stored and shipped better, without bruising. It wasn't until after the Civil War when hybrids arrived from northern China that the "modern" peach was developed. Lettice Bryan devotes an entire chapter to the subject of fruit sauces, both fresh and pickled, to accompany game.

*4 woodcock, picked and cleaned*
*4 tablespoons butter*
*1 cup breadcrumbs*
*salt and pepper*
*1 carrot, chopped*
*1 celery stalk, chopped*
*1 onion, chopped*
*1 cup chicken stock*

## Peach Butter

*1 lb. ripe peaches*
*1 tablespoon butter*
*1 cup sugar (approximately)*
*nutmeg, salt and pepper*

Dry the birds inside and out and sprinkle with salt and pepper. Place a piece of butter in each and brush the outside of each bird with butter. Press breadcrumbs onto the skin. Place the woodcocks in a roasting pan with vegetables strewn around. Pour stock over the vegetables. Roast for 45 minutes at 375°F, basting every 10 minutes. Remove the birds from the oven, strain the stock in the pan and use to make brown gravy. Send the woodcock to the table with peach butter.

*To Make the Peach Butter:* Peel and stone the peaches and simmer them with the butter, the sugar, and enough water to cover until they collapse—about 15 minutes. Don't overcook. Stir often. Season with nutmeg, salt, and pepper. Serve at room temperature. *Serves 4.*

# JUMBERLIE ~ A CREOLE DISH

Adapted from: Mrs. Abby Fisher, *What Mrs. Fisher Knows About Old Southern Cooking,*
1881, p. 119

8 large and garden ripe tomatoes

1 cup rice

1 chicken, jointed and cut into bite-sized
    pieces

2 cups Smithfield ham, chunked into
    bite-sized pieces

1 tablespoon red pepper flakes

1 tablespoon oregano leaf, chopped

1 tablespoon chives, chopped

salt and pepper to taste

With a modesty and lack of pretense that is warmly reassuring, Mrs. Fisher brought her 35 years of Southern cooking experience to her new found home and friends in northern California. And they loved it, feting this former slave and her husband from Alabama with awards at State fairs in 1879 and 1880, and resulting in the publication of this book a year later. As everyone from Mobile knows, the "jumberlie" is the pet name for a celebratory dish that is eaten while you are still waiting for the "jubilee," or one of its many various spellings, which is the explosion of crabs, shrimp, and oysters in the bay. This "jumberlie" cautions patience, and offers its own feast of garden lush tomatoes, chicken, and sweet ham.

 In a large stockpot with boiling water, scald the tomatoes quickly, then skin and chop each one into small dice.

In the scalding stockpot, cook the rice at a mild simmer for 20 minutes, then strain and reserve the rice.

In a 9" casserole dish, combine rice, tomatoes, chicken pieces, ham, herbs and spices. Season to taste with salt and pepper. Cover tightly and bake at 350°F for 25 minutes. "Do not put any water on it," Mrs. Fisher insists. *Serves 4.*

# CARMENCITAS

Adapted from: Encarnación Pinedo, *El Cocinero Español*, 1885, p. 135

These individual patties, or "corn cakes" are a far cry from the enormous casserole that Encarnación Pinedo made for her little cousin Carmencita, but they walk the same walk, and they talk the same joy of corn and picadillo. What's even more modern is that they allow for individual servings, like crab cakes with sour cream on the side.

*4 eggs, separated*
*2½ cups pork chops, trimmed of bone, cubed*
*1 cup onions, chopped*
*4 chili serranos, seeds and stems removed, chopped (alt: Anaheim peppers)*
*4 garlic cloves, chopped*
*2 tablespoons roasted red peppers*
*2 tablespoons butter*
*4 tablespoons peanut oil*
*½ cup flour*
*½ cup peanut oil*
*1 cup yellow cornmeal*
*2 tablespoons fresh basil*
*2 teaspoons sugar*
*1 tablespoon salt*
*¼ cup raisins*
*3 teaspoons cumin, ground*
*salt and pepper*
*1 cup golden hominy, drained*

 In a food processor, process the egg whites for 3 seconds. Add the pork chops, onions, chili serranos, garlic, and roasted red peppers and grind to a uniform size.

In a large skillet, melt the butter and peanut oil, then over moderately high heat, brown the meat and pepper mixture until it is cooked, about 15 minutes. Remove the mixture to a large bowl and dust the meat with ½ cup of flour. Reserve. In the same skillet, add ½ cup of oil; when hot, add the cornmeal. Stir constantly over medium heat until warmed and softened, but not scorched. Reserve.

In the processor bowl, beat the egg yolks, add the basil, sugar, salt, raisins, cumin, salt and pepper, and whirl for 3 seconds. Add the hominy and process to reduce the grain size by half. Combine this mixture with the cornmeal and the meat mixtures; mix all thoroughly. Form 8 (or more) individual corn cakes, and bake at 375°F, turning once, until brown. Serve with sour cream. *Serves 4.*

# PORK LOIN EN MOLE

Adapted from: Encarnación Pinedo, *El Cocinero Español*, 1898, p. 104

2 cups pasilla peppers, deveined and torn into
    rough pieces (alt: poblano peppers)

1 cup cocoa, powdered and toasted

½ cup almonds, ground and toasted

2 tablespoons cinnamon, ground

3 tomatoes, skinned and sliced

peanut oil for frying (alt: lard)

2 cups veal broth

1 lb. pork loin, cut into ¾" medallions

1 cup pork sausages, sliced into 2" sections

2 cups Spanish peanuts, shelled and ground

2 tablespoons sesame seeds

This is a shout from the palace kitchen as one of the first variations of what later was to be universally known as "mole" sauce applied to a pork loin. The intense blending of sweet and pungent flavors that Pinedo and the ranchero cooks achieved in California before the gold rush was made more luxuriant by their liberal and unabashed use of pork lard. In deference to modern sensibilities, we have substituted peanut oil, but the battle goes to the brave who will actually cook these nuts, peppers, and spices until "the fat is absorbed" (and the smoke, presumably, ignored).

 In a shallow baking dish, mix the pasilla peppers, cocoa, and almonds, sprinkled with the cinnamon. Toast for 10 minutes in a 325°F oven. Remove before coloring, then grind the pasilla molina mixture together with the tomatoes in a food processor and reserve.

In a large skillet, heat 4 tablespoons of peanut oil, add the reserved pasilla molina mixture, and fry until the oil is absorbed. Add 2 cups of boiling veal broth and stir to deglaze the pan. Add the sausage and loin meats and simmer until they are cooked through. Remove from the heat and reserve.

In a separate skillet over moderate heat, warm 3 tablespoons of peanut oil, then roast the Spanish peanuts and sesame seeds until the oil is absorbed. Add the seeds and nuts to the sausage mixture, add a pinch of sugar, and over low heat reduce the broth to the desired thickness. Serve over rice. *Serves 4.*

# Rainbow Trout with Oregano and Capers

Adapted from: Encarnación Pinedo, *El Cocinero Español*, 1898, p. 79

These spectacular stuffed trout represent the pinnacle of the cuisine of ancient Alta, California. Lean, fresh, and sparkling from the rivers, this mountain trout provides a vehicle for the subtle stuffing, or "rellenista," which is a blending of olives, peppers, and the balancing earth tones of oregano and capers. Cook with a light hand, using whole hatchery fish and clarified butter, to understand what this old-fashioned food revolution can mean for you.

4 rainbow trout, pan dressed, heads on
salt and freshly cracked black pepper
8 tablespoons clarified butter
2 tablespoons olive oil
½ cup dry sherry

## La Rellenista

¼ cup almonds, ground
¼ cup black olives, pitted
¼ cup poblano peppers, stem, seeds and
    membranes removed, chopped roughly
½ onion, sliced
⅓ cup parsley, chopped fine
2 tablespoons each of fresh oregano and capers
2 tablespoons each of olive oil and vinegar

In a food processor, combine all of the ingredients for La Rellenista and pulse, scraping the sides regularly, to obtain a uniform mixture.

Salt and pepper each fish, inside and out. Divide the Rellenista mixture between the fish and stuff. Then arrange the fish side by side without touching in a shallow ovenproof dish.

Add the clarified butter, olive oil, and sherry. Bake, uncovered, in a preheated 350°F oven for 15 minutes, basting twice. *Serves 4.*

# POACHED SPECKLED TROUT A LA BRIN

Adapted from: François Mignon and Clementine Hunter, *Melrose Plantation Cookbook*, 1956, p. 11

4 lb. speckled trout from the ocean
salt water for purging
½ cup vinegar
1 teaspoon salt
1 onion, sliced
12 black peppercorns
½ teaspoon mace, ground
2 bay laurel leaves
flour for dusting
2 tablespoons butter
2 tablespoons flour
4 tablespoons lemon juice
1 sliced lemon for garnish
cheesecloth

Clementine Hunter was raised in the French antebellum traditions along the Mississippi River and its deep swamp tributaries. This was the Creole culture, speaking French, entertaining in great houses, and cooking with a passion for flavor and detail, always close to the game and fish of the coast and of the bayou. At the time of the dictation of this book, 80 years after her birth, Hunter was nearly blind. She spoke entirely from memory as she described the court bouillon for poaching her fish, and the cheesecloth sleeve she cooked it in, just as we do today if no fish poacher is handy.

The fish should be dressed, scaled, and gilled; place in a pan with sufficient salt water to cover for 30 minutes. In a large fish-poaching pan, prepare the court bouillon, using enough fresh water to cover the fish, the vinegar, salt, onion, peppercorns, mace, and bay leaves. Remove the fish from the brine, rinse and pat dry, and dust with flour. Then wrap the fish in the cheesecloth, securing the bundle with a knot at each end.

Place the fish in the cold court bouillon and bring the heat up slowly to a rousing boil, then simmer for 4 minutes. Remove the fish, discard the cheesecloth, and arrange the fish on a platter.

In a saucepan, make a roux of the butter and flour, add 1 cup of the poaching liquid, and add the lemon juice while whisking. Serve this sauce with the fish, garnished with lemon slices. *Serves 4.*

# FILLET OF KEDGEREE

Adapted from: Rufus Estes, *Good Things To Eat*, 1911, p. 10

When the explorer Henry M. Stanley, Honorary Member of the Royal Geographical Society, Grand Cordon of the Order of the Congo, and Star of Zanzibar, rode the rails to old Chicago in the last decade of the 19th century, he was assigned to the special care of Rufus Estes, Master Porter. Estes was warned of the explorer's heroic achievements, "Dr. Livingston, I presume?" and all that, and he just managed to re-provision the Pullman Galley with a sharp jar of Zanzibar Curry. This is the way a simple fillet of lean white fish, gently washed in bright curry sauce and garnished with croutons of fried bread, put the old explorer at ease.

2 white fish fillets, sea bass or similar, 8 oz. each
1 cup onions, sliced thinly
2 tablespoons butter
3 cups fish stock (alt: chicken stock)
3 tablespoons curry powder (Star of Zanzibar, or better)
1 teaspoon sugar
1 tablespoon lemon juice
½ teaspoon cayenne pepper
1 tablespoon flour and 2 tablespoons butter

In a large saucepan, soften the onions in the butter until lightly browned. Add the stock, curry powder, sugar, lemon juice, and cayenne to the onions and boil for 15 to 20 minutes.

Place the fillets in a sauté pan, and gently pour over the curried stock. Simmer for 10 minutes, until the fish just flakes. Remove the fillets to a serving plate. Reduce the stock to 1 cup. Whisk in the prepared beurre manie (the combined flour and butter) to thicken. Pour the curry sauce over the fish and serve with fried bread croutons and rice in a separate bowl. *Serves 2.*

# PEANUT SOUP

Adapted from: Rufus Estes, *Good Things To Eat*, 1911, p. 4

3 cups raw peanuts, shelled
5 quarts water
1 bay leaf
1 celery stalk with leaves, chopped
1 small onion, sliced
½ teaspoon mace, ground
1 cup heavy cream
salt and pepper

As much a part of Southern ritual dinners 100 years ago as it is part of Kwanzaa ceremonies today, peanut soup is a familiar favorite, still celebrated in South Africa and other communities linking to their indigenous past. Rufus Estes reveals his Southern roots in this recipe, despite his Chicago address, by calling for the flavoring of mace and a staggering preparation time of four to five hours spent watching the pot boil.

Soak the peanuts overnight in 2 quarts of water, stirring once or twice. Discard the water; rinse, drain and reserve the peanuts.

In a large Dutch oven, combine the peanuts, three quarts of water, the bay leaf, celery, onion, and mace and boil slowly for 4 to 5 hours. Drain and reserve the water and the peanuts, separately.

In a food processor, pulse the peanuts to a fine paste. In a large saucepan, combine the peanut paste and 4 cups of the strained peanut water, stirring to combine, and warm over medium heat. Add so much of the reserved peanut water as necessary to reach the desired consistency. Adjust the seasonings with salt and pepper. Add the cream and serve hot with croutons. *Serves 4.*

# BISQUE OF CRAYFISH

Adapted from: Lafcadio Hearn, *La Cuisine Creole*, 1885, p. 22

Lafcadio Hearn was an outgoing personality who drifted into New Orleans from Greece, embraced the food culture, and then drifted on to Japan where he created another line of myths. He knew very well, however, that with crayfish bisque, presentation is nine points of the dish. Purists insist on pulverizing the freshly cooked meat, mixing it with butter and herbs, and then stuffing the hollowed out crayfish carapace with this ambrosia. The stuffed heads are then lightly fried in butter and floated on the separately prepared bisque. This dish was once the basis of the New Orleans restaurant legend.

*50 crayfish, live (alt: 50 fresh frozen, whole)*

## THE STUFFING

*16 empty crayfish carapace with feelers*
*1 cup crayfish tail meat, cooked and shelled*
*½ cup stale breadcrumbs*
*½ cup milk*
*1 stick butter, cut into bits*
*1 teaspoon dried thyme*
*2 sprigs fresh sage*
*2 garlic cloves, minced*
*1 onion, chopped fine*

## THE BISQUE

| | |
|---|---|
| *3 tablespoons butter* | *4 cups oxtail broth* |
| *3 bacon rashers* | *1 teaspoon thyme, dried* |
| *2 onions, sliced thin* | *salt and pepper to taste* |
| *4 tablespoons flour* | *16 crayfish heads, stuffed* |

If using live crayfish, be sure to purge them in salt water (40:1) for half an hour, then drop into boiling water; allow the boil to return, continue for 5 minutes, then allow to rest in the "boil" for 10 minutes. Whether fresh or frozen, peel and separate the meat from all shells. Select the best 16 carapace shells, clean them with the tip of a knife, then boil briefly in a small saucepan to clean. Reserve.

*To Make the Stuffing*: Use 1 cup of the crayfish tails; combine in a food processor with all the other ingredients. Stuff each head or carapace with a dollop of this mixture, then fry them in butter until brown, and reserve.

*To Make the Bisque*: In a large stewpan, fry out the bacon in the butter. Add the onions and continue over low heat until translucent. Add the flour and make a roux, then add the oxtail stock and form a heavy broth. Mince and add all remaining crayfish tails. Adjust the seasonings with salt, pepper, and thyme. Float four heads in each serving. *Serves 4.*

# "Deep Creek" Potatoes

Adapted from: François Mignon and Clementine Hunter, *Melrose Plantation Cookbook*, 1956, p. 16

2 large baking potatoes
olive oil as needed
½ cup heavy cream
2 tablespoons butter
2 teaspoons parsley, minced
4 tablespoons scallions, finely minced
(alt: onions)
1 teaspoon cayenne pepper (optional)
2 egg whites
salt and freshly ground black pepper

One of the charms of *Melrose Plantation Cookbook* is the easy way Clementine Hunter dictates her plantation learned recipes in a way that relates them to the winding river based lifestyle of Natchitoches, Louisiana. The first French settlers entered the area in 1714 and discovered the deep creek meandering beside the tiny moss-draped church of "St. Mary's on the Bayou." By Clementine Hunter's time, not too much had changed.

Split each potato in half on the long axis, then score the exposed meat side with diagonal strikes of the knife. Oil the potatoes on all sides and bake, meat side down, on a lightly oiled baking sheet at 450°F for 50 minutes, or until the shells are crisp.

Remove the potatoes, allow to cool, then spoon out the meat without breaking the shell. Reserve meat and shells separately.

In a large bowl, mash the potato meat with the cream and butter, add then parsley, scallions, and cayenne, as desired, and work until smooth. In a separate bowl, with 1 tablespoon of ice water, whip the egg whites to stiff peaks. Work the beaten egg white mixture into the mashed potatoes carefully, season well with salt and pepper, then fill the empty potato shells with the mixture, brimming above the sides like the banks rising above the creek.

Bake the potatoes in a roasting pan in a preheated 325°F oven for 30 minutes or until the top part of the mixture is golden brown. *Serves 4.*

# MELROSE TOMATO ROBELINE

Adapted from: François Mignon and Clementine Hunter, *Melrose Plantation Cookbook,* 1956, p. 14

Defining "Creole cooking" has always involved a bit of history and a bit of whimsy. We know that the 18th century French plantations along the banks of the Mississippi River always imagined themselves to be situated on the Joyous Coast, part of the north Louisiana tradition of French colonialism, eventually part of the American South. But Melrose Plantation and its legendary reputation for hospitality and food never wavered, even up to the time that Clementine Hunter, the semi-literate granddaughter of slaves, sat down and dictated all she had learned about Creole food in 1956. That was 160 years after the semi-literate Amelia Simmons penned the first American cookbook.

4 large juicy tomatoes

2 teaspoons unsalted butter

2 teaspoons flour

2 teaspoons Worcestershire sauce

1 clove garlic, minced

salt and pepper

1 cup cold rare roasted beef, without gristle or fat

½ cup beef stock

4 eggs

4 slices homemade-type white bread

 Cut off the tops of the tomatoes and remove the pulp with a small spoon. Reserve the shells and tops. Rub the butter and flour together to make a paste, and mix this with the tomato pulp, Worcestershire, garlic, salt and pepper to make a sauce. Reserve.

Mince the beef and moisten with the beef stock; season with salt and pepper. Fill the tomato shells half full with the meat, set in a covered pan, and bake in a 350°F oven for 15 minutes. When the tomatoes are cooked, remove from the oven and drop into each one a raw egg. Replace the tops and cook the filled tomatoes for 5 minutes until the eggs are firm. Pour the tomato sauce over the tomatoes. Set the filled tomatoes on the slices of toasted and buttered bread, and send to table. *Serves 4.*

# CALINDA CABBAGE

Adapted from: François Mignon and Clementine Hunter, *Melrose Plantation Cookbook,*
1956, p. 9

1 large savoy cabbage, stripped of broken or
damaged leaves

## FORCEMEAT

1 cup rice, boiled
1 cup chopped chicken, no skin or fat
1 cup ham, cooked and minced
¼ cup chives, minced
½ teaspoon cayenne (optional)

## WHITE SAUCE

1 tablespoon butter
1 teaspoon flour
1 cup milk
salt and pepper

Even without any textual explanation, foodies will recognize this recipe as French provincial. "Chou farci," or stuffed cabbage, in one form or another was a staple in every French village, and distinct from home to home. The recipe, remembered fondly by a black-authored cookbook describing antebellum food in rural Louisiana, does as much to define Creole cooking as any list of special sauces or ingredients. Wrap the cabbage in cheesecloth or muslin if you prefer, and reduce the cooking liquid to make a sauce.

 Soak the whole cabbage in cold water for 30 minutes. Boil the whole cabbage in water with a tablespoon of salt for 10 minutes. Remove from the boiling water and let it drain until cold.

Make a forcemeat by chopping, dicing, and then grinding into a paste the rice, chicken, ham, chives, and cayenne.

When the cabbage is cold, stand it on stem-end. Then, beginning at the center, gently open the leaves without breaking the ribs. Fill the spaces between the layers of leaves with the forcemeat and then close together.

Tie the cabbage firmly with a cheesecloth, then circle with kitchen twine once or twice and knot securely. Lay the trussed cabbage in a pot of boiling salted water and cook until tender at the stem-end, about 45 minutes.

Prepare a white sauce by melting the butter in a small frying pan and when it is hot—not brown—add the flour and stir until smooth. Slowly stir in the milk, let it boil up once, then remove from the heat. Adjust the seasonings with salt and pepper. Carve the stuffed cabbage in quarters, and then pour the sauce over. *Serves 4.*

# EGGPLANT BOURRE

Adapted from: François Mignon and Clementine Hunter, *Melrose Plantation Cookbook*, 1956, p.15

In a curious blending of cultures, Clementine Hunter chose the Anglo word *eggplant* to describe her favorite vegetable, and the French or Creole word *bourre* to describe how it was stuffed. Every culture from ancient Persia across the Mediterranean and into West Africa will recognize this dish as one of their own, at least in part. This adaptation includes Tabasco to prove it is from Louisiana.

*2 eggplants*
*2 tablespoons onion juice (alt: lemon juice)*
*salt and pepper*
*4 tablespoons stale breadcrumbs*
*2 tablespoons capers, finely chopped*
*6 anchovy fillets, drained and chopped (optional)*
*4 tablespoons cold boiled tongue, chopped (alt: smoked bacon, cooked dry)*
*3 cups chicken stock*

## PIQUANTE SAUCE

*3 tablespoons butter*
*1 tablespoon Tabasco*
*1 teaspoon vinegar*
*1 teaspoon Kitchen Bouquet*
*1 tablespoon tomato catsup*
*1 teaspoon prepared mustard*
*salt and pepper to taste*

Cut each eggplant in half on the long axis. Cut out the meat carefully, leaving the walls strong. Chop the eggplant meat and place it in a saucepan, with water to cover. Add the onion juice, salt and pepper, and simmer for 15 minutes. Remove from the fire and drain.

In a mixing bowl, combine the cooked eggplant meat, breadcrumbs, capers, anchovies, and tongue (or bacon bits), and mix well, using the back of a fork. Adjust the seasonings with salt and pepper. Pack this forcemeat neatly into each half eggplant. Place the 2 parts of each eggplant back together, pin with skewers, and secure with kitchen twine. Place both reconstructed eggplants in a covered roaster, pour 2 to 3 cups of stock to cover the bottom of the roaster to a depth of 1", and bake in a 350°F oven, turning the eggplant as needed, for 30 minutes, or until both sides of each eggplant are well done. Remove the skewers and strings and put the eggplant halves on warmed serving plates.

*To Make the Piquante Sauce*: Melt 3 tablespoons of butter in a saucepan with the vinegar, Tabasco, Kitchen Bouquet, catsup, and mustard. Adjust the seasonings with salt and pepper, simmer for 10 minutes, and pour over the eggplant halves. *Serves 4.*

# Fried Tomatoes in Deepest Winter

Adapted from: Mrs. Lettice Bryan, *The Kentucky Housewife*, 1839, p. 217

Fried Tomatoes in Deepest Winter:
Select them large and ripe, take off the peelings, cut them in thick slices, and season them with salt and pepper.

Have ready a plate of finely grated bread, dip each side of the sliced tomatoes in it, taking care to make as much of the bread adhere to them as possible, and fry them brown in butter, which should be hot when they are put in.

Serve them warm; mince very fine an onion or two, fry them in the gravy, and transfuse the whole over the tomatoes.

Lettice Bryan

To Preserve the best tomatoes until February:
Select those that are large and ripe, but firm, and perfectly free from blemish.
Wipe them clean with a cloth, taking care not to bruise them in the least;
Put them in a jar of the best vinegar, with a large handful of salt.
Add no spices, as the design is to retain the pure flavor of the tomatoes.
They will be fine for soups and gravies, and may be dressed in any way that fresh ones can except for preserves or jellies.
The jar should be closed securely.

# SCOTCH OAT CAKES

Adapted from: Rufus Estes, *Good Things To Eat*, 1911, p. 81

The humble "Oat Cake" is a thing of beauty to a true Scot. Made from the freshest ground oatmeal, the cake is always fried on a griddle, or over a hot fire. Rufus Estes, eager to avoid any criticism from his clientele with experience shooting grouse in the Scotch Highlands, followed the oldest traditions to serve these hot breads for breakfast as the Pullman sped its passengers across the American countryside. He might have ground his oats in one of the new hand operated mills, or bought them by the barrel. The trick is to double cook the cakes, which must be toasted after cooking and drenched in butter and honey, or, as in Scotland, served with herring.

*2 cups oatmeal (not instant)*
*¼ teaspoon baking powder*
*½ teaspoon sea salt*
*1 tablespoon unsalted butter, melted*
*8 teaspoons boiling water*

Pulverize the oats in an electric blender for about 10 seconds. Reserve ¼ cup for rolling. Mix the oats with the baking powder and salt. Stir in the butter and enough of the hot water to make a firm paste. Gather the mixture into a ball and roll it out on a counter dusted with more pulverized oats. Roll to a thickness of ⅛". Cut out 8 wedges. Bake the cakes on a hot greased griddle for about 10 minutes over a low heat, being careful not to burn. Do not turn. Leave them to cool and crisp. When you are ready to serve, toast lightly for 5 minutes and serve piping hot. *Makes 8 cakes.*

# BOLLILOS

Adapted from: Encarnación Pinedo, *El Cocinero Español*, 1898, p. 61

## LEVADURA

3 large potatoes
½ cup flour
¼ cup sugar
1 teaspoon salt
1 cup water

## DOUGH FOR BOLLILOS

1 cup starter
4 cups all-purpose flour
1 teaspoon salt
1 tablespoon sugar
1 cup warm milk
4 tablespoons unsalted butter,
     at room temperature

In 1864, Maximilian and Carlota were installed as Emperor and Empress of Mexico by Napoleon and thereafter bakeries adopted French techniques to produce such delicacies as meringues, puff pastry, and French bread, which the Mexicans called "bollilos." Encarnación uses a potato starter, more pioneer American than French, to bake up this elegant hard roll standard of Mexican cuisine.

*To Make the Starter:* Peel the potatoes, wash, dry, and grate them into a bowl. Add the flour, sugar, salt, and water and beat to combine. Cover the starter and allow it to work at room temperature for 12 hours, stirring it down every 3 hours. At the end of the 12 hours, it should be puffy and bubbly, indicating that it is active.

*To Make the Bollilos:* Take 1 cup of the starter (the rest can be renewed with the addition of ½ cup flour and ½ cup warm water). Mix the starter with the flour, salt, sugar, milk, and 2 tablespoons butter, forming a smooth dough. Knead the dough on a floured counter, adding more flour as needed to make a satiny dough that springs back from the hands. Place the dough in an oiled bowl and cover. Let rise until doubled. This may take 2 to 3 hours.

Punch down and let stand for 5 minutes. Divide the dough into 24 pieces, using a sharp knife. Roll the pieces until they are 1" thick and oval in shape. Spread the rest of the butter over the dough pieces, fold them in half, and pinch to seal. Put each bollilos on a baking sheet to rise. After 1 hour, the bollilos will be ready to bake. Bake in a 400°F oven for 20 minutes, brushing with egg yolk before baking.

*Makes 24 bollilos.*

# PAIN PERDU

Adapted from: Lafcadio Hearn, *La Cuisine Creole*, 1885, p. 204

Whether it is said in French "pain perdu" or Old English "pandery," the lost bread referred to the hard crusts cut away from the loaf of manchet, and discarded to pamper refined tastes. Old English cookbooks, like Gervase Markham's, recognized there was still good food value in the cut-away crusts and referred to a dish made from the leavings as "Poor Knights of Windsor." The "French toast" many children had on Sundays was the same: crusts, dipped in egg, fried in butter and dusted with sugar. As a dessert dish, "pain Perdu" made its way into the lexicon of Creole classics in America, and was often served with syrup, bananas, and cinnamon sugar. Topped with whipped cream, it is a delicacy.

*1 loaf of stale French bread, sliced into 2" thick slices (see p. 44)*
*2 eggs, beaten with 1 cup milk*
*melted butter*
*½ cup cinnamon sugar*
*sliced bananas and strawberries*
*whipped cream*

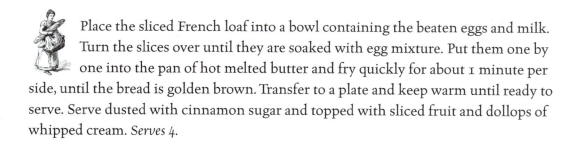

Place the sliced French loaf into a bowl containing the beaten eggs and milk. Turn the slices over until they are soaked with egg mixture. Put them one by one into the pan of hot melted butter and fry quickly for about 1 minute per side, until the bread is golden brown. Transfer to a plate and keep warm until ready to serve. Serve dusted with cinnamon sugar and topped with sliced fruit and dollops of whipped cream. *Serves 4.*

# FRIED CALIFORNIA CAROLAS

Adapted from: Mrs. Abby Fisher, *What Mrs. Fisher Knows About Old Southern Cooking*, 1881, Recipe no. 67

5 eggs
2 cups sugar
4 cups flour
1/3 cup milk
1 teaspoon baking soda
1 teaspoon salt
1/3 cup orange juice
2 tablespoons grated orange zest
1 teaspoon butter
fat for frying
cinnamon sugar

Dutch Americans first introduced the cruller to New York. The twisted doughnut was named for its shape, as *cruller* means, "to curl." But the cruller became known by a slew of different names as it was prepared and eaten all over the country. They were served at wedding feasts throughout the 18th and 19th centuries as wedding knots or love knots, in which variation the dough was twisted and tied. Mrs. Fisher's Californian interpretation adds orange to the batter.

Beat the eggs with the sugar until the batter is frothy and light. Over the egg mixture, sift in the flour. Dissolve the soda in the milk, and beat this mixture into the eggs and flour until smooth. Add the salt, orange juice, zest, and softened butter to make a dough.

The dough should be soft but not so sticky that you cannot roll it out. Cut strips of uniform length, about 5" long and 1" wide, twist each roll into a corkscrew and drop at once into deep hot fat (a deep fat fryer works best). As each carola—or cruller—browns, remove it from the oil, drain, and dredge in powdered cinnamon sugar. Serve right away. *Makes 3 dozen carolas.*

# Adam's Fig Cake

Adapted from: François Mignon and Clementine Hunter, *Melrose Plantation Cookbook*, 1956, p. 28

In 1956, Clementine Hunter reminisced about her years in the kitchen in the late 19th century and recalled the dishes she and her mother had cooked half a century earlier. "Fig Cake," with silver and gold layers, was one of their favorites, and not the least of its magical qualities was that it called for the newfangled baking powder. Egg whites were beaten into the white or silver layer, and egg yolks into the golden, and fresh figs, snatched from under the mockingbird's eye in a southern garden, completed the array. This is the way they did it at Tara.

## Silver Part

2 cups sugar

⅔ cup butter

⅔ cup milk

3 cups flour

3 teaspoons baking powder

8 egg whites

## Gold Part

1 cup sugar

¾ cup butter

1 cup milk

1 cup flour

1 teaspoon baking powder

1 teaspoon allspice

2 teaspoons cinnamon, ground

7 egg yolks, beaten

2 cups of figs, cut in halves

 To make 2 silver cakes, cream the sugar and butter until fluffy, add the milk, and then the sifted flour and baking powder. Finally, stir in the stiffly beaten egg whites. Place half the batter in each of 2 buttered 13"x9" baking pans, and bake in a 325°F preheated oven until done.

To make 1 gold cake, cream the sugar and butter until fluffy, add the milk, and then the sifted flour, baking powder, and spices, alternately with the egg yolks. Place half the batter in a 13"x9" baking pan. Sprinkle the figs with flour and spread them on the batter, then pour the remainder of the batter over the figs. Bake in a 325°F preheated oven until done.

After the cakes are done, remove from the pans and cool. Place the gold between the silver layers, and cover with frosting. *Makes 1 cake.*

# Lemon Meringue Pie

Adapted from: Lafcadio Hearn, *La Cuisine Creole*, 1885, p. 191

1 pie crust, prebaked (see p. 50)

## Lemon Filling

1 cup sugar

¼ cup cornstarch

½ teaspoon salt

1½ cups water

6 egg yolks

½ cup lemon juice and 1 tablespoon zest

2 tablespoons unsalted butter

## Meringue

⅓ cup water

4 egg whites

½ cup sugar

¼ tsp cream of tartar

1 tablespoon cornstarch

Queen Marie Antoinette had a number of unfortunate indulgences and one was the meringue, which was developed by a Swiss pastry chef named Gasparani who baked the sweets for the ill-fated Queen. In 19th century cookbooks, the meringue was called a sugar puff but when it topped a lemon pie, it generally was not given any name at all. Oftentimes, a frustration for meringue cooks is the tendency of the meringue to weep and form an unattractive puddle of moisture that turns even a fine crust soggy within hours. Our solution is to beat in a little cornstarch to stabilize the delicate foam of the egg whites—and we've brought Lafcadio Hearn's recipe into the modern era by also insisting that the filling be poured into the pastry case when piping hot.

 *To Make the Filling:* Mix the sugar, cornstarch, salt, and water and bring to a boil. When it turns translucent, add the egg yolks, beating well. Then add the lemon juice and zest, and finally the butter.

*To Make the Meringue:* Mix the cornstarch with the water and bring to a simmer, stirring. Beat the egg whites until foamy. Fold in the sugar and cream of tartar. Add the cornstarch and continue whisking.

*To Assemble:* Pour the hot filling into the pie crust and cook in a 325°F oven alone for 5 to 10 minutes to give it a head start, and to reduce the risk of overbrowning the meringue. Then remove the pie from the oven, mound the meringue over the top, and continue baking for 10 minutes, or until the meringue is pale golden brown. Serve same day. *Makes 1 pie.*

# BANANAS FOSTERCHILD

Adapted from: Rufus Estes, *Good Things to Eat*, 1911, pp. 46–47

You were trendy if you cooked bananas in the late 19th century. The fruit was still considered something of a luxury when it began turning up in cookbooks in the 1880s. At first, cooks weren't sure how to use the fruit and most recipes were simple substitutes, but at the turn of the century, cooking schools began to experiment and included bananas in ice cream, cakes, and, as seen here, fried in this dessert. Glassware and chinaware manufacturers had a field day. With its unique shape, the banana merited a special serving dish. The famous Bananas Foster, flambéed in rum and served over ice cream, did not appear in New Orleans at Brennans until the 1930s, but Rufus Estes had already taken the fantastic fruit idea and dressed it up when he ran the dining car kitchen for the Pittsburg and Gould Railroad tycoon, Arthur Stillwell.

*4 large firm bananas*
*½ cup powdered sugar*
*½ cup lemon juice*
*1 egg, beaten*
*1 cup fine cracker or cookie crumbs*
*peanut oil for frying*

## SAUCE

*4 tablespoons unsalted butter, melted*
*2 tablespoons Cointreau liquor*
*2 tablespoons brown sugar*

Peel the bananas and scrape off the long strings. Sprinkle with powdered sugar and moisten with lemon juice. Let stand 20 minutes. Dip each banana in egg and roll in crumbs. Fry each banana in deep oil. Remove and drain and serve each banana topped with the sauce.

Make the sauce by mixing together the butter, sugar, and Cointreau. Pour over the bananas for serving. Cold vanilla ice cream may also accompany the bananas. *Serves 4.*

# PEACH MARMALADE

Adapted from: Mrs. Abby Fisher, *What Mrs. Fisher Knows About Old Southern Cooking*, 1881, Recipe no. 99

3 pounds peaches
2 cups sugar
¼ cup lemon juice
½ cup lemon peel

Early marmalade eaters ate either "quince jam" or "marmalada." Orange marmalade only became a *sine qua non* in England in the middle of the 19th century when Mrs. Beeton gave multiple recipes in her famous book of Household Management. On arriving in California following the Civil War, Mrs. Fisher made preserves her trademark, and she won numerous medals for them. The peaches used in this marmalade are slow baked with no water added, so the fruit develops an intense flavor that is delicious eaten with toast or on hot breads.

Peel and stone the peaches, halve them, and put them in a casserole dish. Sprinkle with the sugar and lemon juice and leave them overnight. The next morning, add the peel and stir to combine. Put the fruit in a deep pan and cook slowly over low heat for 2 hours, stirring from time to time to prevent scorching. Use a spoon to ladle the marmalade into hot sterilized jars. Seal and store in a dark place for a week before using. *Makes 3 cups.*

## Chapter Eight
# Voices of Authority

Pierre Blot, *What to Eat and How to Cook It*, 1863
Mary Lincoln, *Mrs. Lincoln's Boston Cook Book*, 1884
Fannie Merritt Farmer, *The Boston Cooking-School Cook Book*, 1896
Sarah Tyson Rorer, *Mrs. Rorer's New Cook Book*, 1902
Sara Bosse and Onoto Watanna, *Chinese-Japanese Cook Book*, 1914
Maria Parloa, *Miss Parloa's New Cook Book*, 1880

The 20th century ushered in a new era for the professional cookbook writer. Personalities such as Fannie Farmer, Sarah Rorer, Mary Lincoln, and Maria Parloa became household names on the basis of their expertise. They launched the domestic science movement and, through effective advertising, sold vast numbers of books. Fannie Farmer's *The Boston Cooking-School Cook Book*, for example, sold over four million copies in its publishing lifetime.

The advertising industry took advantage of new demands and interests among their female readers. Daily newspapers and weekly and monthly magazines flourished with a readership that mounted into the millions. Free rural route delivery from 1893, meant that readers in the country were not left behind their urban neighbors. Income from advertisements rose. There was plenty to sell and plenty to buy. The American public became consumers rather than producers. This would have a direct influence on the cookbooks written in the early 20th century, many of which featured brand-name products in their recipes.

Mr. Kellogg and Mr. Post marketed packaged breakfast cereals such as cornflakes and grape nuts and convinced a public used to eating mush and hot breads that there was a new and better (read more convenient) way to breakfast. When Mr. Heinz bottled his ketchup in 1892, he initiated a decline in the centuries old tradition of home preserving. When the Fleischmann brothers began to sell cakes of yeast in the 1880s, they ushered in a small revolution in baking practices that had not changed since those described by Gervase Markham in 1615. Prior to the widespread availability of store-bought yeast, the cultivation of a yeast starter from wild ingredients was the most fundamental and important housekeeping skill that a young woman learned.

The American kitchen had emerged from the dark ages. The open hearth had finally given way to the iron stove in all but the most rural areas. The iron monster was still a creature to be tamed, and cookbooks included instructions on how to master the temperamental flues and dampers. Tedious kitchen tasks could be short circuited with the use of labor-saving tools, such as rotary egg beaters and hand-operated food mills.

Finally, and not the least important, a reliable and speedy transportation system made it possible for customers in Miami and Seattle to eat the same foods. Miami took to the rails in 1896 and was soon exporting tomatoes and pineapples to the folks in winter bound Seattle, who had their own railway depots in 1893. For the first time, cookbooks could become truly national in scope.

Meanwhile, the humble measuring cup turned recipe writing on its head. No longer need the housewife ponder the nuances of instructions like "butter the size of an egg," or "as much flour as needed." When the famous cooking schools in Boston, Philadelphia, and New York decreed that the cup was the standard measuring unit, recipe writers adopted the measurement right away. It was Fannie Farmer who took accuracy a step further and invented the level spoonful. She quickly became known as the Queen of Level Measurements.

This insistence on accuracy was all part of the trend away from calling cooking an art. The domestic science movement left nothing to chance. Any novice could read directions from one of Fannie Farmer's cookbooks and turn out something passably good.

Fannie Farmer took on the Boston Cooking School in 1894, from her teacher Mary Lincoln, who had left to pursue a lucrative career on the lecture circuit. Fannie's first book borrowed heavily from Mrs. Lincoln's well respected *Mrs. Lincoln's Boston Cook Book*. In itself this was not an outrage, because recipes were still regarded as more common property than anything else. Fannie's personality was irrepressible however, and her next effort (and the one that was to launch her career), *The Boston Cooking-School Cook Book* was full of her own ideas. She guessed rightly that readers would clamor for the chance to prepare the salad eaten at the famous hotel, the Waldorf, or the ice cream fantasy "Nesselrode" that was enjoyed by Queen Victoria. Miss Farmer also laid down the law about food presentation, which was increasingly elaborate and genteel.

Sarah Rorer came to the domestic science movement because she was frustrated with what she saw as her limited role as a housewife. She dressed to the nines to take to the lecture podium circuit where she talked about diet and good health, and where she gave demonstrations. Mrs. Rorer was one of the earliest exponents of the celebrity endorsement, one of the most interesting being "Cottolene," a vegetable shortening that was promoted as the healthy alternative to lard in the diet.

Mrs. Lincoln, meanwhile, was not eclipsed by the meteoric rise to fame of her former student, Fannie Farmer. Keeping her name in the forefront, she became the spokesperson for Jell-O and started her own baking powder company. Maria Parloa, the last of the great celebrity lecturers and cookbook authors in this chapter, was equally at home endorsing Walter Baker's Chocolate and writing a pamphlet full of recipes for indulgent chocolate confections, whilst at the same time honestly singing the praises of the healthful properties of the candy.

The self-styled Professor Pierre Blot, who ran the first French cooking school in America, published *What to Eat and How to Cook It* in 1863. The recipes he wrote were a mixture of French technique and American method, and were a hit amongst the growing numbers of middle class American women who were eager to expand their repertoire with a little Gallic flair.

A cook's training had historically been at the apron strings of her mother, assisted perhaps by a handwritten notebook of familiar receipts, but, a century after Amelia Simmons wrote *American Cookery*, all that had changed. The art of cookery was now accessible to all who turned to the printed page.

# Chicken a la King

Adapted from: Fannie Farmer, *The Boston Cooking-School Cook Book*, 1896, p. 221

Spectacular events were a commonplace on Coney Island in the last quarter of the 19th century. Gigantic luxury hotels, racecourses, and railroads all catered to the vacation whims of the millionaire elite that came down for the summer. Not the least spectacular was the forced relocation of the mighty Brighton Beach Hotel in 1888, due to an eroding beachfront. All those palaces and fortunes, the August Belmonts, the Diamond Jim Brady's, even the Brighton Beach Hotel itself, are now gone. But what remains, and will probably survive the millennium, is the spectacular and durable dish called "Chicken a la King," created by Chef Greenwald at the Brighton Beach Hotel for Mr. E. Clark King, a fellow hotelier who trumpeted the Coney Island glamour. This is the authentic version.

1 cooked roast chicken
4 tablespoons butter, divided
2 tablespoons flour
1 cup cream
1 cup chicken stock
1 cup mushrooms, sliced
1 green pepper, sliced
¼ cup sherry
1 tablespoon pimientos
salt, pepper, and paprika
2 egg yolks

 Remove the chicken from the bones and chop into bite-sized pieces. Make a cream sauce with 2 tablespoons butter, the flour, the stock, and cream and whisk until smooth. Cook the mushrooms and green pepper in 2 tablespoons butter for 5 minutes, then add to the sauce and stir in the sherry. Add chicken and pimiento to the sauce and season well with salt, pepper, and paprika. Just before serving, add the yolks off the heat and cook for 1 minute. Serve mounded in patty shells, surrounded by vegetables of your fancy, like asparagus tips. *Serves 4.*

# THE CROWN ROAST OF LAMB

Adapted from: Fannie Farmer, *The Boston Cooking-School Cook Book*, 1896, p. 196

2 lamb loins, frenched by the butcher or
    prepared as below

1 piece salt pork, sliced into 16 slices

2 tablespoons thyme, chopped and mixed with
    2 tablespoons olive oil

salt and pepper

1 medium onion

2 tablespoons butter (approximately)

16 oz. can of chestnuts

1 cup good chicken stock

1 tablespoon rosemary, chopped

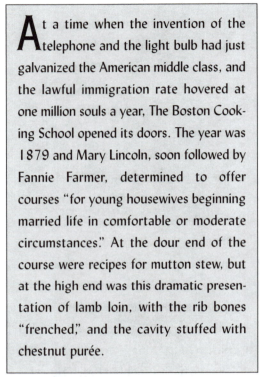

At a time when the invention of the telephone and the light bulb had just galvanized the American middle class, and the lawful immigration rate hovered at one million souls a year, The Boston Cooking School opened its doors. The year was 1879 and Mary Lincoln, soon followed by Fannie Farmer, determined to offer courses "for young housewives beginning married life in comfortable or moderate circumstances." At the dour end of the course were recipes for mutton stew, but at the high end was this dramatic presentation of lamb loin, with the rib bones "frenched," and the cavity stuffed with chestnut purée.

Strip the flesh from the bone between the ribs, as far as the lean meat, if the butcher has not done so. Shape each loin into a semicircle, having the ribs facing outside, so that the roast resembles, in shape, a crown. Skewer the pieces together. Trim the bones evenly so they are of the same height and wrap the tip of each bone in a strip of salt pork. Cap it with a piece of foil. Sprinkle the lamb with the fresh herbs and oil mixture, and a generous seasoning of salt and pepper. Roast the lamb in a 425°F oven for 1 hour, or rare. A thermometer inserted will read 135°F. Remove the crown from the oven. Remove the foil and pork from the tips. Use the pan drippings to make a gravy. Fill the center of the crown with the Chestnut Purée and serve, carving 2 ribs per person.

*To Make the Chestnut Purée*: Sauté the onion in a little butter until soft, add the chestnuts, and cook for 10 minutes, seasoning well. Add the chicken stock and beat until a smooth purée is formed. Finally, fold in the chopped rosemary. The purée can be formed in the food processor if you wish. Serve the purée mounded in the middle of the crown. *Serves 4 to 6.*

# CHOP SUEY

Adapted from: Sara Bosse and Onoto Watanna, *Chinese-Japanese Cook Book*, 1914, p. 52

"Bits and pieces," as some have translated the Chinese phrase, was a clever piece of public relations. In 1896 the Chinese ambassador, Li Hung Chang, visited New York. The local newspapers and the people were fascinated by his presence—his bright yellow jacket and his retinue of private chefs. Li Hung Chang wouldn't eat the local food, but he left this recipe, allegedly made up for the occasion, that has enlivened American Chinatowns from New York to San Francisco to the present. In this form, the dish is not known or offered in ancient China.

1½ lb. chicken breast, sliced in ½" slices
1 tablespoon chicken fat
1 pound mushrooms
2 celery sticks
1 dozen water chestnuts
2 onions
1 can bamboo shoots
2 pounds bean sprouts
2 tablespoons soy sauce

Wash and dry the vegetables and slice into ½" slices. Slice the chicken breast on the diagonal into thin strips. In a wok, heat 1 tablespoon chicken fat or vegetable oil until smoking hot. Stir in the chicken breasts and cook for 1 minute until they become transparent. Remove to one side of the wok and in the middle, tip in the vegetables, stirring hard for 2 minutes until they are crunchy. Recombine the chicken with the mixture, stir in the soy sauce and cook for 30 seconds more. Serve at once with Chinese Rice and soy sauce. *Serves 6.*

# WHOSE HAMBURGER?

Adapted from: Fannie Farmer, *The Boston Cooking-School Cook Book*, 1896, p. 178

1 pound lean raw beef
salt and pepper
1 teaspoon onion juice
2 shallots, finely chopped and cooked

## BURGER BUNS

⅓ cup milk
¼ cup sugar
2 packets instant dry yeast
1 tablespoon salt
5 cups flour
5 tablespoons butter
1½ cups hot water

The St. Louis World's Fair of 1904 was a grand event. There are hundreds of stories of "dishes" invented and promoted there. Ice cream, hotdogs, Dr. Pepper, iced tea, cotton candy, and even hamburgers are alleged, by one faction or another, to have made their debut at the Fair. The origins of the hamburger, in particular, have been the subject of fierce debate. Louis Lassen of New Haven, Connecticut ,has his supporters, as does Fletcher Davis of Athens, Texas. There may be others—it was a very big fair—and 1904 was a long time ago. Fannie Farmer, writing authoritatively in 1896, gives this recipe but doesn't take sides in the finger pointing.

Mix the beef, seasonings, onion juice, and shallots together and form into patties. Chill until needed, then broil under high heat for 2 minutes a side. Serve in home made burger buns with desired relishes and toppings.

*To Make the Buns*: Combine the milk, sugar, yeast, salt, and 2 cups of flour in a large bowl. Cut in the soft butter. Stir the hot water into the mixture, blending well. Blend in as much of the remaining flour as needed to form a soft dough and knead for 10 minutes. Set the dough in a large greased bowl, cover, and let rise for an hour.

Punch down the dough and form it into bun shapes, rolling the dough to make a bun of ½" thickness. Cover and let rise for 30 minutes until puffy. Bake in a preheated 375°F oven for 20 minutes. The buns should not be allowed to color. Cool on wire racks before splitting and using. *Makes 16 buns.*

# CHAFING DISH LOBSTER NEWBURG

Adapted from: Fannie Farmer, *Chafing Dish Possibilities*, 1898, p. 116

Any self-respecting 19th century kitchen was home to a chafing dish. Imagine a frying pan on legs, heated over hot coals, and you have an idea of the versatility of the chafing dish. This piece of equipment was essential to the completion of a delicate sauce because the dish could be cooked away from direct heat or flames. In the late 19th century, the chafing dish took on a different role. It became an elegant serving dish for a dainty supper, and often turned up in silver with fine wooden handles. Fannie Farmer, always quick to embrace a new trend, wrote an entire book called *Chafing Dish Possibilities*.

*1 large lobster*
*6 tablespoons sherry*
*2 tablespoons butter*
*1 tablespoon flour*
*2/3 cup cream*
*salt, pepper, and fresh ground nutmeg*
*3 hard-boiled egg yolks*
*toast*

 Remove the meat from the lobster and chop into bite-sized pieces. Sprinkle with the sherry and set aside. In a chafing dish or the top of a double boiler, melt the butter and add the flour, cooking to form a roux. Stir in the cream and seasonings. Put the lobster and its juices back in the dish, pour the sauce over, and keep warm until you are ready to serve. Accompany with toast points and lemon, and hard-boiled egg yolks sprinkled over. Adding the sherry to the meat rather than stirring it into the sauce keeps the flavor intact. *Serves 4.*

# SALMON GENOVESE

Adapted from: Pierre Blot, *Hand-book of Practical Cookery*, 1868, p. 145

2-lb. to 3-lb. salmon steak, skin on
1 cup fish broth
1 cup claret
bouquet garni (thyme, tarragon, parsley
　and basil)
12 mushrooms
4 tablespoons butter
3 tablespoons flour
salt and pepper
2 tablespoons lemon juice from 1 large lemon

Pierre Blot remains an enigmatic figure in American culinary history. What we can say, based upon the extensive media coverage his classes received, is that he was a celebrity in his time. When his school opened on March 24, 1865, he garnered a lengthy article in the *New York Times* who spoke of him as being "a household name." What happened after has never been fully established, but when he died only a few years later, in 1874, it was in sad obscurity. Thanks to the exhaustive work of Jan Longone, food historian, Monsieur Blot's place in the food history of the late 19th century has been rediscovered and we can cook the classic dishes he recommended, such as this Salmon Genovese.

 Place the salmon steak, skin side down, in a kettle and cover with the fish broth and claret. Bury the bouquet garni beneath the fish, season with salt and pepper, and cover. Bring the pot to a gentle boil and simmer, covered, for approximately 20 minutes, allowing 10 minutes per pound. The fish is done when the flesh flakes away to the pressure of a sharp knife tip inserted between skin and meat. Carefully remove the fish to a warm plate and remove the bouquet garni from the kettle.

Reduce the stock to 1 cup by boiling it briskly over moderate heat. Meanwhile, sauté the mushrooms in a little of the butter and add to the reduced stock. Make a roux with the remaining butter and flour. Over low heat, whisk in the roux to the reduced stock and mushrooms, season with salt and pepper, and simmer gently for 5 minutes. Squeeze in the lemon juice. Serve the salmon in thick slices, with the sauce poured over. *Serves 6.*

# TERRAPIN SOUP

Adapted from: Mary Lincoln, *Mrs. Lincoln's Boston Cook Book*, 1884, p. 196

There are only two lawful turtles that can be eaten in America today, the snapping turtle (Family: *Chelydra*) and the soft-shell (Family: *Trionyx*), and they are each wonderful in flavor and delicacy. The land tortoises (Family: *Testudinidae*) and the marine turtles (Family: *Cheloniidae*) are protected. If we can agree that the word "terrapin" is derived from "torope" the indigenous Delaware native word for the turtle-like creature, then that is just about the limit. Unregulated commercial hunting had driven the species to near extinction so that, by the time of Mrs. Lincoln's writing, she considered them an expensive delicacy. Today soft-shell and snapping turtles, alone, are available at gourmet meat stores such as Czimers in Chicago.

Mrs. Lincoln states the following: "Terrapin may be kept alive through the winter, before cooking, soak them in strong salt water. Put them alive into boiling water and boil rapidly 10-15 minutes. Remove the black outside skin from shells and the nails from the claws. Wash in warm water, then put them on again in fresh boiling water and boil them for ¾ of an hour or until the undershell cracks."

1 terrapin
1½ tablespoons butter
1½ tablespoons flour
1 cup cream
¾ cup chicken stock
salt, pepper, and cayenne
½ cup mushrooms
2 tablespoons sherry
2 eggs

Melt the butter, add flour and pour on the cream. Stir to make a smooth sauce. Add the terrapin meat, including the eggs and liver if available. Add the stock. Season with salt, pepper, and cayenne and simmer for 10 minutes. Just before serving, add the mushrooms, the sherry, and the eggs, slightly beaten. Do not allow to return to a boil. *Serves 4.*

# SENATE BETTER BEAN SOUP

Adapted from: Sara Tyson Rorer, *Mrs. Rorer's New Cook Book,* 1902, p. 63

1 pint black beans
2 quarts chicken stock
1 onion
1 ham hock
2 teaspoons salt
1 teaspoon pepper
¼ teaspoon cayenne
1 teaspoon mustard
1 tablespoon flour
1 tablespoon butter
2 eggs, hard-boiled
juice of 1 lemon

It was in 1903 that various U.S. Senators began to realize that there was a political gold mine at their very feet. No one from amongst their midst had yet laid claim to the "bean soup" vote. "Bean soup," so the argument goes, "is unchallengeable evidence of the candidate's warm, common, and humane qualities." Once the issue was raised, no less than half a dozen in the first year, and at least two or three in every year since then, have claimed allegiance to some form of bean soup. The number of declarations seems to go up during election years, but they all have one sad fact in common: the Senators don't know beans about soup. Some have added mashed potatoes, some have claimed or blamed their oratory on the bean's effects, but they have all overlooked the black bean soup as champion.

 Soak the beans in cold water for 4 hours; pick over and drain. Put the beans in a large pot covered with chicken stock, slice the onion and add to the pot along with the ham hock. Bring to a boil, lower the heat and simmer for 4 to 5 hours. Check the liquid level every hour and top up if necessary. Remove the soup from the heat, shred the ham and return to the pot. Purée about half of the beans and blend with the liquid in the pot. Season well with the pepper, cayenne, and mustard. Thicken the soup with a roux made from the flour and butter. Serve the soup ladled in hot bowls and garnished with the crumbled hard-boiled eggs. Squeeze the lemon juice over. *Serves 6.*

# MEG MERRILIES SOUP

Adapted from: Maria Parloa, *Miss Parloa's New Cook Book*, 1880, p. 90

The poet Keats had a soft spot in his heart for the lady poacher called Meg Merrilies, made infamous in his ballad.

*No breakfast had she many a morn,*
*No dinner many a noon,*
*And instead of supper she would stare*
*Full hard against the moon.*

But that was only the beginning for old Meg, who used moonlight to poach up a sack of rabbits, grouse, and other fowl from which she made a vigorous and engaging meal. This imagery was so evocative to 19th Century sensibilities that *Miss Parloa's New Cook Book* dedicated a recipe to "Meg Merrilies Soup."

1 carrot, sliced
1 turnip, sliced
1 stalk celery, sliced
1 tablespoon vegetable oil
1 rabbit, jointed
1 chicken, jointed
1 bouquet garni
8 cups good brown stock
4 onions
4 tablespoons butter

## FORCEMEAT BALLS

2 thick slices white bread, crumbled
1 egg, beaten
½ cup milk
1 tablespoon chopped mixed herbs

redcurrant jelly

Slice the carrot, turnip, and celery and put in a large pot, and sauté in the butter for 5 minutes. Roll the rabbit in flour and salt and pepper, and fry it in a separate pan in oil until well colored; remove it to the soup pot. Repeat with the chicken. Add the bouquet garni, salt and pepper, and stock to cover. Simmer the soup for 1½ hours. Allow to cool. Take the meat from the bones and cut into handsome pieces. Fry the meat in the butter and reserve. Slice the onions and fry in the same butter; add these both to the pan.

Make forcemeat balls from the crumbled bread, egg, and milk seasoned with herbs, and fry them in butter. Take the bouquet garni from the soup and taste carefully for seasoning. Drop the forcemeat balls into the soup about 20 minutes before serving and heat through. Serve very hot with a serving of onions, vegetables, forcemeat balls, and meat in each bowl. Ladle the hot soup over. Garnish with redcurrant jelly. *Serves 8.*

# SARATOGA CHIPS

Adapted from: Fannie Farmer, *The Boston Cooking-School Cook Book*, 1896, p. 280

russet potatoes
vegetable oil for frying
salt and pepper

In late 19th century America, as diners increasingly ate out, restaurants contributed new potato dishes to their menu. Delmonicos did a mouth-watering version with butter and lemon juice; The Ritz Carlton made vichyssoise; The Astor House included a choice of mashed or boiled on their Ladies Ordinary Lunch menu, but at Fleischmanns, the menu offered no less than 16 different treatments of the common spud. The most popular was the "Saratoga Fried Potato," a thin crispy fried chip "born" at a resort at Saratoga Springs in the 1850s. Mr. Lay and his family began to package and distribute the Saratoga fry in the 20th century, and they haven't stopped yet. The success of the Saratoga fry for the home chef depends upon soaking the potato to remove the excess sugars.

 Choose large, unblemished potatoes; peel and drop them into cold water. Slice each potato as thin as possible, using a sharp knife or a mandolin. Soak for 2 hours, changing the water twice. Drain, and plunge into boiling water for 1 minute. Drain again and cover with cold water. Remove the slices and pat them dry. Heat the vegetable oil to 325°F and arrange a plate lined with paper towels. Fry the dried slices in the fat for 5 minutes, until they soften and go limp. Keep them moving in the oil by using a slotted spoon to stir them about. Remove from the oil and put them on the paper towels to absorb the fat. Leave them for at least 15 minutes. Reheat the oil to 350°F and cook for 1 more minute until the chips turn golden. Drain again, sprinkle with salt and pepper, and serve at once.

# Franco~American Potato Salad

Adapted from: Pierre Blot, *What to Eat and How to Cook It*, 1863, p. 194

Potato salad came to this country with the Germans, who ate it warm in a dressing enriched with bacon drippings. The French contributed mayonnaise and garnished the potatoes with parsley. Professor Blot thickens the plot in his popular cookbook that encourages the addition of slices of beets and pickled cucumbers. Mrs. Lincoln, an all-American cookbook author and a niece of the former President, added olive oil, partly for its health benefits, but also because the production of the oil in Florida and California lowered the price to within reach of her readers. This Franco-American salad is something of a compromise, but the all-important constant is the baking of the potatoes in the oven with no added moisture. This technique preserves the flavor and texture of the vegetable in the finished salad.

## Salad

6 russet potatoes
½ cup white wine vinegar
2 cups homemade mayonnaise
½ cup chopped parsley
sliced pickled homemade cucumbers
1 medium onion, sliced

## Mayonnaise

2 egg yolks
1 cup olive oil
½ cup white wine vinegar
2 teaspoons Dijon mustard
salt and pepper

 Scrub the potatoes and prick them with a fork; bake them for about 1 hour in a 400°F oven. They should be tender, but not soft. When the potatoes are cool enough to handle, remove the skins; slice the potatoes ¼" thick and place them in a shallow dish. Pour over the vinegar, turn the slices and allow them to cool to room temperature. Pour over the mayonnaise, add chopped parsley, sliced cucumbers, and onions and turn to coat. Keep the salad cool rather than cold and eat the same day. *Serves 6 as a side dish.*

*To Make the Mayonnaise:* Whisk the eggs in a bowl and add the olive oil slowly, whisking the whole time. When the oil is used up, add the vinegar and combine well. Season with mustard and salt and pepper to taste. Cover and refrigerate until needed. The mayonnaise should be the consistency of thick custard.

# THE AUTHENTIC WALDORF

Adapted from: Fannie Farmer, *The Boston Cooking-School Cook Book*, 1918, p. 494

2 green apples
celery

## MAYONNAISE

2 egg yolks
1 tablespoon Dijon mustard
1½ cups light olive oil
2-3 tablespoons white wine vinegar
salt and pepper

In the same year that Fannie Farmer first published the cookbook that would be dubbed "The Kitchen Bible," the Waldorf Astoria opened in New York and served its eponymous salad. Oscar Tschirky published the recipe and, like all good recipes, it was at once elaborated upon and what had begun as a simple mixture of chopped apples and celery dressed with mayonnaise suffered all kinds of indignities: nuts, fruits, tomatoes, and sundry garnishes still did not dampen the enthusiasm. Miss Farmer's recipe was authentic and although she could not resist a few serving suggestions, the salad's classic ingredients remained intact.

Peel 2 green apples and cut into small pieces. Cut the inner stalks of celery the same way. Mix the salad with the mayonnaise.

*To Make the Mayonnaise:* Warm the eggs and bowl. Then, whisk the egg yolks to thicken slightly, add the mustard and blend. Gradually pour in the olive oil in a slow trickle, whisking constantly. As the mayonnaise thickens, add the oil a little more quickly until it is all used and a thick emulsion results. Beat in the vinegar and salt and pepper to taste. Cover and keep cool until needed and use the same day.

Oscar Wilde wrote: "To make a good salad is to be a brilliant diplomatist—the problem is entirely the same in both cases. To know how much oil one must mix with one's vinegar."

# CHESTNUT GRIDDLE BREAD

Adapted from: Sara Tyson Rorer, *Mrs. Rorer's New Cook Book*, 1902, p. 529

Chestnuts used to be the ultimate "free food." They fell from the unlimited forests of trees and could be picked from the ground at will. Today they are a luxurious treat. To explain why there were plenty of recipes for chestnuts in 19th century cookbooks, and today only the odd one or two for holiday stuffing, you need look no further than the massive blight that hit American trees in the early 20th century and decimated the population. Today's roast chestnuts are from Asian chestnut trees. This griddle bread is made from chestnut flour, which was originally used in Italy in Roman times to make polenta before the introduction of cornmeal.

2 large eggs, separated
½ cup whole milk
⅔ cup chestnut flour
1 teaspoon baking powder
½ teaspoon salt
1 tablespoon butter

To the egg yolks, add a half cup of milk. Mix. Stir in the chestnut flour. Cover and stand overnight in a cool place. The next morning, add the stiffly beaten egg whites, the baking powder, and salt. Make into thin cakes and drop onto a hot buttered griddle. Cook for 2 minutes per side until lightly colored. *Makes 8 griddle cakes.*

# Parker House Rolls

Adapted from: Maria Parloa, *Miss Parloa's New Cook Book*, 1880, p. 381

4 cups all-purpose flour
½ teaspoon salt
4 teaspoons sugar
1 teaspoon instant dried yeast
1¼ cups warm milk
1 large egg
12 tablespoons cold butter, divided

 Combine the flour, sugar, salt, and yeast. Pour in the warm milk and egg, and mix to make a dough. Add half the butter, cut into small pieces, and knead into the dough. Knead the dough for 5 minutes on a floured counter until it is smooth and elastic. Put the dough in an oiled bowl, cover, and let rise for 2 hours until doubled in size. Turn the dough out and let it rest, covered, for 10 minutes to relax the gluten. Roll the dough to ½" thickness and cut out circles about 2" in diameter with a cookie cutter. Cover and let the rolls rest for 5 minutes. Make a crease in each circle using a round wooden spoon handle. Smear a little of the remaining cold butter bits into the crease of each circle and fold the circle in half. Pinch the edges together. Place the rolls almost touching on a baking sheet and cover. Let them rise for another hour and then bake in a 400°F oven for 15 minutes until the rolls are golden brown. Eat warm. *Makes 24 rolls.*

"We are of the opinion that everybody ought to eat as little meat as possible, and drink no wine, beer or any other liquor at breakfast, no matter what the sex or age… the food may be selected from among the following: bread and butter, eggs, omelets, fried fish, fried vegetables or other vegetables, sardines, fruit according to season," wrote Pierre Blot on Breakfast in 1868.

In days when appetites were heartier, and the pace of life more leisurely (at least for some), breakfast was a meal of consequence, rather than a snack eaten on the run. Parker House Rolls always eclipsed whatever else went on the table, even when they were first baked at the Hotel of the same name in Boston, in 1860—the original recipe was quite modest. As the recipe developed, they became sweeter and richer. Maria Parloa's recipe is a classic. Using only a small amount of yeast and slow rises, the rolls develop as much flavor as possible.

# SPIDER CORN CAKE

Adapted from: Mary Lincoln, *Mrs. Lincoln's Boston Cook Book*, 1884, p. 91

The American obsession with accurate measurements began with Mrs. Mary Lincoln, although Fannie Farmer still gets the credit today. Mary Lincoln objected to loose phrases such as "a pinch of salt," "butter the size of an egg" and "nuts of honey." In this time-honored recipe for corn cake, the batter is prepared in a hot spider (a 19th century raised frying pan on legs), but is then baked in a fry pan in the oven. Sour milk was specified and necessary in the days when the only leavening agent was pearl ash, but with the invention of baking soda, sweet milk could be used.

1 tablespoon butter
¾ cup corn meal
¼ cup flour
1 tablespoon sugar
½ teaspoon salt
½ teaspoon soda
½ cup sour milk
1 egg
1 cup sweet milk

Melt the butter in a hot spider or frying pan on the stove. In a separate bowl, combine the dry ingredients. Dissolve the soda in the sour milk. Add the egg to the bowl and beat to combine; add the soda/milk mixture and the sweet milk. Beat the batter for 1 minute then pour into the hot pan. Bake at 350°F for 30 minutes. Serve hot with butter. *Makes 1 loaf.*

# Doughnuts

Adapted from: Mary Lincoln, *Mrs. Lincoln's Boston Cook Book*, 1884, p. 150

1 packet dried active yeast
¼ cup warm water
1 cup milk
1½ sticks butter
1 teaspoon salt
1 teaspoon cinnamon
2 large eggs
4 cups flour
vegetable oil for frying
1 cup sugar

Once, there were no doughnuts in America. Author Washington Irving waxed enthusiastic in 1809 about a delicious kind of cake called "oliykoek," that was baked by the Dutch; he wrote that it was "scarce known in this city." Over time, the doughnut gained a hole (the doughnut cooked much faster with it). How the shape originated isn't known, but the first enterprising man to invent the doughnut cutter was John Blundell who patented a wood mould in 1872. It was this cutter that Mrs. Lincoln instructed her readers to use, although it was soon replaced by a fluted metallic cutter of more modern design.

Whisk the yeast into the warm water and allow to proof. Add the milk and softened butter and beat well. Add the salt, cinnamon, eggs, and about half the flour and beat well. By hand, stir in the additional flour until a smooth satiny dough results. Cover with plastic wrap and allow to rise for 1½ hours until doubled in volume. Turn the dough onto a floured surface and roll it out ½" thick. Cut out doughnuts and set them 2" apart on a baking sheet. Cover lightly and allow to rise for 1 hour. Heat the oil in a deep fryer until the temperature on a thermometer reads 365°F. Fry 4 doughnuts at a time to avoid crowding. Cook for about 3 minutes, using tongs to turn. Place on a wire rack to drain. Put the cup of sugar in a bag and add the doughnuts, a few at a time. Shake to coat with sugar and eat right away. *Makes 24 doughnuts.*

# Devil's Food Cake

Adapted from: Sara Tyson Rorer, *Mrs. Rorer's New Cook Book*, 1902, p. 619

Mrs. Rorer was the first to give us a recipe for "Devil's Food Cake" using the chocolate that was becoming fashionable in her day. Mrs. Rorer believed that "…the more chocolatey the better, and the more devilish the cake!" By 1913, a popular cookbook, *Modern Women of America Cookbook* by Anna Vangalder, would list no less than 23 recipes, some of them colored with red food coloring.

## The Cake

¼ cup Dutch processed cocoa

4 oz. unsweetened chocolate

1½ cups boiling water

¾ cup pastry flour

¾ cup cake flour

teaspoons baking powder

2 sticks unsalted butter

1½ cups brown sugar

4 eggs

½ cup sour cream

1 teaspoon vanilla extract

## The Icing

16 oz. bittersweet chocolate

1½ cups heavy cream

⅓ cup light corn syrup

1 teaspoon vanilla extract

*To Make the Cake*: Combine the cocoa and chocolate in a bowl, pour the boiling water over, and whisk. Combine the flours and baking powder and set aside. Beat the butter until creamy and add the sugar; continue beating until fluffy. Add the eggs 1 at a time. Add the sour cream and vanilla, and beat well. Add ½ of the chocolate mixture and sift in ½ of the flour mixture, folding gently to combine. Repeat with the remaining chocolate and flour. Pour the batter into 2 well-greased round cake pans and bake in a 350°F oven for 20 minutes. A skewer inserted in the middle of the cake will come out clean. Cool on wire racks before icing.

*To Make the Icing*: Bring the cream to a simmer over medium-high heat and pour it over the chocolate in a bowl. Add the corn syrup and let it stand for 5 minutes. Then whisk gently, adding the vanilla. Refrigerate for 1 hour, stirring every 15 minutes. Spread thickly between the cakes and over the sides. Serve the cake the same day it is made. *Makes 1 layered cake.*

# THE REAL LADY BALTIMORE CAKE

Adapted from: Fannie Farmer, *A New Book of Cookery*, 1912, p. 333

## THE CAKE

½ cup butter

1½ cups sugar

1 cup water

3 cups flour

2 teaspoons baking powder

4 egg whites

1 teaspoon vanilla

## THE FROSTING

1½ cups sugar

⅔ cup water

2 teaspoons corn syrup

2 egg whites

⅛ teaspoon salt

1 teaspoon vanilla

¼ cup pecans, chopped

¼ cup figs, raisins, candied cherries, and
candied pineapple, chopped

The real Lady Baltimore was a character in a book of the same name, whose otherwise forgotten romantic plot featured a memorable scene in which the hero ate "Lady Baltimore Cake" and fell in love with both heroine and cake. Whether the author of the book, Owen Wister, had in fact ever eaten such a cake is not recorded, but readers clamored for the recipe and one appeared. The setting for the novel was Charleston, South Carolina, and the cake remained a Southern favorite, offered for consumption at the Lady Baltimore Tearooms, of course. Frosted and filled, it became a favorite recipe for weddings.

 *To Make the Cake*: Cream the sugar and butter until smooth and fluffy. Add the water. Sift the flour with the baking powder and fold into the batter until just combined. Beat the egg whites stiff and fold into the batter. Add the vanilla. Divide the batter between 3 greased cake pans and bake for 20 minutes in a 375°F oven, rotating the pans between shelves. Cool on wire racks.

*To Make the Frosting*: Combine the sugar and water in a small heavy saucepan and heat over medium heat without stirring. Add the corn syrup. When the sugar dissolves and the syrup comes to a boil, continue to boil until the syrup is 240°F on a candy thermometer. Beat the egg whites until stiff, and add salt. Off heat, pour a thin stream of syrup over the egg whites, beating all the time. Add the vanilla. Whisk for 10 minutes until the frosting firms. Add the chopped nuts and fruits.

Use the frosting between the cake layers and to frost the cake. Let the cake stand so that the filling can harden. *Makes 1 cake.*

# CENTURY GINGERSNAPS

Adapted from: Fannie Farmer, *The Boston Cooking-School Cook Book*, 1896, p. 403

Gingersnaps are a variation on the theme of gingerbread, one of the most popular forms of cake and one of the earliest recorded recipes. Amelia Simmons had no less than four receipts for gingerbread in *American Cookery*. The cookie quite likely got its name from the fact that the tops crinkle and the cookie snaps when baked. In her recipe for snaps, Fannie Farmer gives the sage advice not to add unnecessary flour or the cookies will be hard rather than short and crisp.

1 cup molasses
½ cup shortening
3 cups flour
1 cup brown sugar
½ teaspoon soda
1 tablespoon ginger
½ teaspoon salt

Heat the molasses to boiling point and pour over the shortening. Add dry ingredients and beat smooth. Chill the dough for 1 hour. Roll the dough as thinly as possible and cut into rounds. Using a cutter dipped in flour helps to prevent the dough from sticking. Bake in a 350°F oven for 8 minutes. Cool on wire racks. *Makes about 24 cookies.*

# Queen Victoria's Nesselrode Pudding

Adapted from: Fannie Farmer, *The Boston Cooking-School Cook Book*, 1896, p. 379

1½ cups chestnuts, prepared

1 pint sugar syrup

3 cups cream

1½ cups sugar

4 egg yolks

¼ cup pineapple juice

¼ cup maraschino

¼ cup jumbo raisins

1 cup heavy whipping cream

## Nesselrode Sauce

2 egg yolks

½ cup sugar

1 cup boiled cream

¼ cup maraschino syrup

The Victorians did not have freezers, or even river ice boxes, but they did have some decorative ways of keeping ice cream cool. One method was to enclose the frozen dessert known as a "Nesselrode Pudding" in a meringue which acted as an insulator. A famous example was the spun sugar beehive designed by Royal Confectioner, Francatelli, which covered the pudding beneath. The ersatz beehive came complete with pretend bees, also made from confections—and the spectacular result was set on a carved ice stand and presented to Queen Victoria.

Simmer the chestnuts in sugar syrup until they are soft, about 30 minutes. Drain and rub them through a fine-meshed sieve. Simmer the raisins in the same syrup, drain and set aside. Heat the cream in a small pan and stir in the 1½ cups sugar. Add the egg yolks gradually, whisking to thicken. To this custard, add the chestnut purée and the maraschino and pineapple juice. Add the jumbo raisins. Pour the cream into the freezer and work it with a spatula until it starts to firm, then add the whipped cream and continue working until the cream is frozen. Put the ice cream in a dome-shaped ice cream mould and freeze until needed. Traditionally, the Nesselrode is eaten with the sauce poured over.

*To Make the Sauce*: Make a custard of the egg yolks, sugar, and cream. Cool, stirring constantly. Add the maraschino and put the pan on ice. The sauce should be very cold but not frozen. *Makes 1 Nesselrode pudding.*

# New World Apple Pie

Adapted from: Sara Tyson Rorer, *Mrs. Rorer's New Cook Book*, 1902, p. 590

Cottolene was a manufactured shortening made from cotton seed and represented to be better than lard as a cooking oil. It might well be, and the indigestive aspects and other health hazards of eating lard are now well-known. Mrs. Rorer certainly thought so, and was among the first to lend her prestige and endorsement to the product. She joined some powerful company—Huey Long, "The Kingfish" of Louisiana politics and a depression era politician of enormous power, took his first job as a traveling Cottolene salesman. Today we recommend Crisco.

## A More Friendly Pastry

2 cups flour
½ teaspoon salt
1 cup Crisco (formerly Cottolene)
8 tablespoons ice water

## Filling

6 Granny Smith apples, peeled and sliced
1 cup brown sugar
1 teaspoon cinnamon
1 teaspoon nutmeg
1 tablespoon butter
1 tablespoon lemon juice
1 egg white, beaten, for glaze

*To Make the Pastry*: Tip the flour and salt onto a cool counter and add the cold shortening. Use a knife to cut the shortening into the flour. Make a well in the center and tip in the water. Knead together lightly to make a soft dough. Wrap and refrigerate for 1 hour.

*To Make the Pie*: Roll out half the cold dough to a large circle big enough to fit a pie plate. Line the plate. Tip in the sliced apples, the sugar, and spices. Dot little pieces of butter on top and sprinkle over the lemon juice. Roll out the remaining pastry and place on top. Seal the edges, and make slits in the top lid. Brush with the egg glaze. Bake for 30 minutes in a 375°F oven, then cover the pie and finish baking at 350°F for another 20 minutes. *Makes 1 pie.*

# PEANUT BUTTER WAFERS

Adapted from: Sara Tyson Rorer, *Mrs. Rorer's New Cook Book*, 1902, p. 736

½ cup peanut butter (see below)
½ cup peanut meal (see below)
1 cup sugar
½ teaspoon soda
½ cup warm water
3 cups graham flour
½ teaspoon salt

With the increased interest in nutrition that came on the heels of the domestic science movement, cookbooks burst with chapters on food values and diet plans. Sara Rorer, with her interest in vegetarianism had chapters on vegetables (broken down into starchy and non-starchy), mushrooms, and nut cookery. Making peanut butter became something of a fad—this, of course, was before the butter was officially named "health food" at the St. Louis World Fair in 1904. "Skippy" and "Jif" took it from there, but Mrs. Rorer had shown the way.

To make the peanut meal, grind just over ½ cup peanuts in a food processor until mealy; set aside. To make peanut butter, roast the shelled peanuts in the oven until they are golden and fragrant, about 15 minutes. Watch carefully. Put the peanuts in the food processor and purée until smooth.

Beat the peanut meal with the peanut butter in the processor, then add the sugar. Dissolve the soda in the warm water, and add to the nut mixture. Then work in 3 cups of graham flour and salt. The dough should be rather hard. Place the dough on the counter and cover it with a large Ziploc bag. Roll out into a thin sheet. The bag will prevent the dough from sticking. Cut into small squares and bake on a greased baking sheet in a 325°F oven for 1 hour. *Makes 24 wafers.*

# THE SCHOOL OF LIFE FUDGE

Adapted from: Sara Tyson Rorer, *Mrs. Rorer's New Cook Book*, 1902, p. 629

Because "fudge" could be made surreptitiously in the dormitory at Vassar, it became an overnight sensation with the students at all of the "Seven Sisters" women's colleges of the 1890s. The name was already popular on campus, used as slang for "almost swearing" or "almost cheating." As a result, "fudging" became a popular pejorative. In 1908, the Walter Baker Company published recipes for "Vassar Fudge," "Smith College Fudge," and "Wellesley Marshmallow Fudge."

3 cups sugar
4 tablespoons unsalted butter
4 ounces chocolate
½ cup milk
1 teaspoonful vanilla

Warm the sugar, butter, chocolate, and milk in a saucepan over low heat until melted. Boil, stirring constantly, until the mixture reaches soft-ball stage. A candy thermometer will read 230°F. (If you are making fudge in a dorm room, use the soft-ball test. Drop a small ball of the mixture into a cup of cold water. If the mixture hardens, it is ready.) Take the pan off the fire, add the vanilla, then turn it into a shallow pan. When cold, cut into squares. *Makes approx 24 squares.*

# Eggs a la Bennett

Adapted from: Sara Tyson Rorer, *Mrs. Rorer's New Cook Book*, 1902, p. 66

4 eggs, hard-boiled
5 tablespoons butter
½ teaspoon salt
1 tablespoon chives, finely chopped
1 teaspoon anchovy sauce
½ cup breadcrumbs
pepper

## Mornay Sauce

6 tablespoons butter
2 tablespoons flour
1 cup milk
salt and pepper

Sarah Rorer was a 19th century culinary celebrity with "box office" appeal. Her lectures stressed the importance of diet in health without recourse to hysteria, and attracted audiences numbering in the thousands. In 1886, she put her theories in print in *Mrs. Rorer's Philadelphia Cookbook*. Between its greaseproof covers, she held forth about the importance of cooking green vegetables only until they were tender; she talked about macaroni as the bread of the Italian laborer and wondered why it should not be eaten by American families; she extolled the virtues of eating salads and plain food. Amongst her best recipes were simple ideas for baking eggs for a healthy meatless supper. "Eggs a la Bennett" appears here verbatim.

*To Make the Mornay Sauce:* Melt the butter in a saucepan, and beat in the flour until smooth. Gradually whisk in the milk, stirring to make a satiny sauce. Season to taste with salt and pepper.

Cut the eggs in halves lengthwise, remove the yolks and rub them with half the butter, salt, chives, and anchovy paste. Fill the egg whites with this mixture. Cover the bottom of a baking dish with the mornay sauce, stand in the eggs, sprinkle with the breadcrumbs and pepper, and baste with the remaining butter. Sprinkle Parmesan over all. Brown under the broiler for 5 minutes just until brown. *Serves 4.*

# COOKBOOK CHRONOLOGY

1615    Markham, Gervase, *The English Huswife, Containing the Inward and Outward Virtues Which Ought to Be in a Complete Woman.* London.

1651    La Varenne, François Pierre (de), *Le cuisinier françois.* Paris (*The French Cook.* London, 1653).

1667    Molen-Willebrands, Ed., *Der verstangige kock,* Amsterdam ("*The Sensible Cook and Housekeeper*").

1671    Dame Alys Katharine of Asthorne Glen, *The Compleat Cook.* London.

1727    Smith, Mrs. Eliza, *The Compleat Housewife, or Accomplish'd Gentlewoman's Companion.* London and Williamsburg, Virginia, 1742.

1747    Glasse, Hannah, *The Art of Cookery Made Plain and Easy.* London and Alexandria, Virginia, 1805.

1749    Washington, Martha, *The Booke of Cookery.* (Reprint, 1981 transcribed by Karen Hess, Columbia Univ. Press).

1765    Carter, Susannah, *The Frugal Housewife, or, Complete woman cook.* London: F. Newbery and Boston: Reprinted by Edes and Gill, 1772.

1796    Simmons, Amelia, *American Cookery, or the art of dressing viands, fish, poultry, and vegetables, and the best modes of making pastes, puffs, pies, tarts, puddings, custards and preserves, and all kinds of cakes, from the imperial plum to the plain cake: Adapted to this country, and all grades of Life.* Hartford: Printed for Simeon Butler, Northampton.

1798    Briggs, Richard. *The New Art of Cookery; According to the Present Practice; Being a Complete Guide to all Housekeepers, on a Plan Entirely New....* Boston: For W. Spotswood.

1805    Glasse, Hannah, *The Art of Cookery Made Plain.* Alexandria, Virginia.

1807    Rundell, Maria Eliza, *A New System of Domestic Cookery, Formed Upon Principles of Economy, and Adapted to the Use of Private Families. By a Lady.* Boston: W. Andrews.

1813    Ude, Louis Eustache, *The French Cook.* London: Cox & Baylis.

1824    Randolph, Mary. *The Virginia Housewife: or Methodical Cook*. Baltimore: Plaskitt, Fite, Baltimore.

1825    Savarin, Brilliat, *Le Philosophie de Gout*, Paris. (*Physiology of Taste.*)

1827    Roberts, Robert, *The House Servant's Directory, or A Monitor for Private Families: Comprising Hints on the Arrangement and Performance of Servants' Work*. Boston: Munroe and Francis; New York: Charles S. Francis.

1828    Leslie, Eliza, *Seventy-Five Receipts for Pastry, Cakes and Sweetmeats*.

1829    Kitchiner, Dr. William, *Aspicius Redivivus, or the Cook's Oracle*. London, Simpkin and Marshall, and G.B. Wittaker.

1832    Child, Lydia Maria, *The Frugal Housewife, Dedicated to Those Who Are Not Ashamed of Economy*. Boston: Carter and Hendee.

1832    Lee, Mrs. N.K.M., *The Cook's Own Book; Being A Complete Culinary Encyclopedia... With Numerous Original Receipts And A Complete System Of Confectionery. By A Boston Housekeeper*.

1837    Graham, Sylvester, *A Treatise on Bread, and Bread Making*. Boston.

1837    Leslie, Eliza. *Directions for Cookery, in its Various Branches*. Philadelphia: E.L. Carey & Hart.

1839    Bryan, Mrs. Lettice, *The Kentucky Housewife Containing Nearly Thirteen Hundred Full Receipts*. Cincinnati, OH: Shepard & Stearns.

1840    "anon", *La Petite Cuisinière Habile*, New Orleans.

1841    Hale, Sarah Joespha, *The Good Housekeeper, or The Way to Live Well and to Be Well While We Live*. Boston: Weeks, Jordan & Company.

1841    Girardey, George, *Manual of Domestic Economy, or House-Keeper's Guide. Comprising a Very Large Collection of Original Receipts, Derived from the Practical Experience of the Author*. Dayton, Ohio: John Wilson, Printer.

1841    Beecher, Catharine, *A Treatise on Domestic Economy for the Use of Young Ladies at Home and at School*. Boston: Thomas H. Webb & Co.

1842    Hardin, Philomelia, *Everybody's Cook and Receipt Book: But More Particularly Designed for Buckeyes, Hoosiers, Wolverines, Corncrackers, Suckers, and All Epicures Who Wish to Live with the Present Times*. Cleveland.

1845    Acton, Elizabeth 'Eliza', *Modern Cookery for Private Families*. London: Longmans.

1845    Crowen, Mrs. T. J., *Every Lady's Book*. New York, J.K. Wellman.

1845    Kingsmill, Louisa, handwritten manuscript only, Canada.

1845    Howland, Esther Allen. *The American Economical Housekeeper, and Family Receipt Book*. Cincinatti: H.W. Derby.

1846    Beecher, Catharine, *Miss Beecher's Domestic Receipt Book: Designed as a Supplement to her Treatise on Domestic Economy*. New York: Harper.

1847    Rutledge, Sarah, *The Carolina Housewife*. Charleston.

1847    Crowen, Mrs. T. J., *American Lady's Cookery Book*. New York: Dick & Fitzgerald.

1848    Peters, Gustav, *Die Geschichte Hausfrau*. Germany (*The Practical Housewife*, translated by William Woys Weaver, 1983, U. Pennsylvania).

1851    Soyer, Alexis, *The Modern Housewife: Or, Ménagère. Comprising Nearly One Thousand Receipts....* London, Simpkin, Marshall, & Co.

1854    Leslie, Eliza, *Miss Leslie's New Receipts for Cooking . . .* (38th edition). Boston.

1857    Collins, Angelina Maria, *The Great Western Cook Book, or Table Receipts, Adapted to Western Housewifery*. New York: A.S. Barnes & Company.

1860    Hale, Sarah J., Ed., *Godey's Lady's Book*, 1860-1865, Philadlephia.

1861    Collins, Mrs. Anna M., *Mrs. Collins' Table Receipts; Adapted to Western Housewifery*. New Albany, Indiana.

1861    Beeton, Mrs., *Mrs. Beeton's Book of Household Management*. London.

1863    "committee", *Confederate Receipt Book. A Compilation of Over One Hundred Receipts, Adapted to the Times*. Richmond, Va: West & Johnson.

1863    Blot, Pierre, *What to Eat and How to Cook It. Containing over One Thousand Recipes systematically and practically arranged, to enable the Housekeeper to prepare the most difficult or simple Dishes in the best manner*. New York: D. Appleton & Company.

1864    Chase, Dr. Alvin Wood, *Dr. Chase's Recipes, or, Information for Everybody*. Tenth Edition. Ann Arbor, MI: Chase.

1864    Moss, Maria J., *A Poetical Cook-book*. Philadelphia, C. Sherman.

1865    Goodfellow, Mrs., *Mrs. Goodfellow's Cookery as it should be.: A new manual of the dining room and kitchen ...* Philadelphia: T. B. Peterson & brothers.

1867    Blot, Pierre, *Hand-book Of Practical Cookery, For Ladies And Professional Cooks. Containing The Whole Science And Art Of Preparing Human Food*. New York.

1871    Porter, Mrs., *Mrs. Porter's New Southern Cookery Book, and Companion for Frugal and Economical Housekeepers.* Philadelphia: J.E. Potter.

1871    Levy, Mrs. Esther, *Jewish Cookery Book: On Principles of Economy, Adapted for Jewish Housekeepers, With the Addition of Many Useful Medicinal Recipes, and Other Valuable Information, Relative to Housekeeping and Domestic Management.* Philadelphia.

1873    Harland, Marion, *Common Sense in the Household: A Manual of Practical Housewifery.* New York: Scribner, Armstrong & Co.

1873    "committe", *The Presbyterian Cookbook.* Compiled By The Ladies Of The First Presbyterian Church, Dayton, Ohio. Dayton, Ohio: Oliver Crook.

1876    *The National Cookery Book ... Original Receipts for the Women's Centennial Committees of the International Exhibition of 1876.* Philidelphia.

1877    Wilcox, Mrs. Esther, *Buckeye Cookery and Practical Housekeeping.* Minneapolis, MN: Buckeye Publishing Co..

1880    Parloa, Maria, *Miss Parloa's New Cookbook: A Guide to Marketing and Cooking.* New York: C.T. Dillingham.

1881    Fisher, Abby, *What Mrs. Fisher Knows About Old Southern Cooking, Soups, Pickles, Preserves, Etc.* San Francisco: Women's Co-operative Printing Office.

1884    Lincoln, Mary Johnson, *Mrs. Lincoln's Boston Cook Book: What To Do and What Not To Do in Cooking.* Boston: Roberts Brothers.

1885    Hearn, Lafcadio, *La Cuisine Creole: A Collection of Culinary Recipes, From Leading Chefs and Noted Creole Housewives, Who Have Made New Orleans Famous for its Cuisine.* New Orleans: F.F. Hansell & Bro., Ltd.

1886    Rorer, Sarah J., *Mrs. Rorer's Philadelphia Cook Book.* Philadelphia: Arnold and Co.

1893    *Favorite Dishes. A Columbian Autograph Souvenir Cookery Book. Over Three Hundred Autograph Recipes, and Twenty-three Portraits, Contributed By The Board Of Lady Managers Of The World's Columbian Exposition.* Illustrated By May Root-Kern, Mellie Ingels Julian, Louis Braunhold, George Wharton Edwards. Comp. By Carrie V. Shuman... Chicago [R. R. Donnelley & Sons Co., Printers].

1896    Farmer, Fannie, *The Boston Cooking-School Cookbook.* Boston: Little, Brown.

1896    Tschirky, Oscar, *The Cook Book of "Oscar" of the Waldorf.* New York, Werner Co.

1897    Davidis, Henriette, *Henriette Davidis' Practical Cook Book.* Compiled for the United States from the 35th German Edition. Milwaukee, WI: C.N. Caspar Book Emporium/H.H. Zahn & Co.

1898    Pinedo, Encarnacion, *El Cocinero Espanol* (*The Spanish Cook*).

1898    Farmer, Fannie, *Chafing Dish Possibilities*. Boston: Little, Brown.

1901    Kander, Mrs. Lizzie Black, "*The Settlement*" *Cook Book. The Way to a Man's Heart. Containing Many Recipes Used in the "Settlement" Cooking classes, the Milwaukee Public School Cooking Centers, and gathered from various other Reliable Sources*. Milwaukee: J.H. Yewdale & Sons Co.

1902    Rorer, Sarah J., *Mrs. Rorer's New Cook Book*. Philadelphia: Arnold and Co.

1903    Lummis, Charles F., Ed., *The Landmark Club Cook Book*. Los Angeles: The Out West Company.

1903    Escoffier, Auguste, *Le Guide culinaire*. Paris, Flammarion.

1904    *The Blue Grass Cook Book*, Comp. By Minnie C. Fox, With An Introduction By John Fox, Jr.; Illustrated With Photographs, By A. L. Coburn. New York, Fox, Duffield & Company.

1911    Estes, Rufus, *Good Things to Eat, as Suggested by Rufus; A Collection of Practical Recipes for Preparing Meats, Game, Fowl, Fish, Puddings, Pastries, Etc.* Chicago.

1914    Watama, Onoto, *Chinese-Japanese Cook Book*. By Sara Bosse And Onoto Watanna [pseud.] Chicago, Rand McNally.

1956    Mignon, Francois and Clementine Hunter, *Melrose Plantation Cookbook*. New Orleans, A.F. LaBorde & Sons.

ONLINE BIBLIOGRAPHY

Feeding America: digital lib.msu.edu/cookbooks

The Food Timeline: www.foodtimeline.org

History and Legends of Favorite Foods: www.whatscookingamerica.net/history

Food Reference: www.foodreference.com

Making of America: moa.umdlumich.edu

Civil War Cooking: www.civilwarinteractive.com/cookbook.htm

# RECIPE INDEX